Pension Politics

Population ageing and slower economic growth have raised serious questions about the willingness and ability of governments to maintain current social policies. Within this new reality, discussions on the future of public pensions have been predominant in political debates across Europe.

This book explains why certain countries have been able to radically transform their pension system while others have simply altered parameters. To answer this question an extensive comparative analysis, including more than 60 interviews, was conducted in Belgium, France, Sweden and the UK. This empirical data provides an interesting contrast between reforms. Parametric reforms have stemmed from the creation of pension administrations outside the traditional state apparatus in France and Belgium and the resulting inclusion of social partners; while the state administrations of Sweden and the UK where debates have been internalised have led to programmatic reforms. Two controversial findings of this book include an explanation for the lack of influence on the part of the labour movement in the 1994/98 Swedish reform and a rejection of arguments claiming that policy change will be minimal with coalition governments. Finally, the conclusion seeks to extend the applicability of the model to other industrialized countries.

This book will be of interest to students and scholars of public policy, specifically social policy, political economy, the welfare state and comparative politics.

Patrik Marier is Canada Research Chair in Comparative Public Policy in the Department of Political Science at Concordia University, Canada

Routledge/EUI Studies in the Political Economy of Welfare

Series editors: Martin Rhodes & Maurizio Ferrera
The European University Institute, Florence, Italy

This series presents leading-edge research on the recasting of European welfare states. The series is interdisciplinary, featuring contributions from experts in economics, political science and social policy. The books provide a comparative analysis of topical issues, including:

- reforms of the major social programmes – pensions, health, social security
- the changing political cleavages in welfare politics
- policy convergence and social policy innovation
- the impact of globalisation

Pension Politics

Consensus and social conflict in ageing societies

Patrik Marier

Routledge
Taylor & Francis Group

LONDON AND NEW YORK

First published 2008
by Routledge
2 Park Square, Milton Park, Abingdon, Oxon OX14 4RN

Simultaneously published in the USA and Canada
by Routledge
270 Madison Avenue, New York, NY 10016

Routledge is an imprint of the Taylor & Francis Group, an informa business

Typeset in Times New Roman by
Taylor & Francis Books
Printed and bound in Great Britain by
Antony Rowe Ltd, Chippenham, Wiltshire

British Library Cataloguing in Publication Data
A catalogue record for this book is available from the British Library

Library of Congress Cataloging in Publication Data
Marier, Patrik.
  Pension politics : Consensus and social conflict in ageing societies /
  Patrik Marier.
    p. cm. – (Routledge/EUI studies in the political economy of welfare ;
  11) "Simultaneously published in the USA and Canada by Routledge."
  Includes bibliographical references and index.
  1. Old age pensions–Government policy–Europe, Western–Case studies.
  2. Social security–Europe, Western–Case studies. I. Title.
  HD7105.35.E85E447 2008
  331.25'2094–dc22   2007034962

ISBN 978-0-415-42599-5 (hbk)
ISBN 978-0-203-93121-9 (ebk)

À ma mère

Contents

Tables

Acknowledgements

This book represents close to ten years of research on the topic of pension reforms. The effort and support of numerous professors and friends have not been forgotten. Above all, I was very fortunate to have the guidance of B. Guy Peters at the University of Pittsburgh, who always found time to discuss this project with me even when abroad or between flights. Alberta Sbragia's encouragement and support were second to none. Mark Hallerberg provided detailed and valuable comments on numerous drafts of this manuscript. I would also like to thank Ray Owen, my external reviewer Donald Savoie (from the Université de Moncton) and friends from my graduate programme for their efforts and assistance.

None of the findings in this book would have been possible without the assistance and input of colleagues abroad. In Sweden, I would like to thank Michele Micheletti for allowing me to spend a semester in the autumn of 2000 at the University of Stockholm where I benefited greatly from interactions with Diane Sainsbury and Joakim Palme. In Göteborg, Jon Pierre and the entire department hosted me for a full year in 2001/2; they always involved me in regular departmental activities and even played the role of first-year undergraduates for a practice job talk. In addition to Jon and the other members of the research seminar in public policy and public administration, I received insightful comments on this project from Anna Bendz, Peter Esaiasson, Lennart Lindqvist and Bo Rothstein. In 2006, Torsten Svensson hosted me at Uppsala for two months, allowing me to conduct further interviews in Stockholm, Norway and the UK. His input and that of Christina Bergqvist, Paula Blomqvist, Anders Lindbom and PerOla Öberg were welcome additions. In France, Nicole de Montricher hosted me at CERSA for a brief stay in Paris amidst an office move. In Belgium, I was a guest of the Public Management Institute in Leuwen. Finally, I would like to thank all the policy actors I interviewed during my numerous trips to Europe. This book would not exist without their valuable input.

Throughout the past years, I have been fortunate to interact with gifted welfare state scholars who share a similar passion for pensions and helped me along the way: Daniel Béland, Giuliano Bonoli, Urban Lundberg, Christoffer Green-Pedersen, Markus Haverland, Martin Schludi and Kent

Weaver. Many thanks to my colleagues at Brockport and Concordia for their support. My research assistants – Andrew Bigioni, Michael Braun, Mahsa Hedayati, Anna-Maria Luponio, Jessica Romkey, Suzanne Skinner and Michael Torunian – were extremely helpful in updating the manuscript. I would also like to thank my editor, Jo-Ann Cleaver, for all her time and efforts; the two anonymous referees for detailed comments and critique; and Martin Rhodes and everyone at Routledge. I would also like to acknowledge the financial support of the Social Science and Humanities Research Council of Canada, the political science department at the University of Pittsburgh, the European Union Center at the University of Pittsburgh and the Swedish Institute.

In closing, I would like to thank friends and family members, too numerous to name individually, for their continuing encouragement towards the fulfilment of my academic career.

Abbreviations

AARP	American Association of Retired People
ABFP	Belgian Association of Pension Funds
ABI	Association of British Insurers
ABVV/FGTB	Algemeen Belgisch Vakverbond/Fédération Générale des Travailleurs Belges
ACLV/CGSLB	Algemene Centrale der Liberale Vakbonden/Centrale Générale des Syndicats Libéraux de Belgique
ACV/CSC	Algemeen Christelijk Vakverbond/Confédération des Syndicats Chrétiens (Belgium)
AGIRC	Association Générale des Institutions de Retraite des Cadres (France)
ARRCO	Association pour le Régime de Retraite Complémentaire des Salariés (France)
ATP	Allmän tilläggspension (universal earnings-related pension) (Sweden)
BF	Belgian francs
BNB	Belgian Central Bank
CADES	Caisse d'Amortissement de la Dette Sociale (France)
CANCAVA	Caisse Nationale d'Assurance Vieillesse des Artisans (France)
CBI	Confederation of British Industry
CCSP–CSC	Centrale Chrétienne des Services Publics – Confédération des Syndicats Chrétiens (Belgium)
CFTC	Confédération Française des Travailleurs Chrétiens (France)
CFDT	Confédération Française Démocratique du Travail (France)
CFE–CGC	Confédération Française de l'Encadrement – Confédération Générale des Cadres (France)
CGP	Commissariat Général du Plan (France)
CGSP/ACOD	Centrale Générale des Services Publics/Algemene Centrale der Openbare Diensten (Belgium)
CGSS	Caisse Générale de Sécurité Sociale (France)
CGT	Confédération Générale du Travail (France)

CNAPVL	Caisse Nationale d'Assurance Vieillesse des Professions Libérales (France)
CNAV	Caisse Nationale de l'Assurance Vieillesse (France)
CNBF	Caisse Nationale des Barreaux Français
CNPF	Conseil National du Patronat Français (previous name of MEDEF)
CNRACL	Caisse Nationale de Retraites des Agents des Collectivités Locales (France)
CNRCC (CCI)	Caisse Nationale de Retraite du Personnel des Chambres de Commerce (Chambre de Commerce et d'Industrie) (France)
COR	Conseil d'Orientation des Retraites (France)
CPP	Canada Pension Plan
CPS	Centre for Policy Studies (UK)
CRAM	Caisse Régionale d'Assurance Maladie (France)
CRAV	Caisse Régionale d'Assurance Vieillesse (France)
CREPA	Caisse de Retraite du Personnel des Avocats et des Avoués près les Cours d'Appel (France)
CRPCCMPA	Caisse de Retraite et de Prévoyance de la Chambre de Commerce Maritime et des Ports Autonomes (France)
CRPNPAC	Caisse de Retraite du Personnel Navigant Professionnel de l'Aéronautique Civile (France)
CSG	Contribution Sociale Généralisée (France)
CVP	Christelijke Volkspartij (Christian Democrats) (Belgium)
DG	director-general
DHSS	Department of Health and Social Security (UK)
DSS	Direction de la Sécurité Sociale (France)
DWP	Department for Work and Pensions (UK)
ECJ	European Court of Justice
EMU	Economic and Monetary Union
ENA	École Nationale d'Administration (France)
EU	European Union
FEN	Fédération de l'Éducation Nationale (France)
FO	Force Ouvrière (France)
FPB	Federal Planning Bureau (Belgium)
FSCSP/FCSOD	Fédération des Syndicats Chrétiens des Services Publics/ Federatie van de Christelijke Syndicaten der Openbare Diensten (Belgium)
FSU	Fédération Syndicale Unitaire (France)
FSV	Fonds de Solidarité Vieillesse (France)
GDP	gross domestic product
GMP	guaranteed minimum pension (Sweden)
GNP	gross national product
IG	Genomförandegruppen (Implementation Group) (Sweden)
INSEE	Institut National de la Statistique et des Études Économiques (France)

ISO	International Organization for Standardization
IoD	Institute of Directors (UK)
LO	Landsorganisationen (Swedish blue-collar union)
MALTESE	Model for Analysis of Long-Term Evolution of Social Expenditure (Belgium)
MEDEF	Mouvement des Entreprises de France
MIG	minimum income guarantee (UK)
MSA	Mutualité Sociale Agricole (France)
NAPF	National Association of Pension Funds (UK)
NHS	National Health Service (UK)
OECD	Organization for Economic Co-operation and Development
OMC	Open Method of Co-ordination
ONP	Office National des Pensions (Belgium)
payg	pay-as-you-go
PCF	Parti Communiste Français
PPG	Pension Provision Group (UK)
PPI	Pensions Policy Institute (UK)
PPM	Premiepensionsmyndigheten (Premium Pensions Administration) (Sweden)
PRL	Parti Réformateur Libéral (Belgian French Liberals)
PS	Parti Socialiste (France and Belgium)
PSC	Parti Social Chrétien (Belgium)
PVV	Partij voor Vrijheid en Vooruitgang (Belgium)
RATP	Régie Autonome des Transports Parisiens (France)
RDS	Remboursement de la Dette de la Sécurité Sociale (France)
RFV	Riksförsäkringsverket (National Social Insurance Board) (Sweden)
RPR	Rassemblement pour la République (France)
RVP	Rijksdienst voor Pensioenen (Belgium)
S2P	State Second Pension (UK)
SACO	Sveriges Akademikers Centralorganisation
SAF	Svenska Arbetsgivareföreningen
SAP	Sveriges Socialdemokratiska Arbetareparti
SEK	Swedish krona
SERPS	State Earnings-Related Pension Scheme (UK)
SLFP/VSOA	Syndicat Libre de la Fonction Publique/ Vrij Syndicaat voor het Openbaar Ambt (Belgium)
SN	Svensk Naringsliv (Confederation of Swedish Enterprise)
SNCF	Société Nationale des Chemins de Fer Français
SOU	Statens Offentliga Utredningar (State Public Inquiry) (Sweden)
SP	Socialistische Partij anders (Belgium)
SSAC	Social Security Advisory Committee (UK)
TCO	Tjänstemännens Centralorganisation (Sweden)
TUC	Trades Union Congress (UK)

UDF	Union pour la Démocratie Française
UK	United Kingdom
UMP	Union pour un Movement Populaire (France)
UNSA	Union Nationale des Syndicats Autonomes (France)
UPEA	Belgian Association of Insurance
UTMI	Union des Travailleurs Manuels et Intellectuels (Belgium)
VLD	Flemish Liberals (Belgium)
VOB/FEB	Verbond van Belgische Ondernemingen/Fédération des Entreprises de Belgique
VU	Volksunie (Belgium)
WAP/LPC	Wet op Aanvullende Pensioenen/Loi sur les Pensions Complémentaires (Belgium)
WGOP	Working Group on Pensions (Sweden)

Introduction
Policy change in difficult times

Introduction

The current era will be remembered as one of welfare retrenchment that put a halt to decades of welfare expansion. Numerous attacks were made on the welfare state, and analysts have vehemently debated the importance and magnitude of the reforms introduced in industrialized countries. Public pension systems are cited as being notoriously resistant to change during those debates. Their maturity and popularity leave reform-minded politicians little scope for revision (Pierson 1996; Bonoli 2000). These hurdles did not, however, stop British and Swedish politicians in their successful attempt to enact various reforms. Ironically, they faced less opposition than their French, Belgian and German peers, even though they proposed reforms far more limited in scope. The French government had to face millions of protesters in its numerous attempts to reform the welfare state. This puzzling outcome is the focus of this study, which attempts to delineate those factors that impede and/or facilitate policy change. Within the broader category of policy change, pension reform was chosen as the focus owing to its complex and numerous attributes.

The approaching retirement of the baby-boomers accompanied by slow economic growth in industrialized countries pressured governments to find solutions to avoid vast increases in pension expenditures. Despite the urgency portrayed by the mass media owing to the alleged lack of action on the part of governments, the so-called pension 'time bomb' is far from being an unexpected surprise. As early as 1975, a leading political scientist in the study of welfare states claimed that 'if there is one source of welfare spending that is most powerful – a single proximate cause – it is the proportion of old people in the population' (Wilensky 1974: 47).

The impact pensions have on the public purse should not be underestimated; they constitute the single biggest item of all social expenditures, and already account for more than 10 per cent of gross domestic product (GDP) in nine European Union (EU) member states (Austria, Denmark, Finland, Germany, Greece, France, Italy, Luxembourg and Sweden) (Economic Policy Committee 2000: 27). As a result, reforming public pensions has featured prominently in the political agendas of most governments for the past two decades. Nonetheless, it has proven very difficult to transform pension reform from an agenda item into actual legislation. This outcome reflects both the complexity of the issue at hand and the popular support that pension programmes enjoy. Knowing upcoming demographic trends is not enough to predict the costs of pension programmes given the impact that intimately related factors such as economic growth, unemployment, inflation and immigration will have. For example, income from increased economic growth could partly offset the cost of benefits for a larger proportion of retired individuals, hence generating consensus regarding the extent of the sickness can be as difficult as agreeing on the cure.

Why study public pensions?

Regardless of the economic and/or demographic evidence presented, reforming public pensions is first and foremost *a political problem*. Who gets what, and when, is a controversial political question. The extent to which pensions should be reformed addresses this fundamental question. The study of pensions entails the analysis of five key political conflicts. First, the population shift occurring in many countries has the potential to generate intergenerational conflicts. As a result of population ageing and high unemployment, many countries have now reached the point where the employed population supports a larger, inactive population, thus placing a significant financial weight onto the shoulders of the former. Despite this imbalance, it is widely believed that pensioners deserve their benefits, even by the younger generations who pay the costs. Consequently, pension retrenchment is an unpopular initiative. Nonetheless, one must consider the fact that more than 50 per cent of the social budget is currently allocated to the elderly (Pierson 1998), an inequity that jeopardizes other social programmes like day care and social housing.

Second, intra-generational conflicts are also present. Pension reforms impact individuals differentially, even when they belong to the same age cohort. Continental countries tend to have a plethora of public pension programmes, each tailored to employees' occupational status and each resulting in different rules and benefits. While seeking to reform these schemes, governments experience organized resistance from groups claiming special circumstances, the most common being civil servants who link their pension to their status as civil servants. As is delineated by this study, occupational divides may even exist within universal systems, since uniform rules still tend to privilege certain categories of workers. For example, the former Swedish pension system granted more generous benefits to white-collar workers with shorter careers and faster rising wages than it did to blue-collar workers who maintained a steady income (see Chapter 4).

Third, reforming public pensions relates to the role of the state in providing adequate support for its elderly. Governments have been under both ideological and financial pressure to reduce the size of the state's contribution by encouraging and often subsidizing private pension plan savings. The traditional model has business owners seeking tax reductions in order to remain competitive in a global economy, while unions seek to retain what they consider to be their earned and promised financial entitlement. In addition, financial pressure is strong within the European Union; under the terms of the Maastricht Treaty, its members are required to limit their public deficits to 3 per cent or less. Yet pension expenditure is predicted to grow tremendously in most member states if legislation is not changed. Should the private sector take more responsibility for this problem? The crash of 1929 was actually a key reason behind the expansion of pay-as-you-go (payg) public schemes. The recent poor performance of the stock market coupled with corporate scandals in the United States is once again raising concerns regarding the private sector's ability to deliver safe and generous pensions.

Fourth, reforming public pensions involves gender issues concerning equal treatment of men and women. The application of a similar retirement age for both genders, the result of an old EU directive, provoked heated debate regarding the adequacy and fairness of such measures. Should the state correct for the inequalities produced by the labour market? Are pension policies the appropriate corrective measure for that inequity? Given that low fertility levels contribute significantly to the pension imbalance, women face pressure to actively participate in the labour market while they also still bear most of the responsibility for childcare.

Fifth, the literature on neo-institutionalism analyses the important role institutions play in shaping political conflicts, positing that institutions influence and shape political power. What is the extent of their role in the field of pension policies? A key question is to determine whether or not specific institutional constellations are better equipped to reform pensions.

Finally, alternative solutions that could partly resolve the potential increase in public pensions without changing them remain quite controversial. The 'new' countries such as Canada, the United States and Australia face less pressure owing to their high immigration levels. However, an increase in European immigration levels risks generating even more support for parties on the extreme right than such parties have already garnered this past decade in many countries.

Who matters in the policy process, and how?

In his seminal work on welfare-state retrenchment, Pierson (1994, 1996, 1998, 2001) built upon the argument that 'policy creates politics' (Lowi 1972) as he examined the structure of policy programmes and their institutional environment. Public pensions represent a prime example of an instance wherein public policy creates politics; many beneficiaries have organized themselves politically in order to protect their interests. For example, no American politician can afford to ignore the American Association of Retired People (AARP), with its 30 million members (and votes) (Pierson 1994). Political institutions often require super majorities to enact legislation, and the structure of pension programmes, where current contributions finance current retirees, accentuates the difficulty of implementing meaningful reforms. Taking these elements into account, Pierson (1994) argues that the main components of the welfare state have survived the repeated reform attempts of both Thatcher and Reagan. He dismisses the claim that the Conservative record reflects radical change (Pierson 1994: 5).

Illustrative of the strength of Pierson's argument, numerous critics have challenged his theoretical claims and his conclusion that the welfare state is an immovable object (Pierson 1998). First, Cox and Bashevkin emphasized the role that ideas and public discourse play in successful welfare reforms. Cox (2001), for example, argues that Dutch and Danish politicians succeeded because they linked their proposals to national frameworks like the Constitution, something German politicians did not do. Bashevkin (2002) expands on that argument by saying that politicians created negative images of citizens relying on welfare – an image of dependence, for example. In both cases, the welfare state is not perceived as being immovable, and change is considered a function of discourse.

Second, the structure of pension programmes and the timing of their implementation have also been used to account for the scope of change (or lack thereof) introduced in industrialized countries. It has been far easier to encourage the privatization of pensions when the private sector already occupies a privileged place (Myles and Pierson 2001). Even though the private sector may be ill equipped to provide sufficient benefits in the long run, countries relying on a large public system find it extremely difficult to change it (Bonoli 2003).

Third, the bureaucracy has been (nearly) dismissed as an important actor in studies focusing on welfare retrenchment (Pierson 1996), despite a long tradition associating it with expansion (Heclo 1974; Rothstein 1996). Marier (2005) demonstrates that bureaucracies can either accentuate (or reduce) the difficulties associated with policy change in the realm of the welfare state in his comparison of reform initiatives in France and Sweden.

Fourth, owing to his focus on conservative parties, Pierson (1994, 1996) ignored ideological differences among political parties. Numerous authors claimed that parties approach welfare retrenchment differently (Levy 1999; Green-Pedersen 2001; Swank 2002). For example, Levy (1999) argued that the Socialist Party in France introduced welfare reforms that turned 'vice into virtue'. While those covered by the French occupational system faced a reduction in their benefits, individuals with inadequate coverage saw the amount of their benefits increased. Finally, a European response to Pierson emphasized the role of unions owing to their privileged position within the policy process (Bonoli 2000; Anderson 2001; Béland 2001; Natali and Rhodes 2004). Moreover, elderly union members tended to use these channels to exert influence. Most unions included a pensioner segment within their organization. Italy represents the most extreme case, as more than 50 per cent of all its elderly belong to a pensioner union (Campbell and Lynch 2000). This literature on the power of unions emphasized the need to co-operate with the labour movement when effecting social policy change. As Bonoli (2000) stressed, governments attempted to grant concessions to unions in order to receive their political support in a *quid pro quo* fashion.

The argument in brief

This book offers an alternative approach to explain why some countries restructured their entire pension systems while others simply tinkered with the rules. It is argued that we can find the answer to this puzzle by considering the relationship between the state (politicians and bureaucrats) and the social partners (unions and employers). Their relationship is structured by two important institutional variables considered to be determining factors for the type of pension reforms introduced. These two institutional factors are then ranked according to two ordering principles.

The first such principle states that the institutionalization of the social partners in the management of public pensions grants them a place within the pension reform process, thus constraining the government's ability to enact reforms. In this case, pension programmes tend to have been built *outside* the state, and the social partners are confined to managing them. The social partners' financial contribution is also quite substantial in these pension schemes. Thus, social partners represent a 'veto point' (Immergut 1992) in the process. In cases where the state manages and bears most of the financial responsibilities, public pension schemes are considered to be *within* the state. The influence and power of unions are limited to their ties with the Social Democratic Party, which acts as a filtering influence. A similar logic applies to employers and right-wing parties. This situation occurred because unions and employers did not fear the state and/or trusted that the state would administer this programme properly without seeking to diminish their power and responsibilities. In order to have a strong influence over the public pension schemes, social actors must find a way to influence the state.

The second ordering principle is inspired by Tsebelis' (1999, 2002) examination of veto players. His theory predicts that the larger the government coalition, the more likely it is to have stable policies. In this case, it implies a lack of pension reform or a minor tinkering with the rules. Thus, single-party governments should be better equipped to introduce substantial pension reforms. This book argues that Tsebelis' conclusions only apply once the first ordering principle is in place. Coalition governments have many tools at their disposal to successfully tackle major policy challenges such as pension reform; the ability to negotiate binding agreements, for example. However, the institutionalization of social partners complicates the implementation of coalition agreements because it allows unions and employers to interfere with the negotiation process. Thus, it is argued here that a coalition government might be able to carry on more substantial reforms than a coalition government and/or a single party government that must negotiate with social partners in an institutionalized relationship (see Chapter 1).

Methodology

Different approaches were considered when this study was planned, ranging from the single case study to the statistical method wherein all industrialized countries could have been analysed. The case-study method was rejected because it does not provide the kind of generalization that is realized by analysing many cases. Further, many case studies have already been conducted and reported in the current literature. The statistical method was rejected because of a lack of valid, comparable data. The European Commission began gathering genuinely comparable data only a few years ago, and it remains extremely difficult to gather similarly derived and presented data from many EU countries. Moreover, the use of the statistical method for the study of pensions is quite unreliable. As stated earlier, the need (and therefore success) of public pension reform is highly dependent on factors such as unemployment, fertility rates, immigration and economic growth that are not directly related to a pension programme, and it takes many years, if not decades, to truly assess the financial impact of this type of reform.

This study focused on four cases, each representing a different scenario based on the combination of the two ordering principles presented on p. 5. This has the advantage of generating multiple comparisons and controls, which can help to test hypotheses more rigorously than using only one or two cases. Another important advantage of using four cases is that one can go beyond comparing within the limits of the three welfare regimes (Esping-Andersen 1990), a method frequently used in previous studies.

The four countries chosen for comparison are Belgium, France, Sweden and the United Kingdom. European cases were selected because they face the greatest pressures to reform and because they also have the oldest populations among industrialized countries (with the exception of Japan), while they all face the same pressure to limit their public expenditures owing to the Maastricht Treaty requirements.[1]

The evidence presented is the result of more than 60 interviews conducted with European actors involved in the policy process (mostly Members of Parliament who were involved in pension committees, ministers, bureaucrats and representatives of unions and employers). Policy documents from these groups were also studied and analysed alongside official publications. Finally, a careful review of the four countries' national newspapers was conducted.

Overview

Chapter 1 presents the main analytical framework employed, as summarized on pp. 5–6. To enhance the discussion, the argument presented is compared to current theories prevalent in the literature. Finally, a series of hypotheses is introduced to test the theory used for this study.

Chapter 2 focuses on the case of France and analyses the various attempts to reform pensions in the past 20 years. It represents the scenario where a single-party government must include social partners in order to enact successful reforms. More than 10 commissions have been mandated since the mid-1980s, and both the Balladur government of 1993 and the Raffarin government of 2003 generated successful attempts to reform the system following the white-collar union's (silent) endorsement. Another serious attempt was made in December 1995 by the Juppé government, but it was made without consulting social partners and thus resulted in the most disruptive protests since the events of 1968.

Chapter 3 presents the Belgian case, which is the case nearest to the status quo. The only significant reform occurred in the mid-1990s under pressure from the European Union to alter its system so that it would not violate the directive regarding the equal treatment of men and women. Minor reforms have been introduced over the past few years designed to encourage the development of occupational pensions within the private sector. Unions played a large role by significantly limiting the coalition governments' ability to act. Their involvement in this process forced the government to adopt a small-step-by-small-step approach.

The case of Sweden is discussed in Chapter 4. A long process beginning with a parliamentary committee in 1984 produced a complete overhaul of the system with the agreement of five major parties within Parliament. The political parties were able to shield themselves from other social actors by restricting their access during the sessions of the Working Group on Pensions (1991–4), which served as a stepping-off point for the five-party accord. The agreement they developed successfully withstood criticism from political parties and social actors, and implementation began in 1995. Last-minute meetings saved the agreement from collapsing in 1998. The unions and employers were not actively involved during the negotiations and were unable to interfere substantially with the process, as they were faced with a *fait accompli*.

Chapter 5 analyses the British case, where the most radical reforms of all the countries were introduced by the Thatcher government. These were then followed by a series of reforms implemented by the Blair government to alter the long-term consequences of inadequate savings for future retirees. The extent of Thatcher's reforms resulted in the nearly impossible feat of restoring a viable public system. The new alternatives presented by the Blair government confirm that the presence of the private sector will not be challenged. Unions and, to a lesser extent, employers were excluded from the operational group that presented most of the reforms.

Finally, the Conclusion (Chapter 6) reviews and compares the four cases as it presents a detailed analysis of the hypothesis developed in Chapter 1. It also reflects on the applicability of the theoretical framework to other cases. The last segment offers fruitful possible avenues for further research and inquiries.

1 The origins of diversity in pension reform processes

A theoretical approach

Introduction

The literature on the welfare state stresses the difficulties (even the incapacity) of its institutions to adapt to the new socio-economic realities of the twenty-first century (Pierson 1998; Ferrera and Rhodes 2000; Kuhnle and Alestalo 2000). Public pensions are no exception. Prior to World War II few industrial workers reached the age of retirement, and many actually opposed the creation of contribution-based old-age pensions on the basis that few believed they would live long enough to collect them. They referred to them as 'the pension for the dead'. Owing to recent improvements in the average citizen's quality of life and overall health, old age is now much more commonly attained, and an ever-increasing percentage of the population lives long enough to collect substantial pension benefits. Public pension systems were not designed, however, with this socio-economic eventuality in mind, leaving politicians and state officials struggling to reform a programme that is continuously expanding, even as governments experience ever-increasing budgetary constraints.

This chapter introduces a new explanatory framework that accounts for the different success rates accompanying various types of pension reforms introduced in the four countries studied (Belgium, France, Sweden and the United Kingdom (UK)), a framework that can then be used to understand this complex process in other industrialized countries. For example, why was Sweden able to radically transform its pension system, while France struggled to introduce relatively minor parametric changes? The typology suggested here differs from others commonly used by emphasizing the role of politicians, civil servants and social partners within the institutional structure of public schemes. The institutional structure matters because it grants specific roles to various actors and generates opportunities to veto suggested reform initiatives (Immergut 1992). Further, it is argued that these structured relationships are tied to state formation and to the creation of pension programmes, both of which shape the policy environment. Strongly rooted in the neo-institutionalist literature, this chapter argues that the electoral system and the management of public pensions are the two dimensions that should be examined in order to comprehend the varying degrees of success different countries experience as they attempt to implement substantial pension reforms.

The institutionalization of social partners and the state, and its influence on public pension reforms

This study contributes to the debate on the retrenchment of the welfare state by comparing pension reform attempts in Belgium, France, Sweden and the United Kingdom. It contributes to our theoretical understanding of the process by emphasizing the importance of electoral and pension institutions in any consideration of the 'nature' of the state with respect to analysing both formal and informal relationships within it. This research answers three broad questions: (1) which factors affect the different avenues chosen to reform pensions? (2) How should we account for the inclusion/exclusion of social partners in the process? And a last, related, question, (3) how does the inclusion or exclusion of social partners impact the result of an attempted reform? Thus, the main focuses are the process by which pension reforms are enacted and the outcome of such processes. This research does not seek to challenge the difficulties associated with retrenchment politics. Retrenchment is a more difficult enterprise than expanding welfare rights and benefits. Consequently, governments prefer to retrench public pension programmes via 'stealth' methods such as obfuscation, division and/or compensation strategies in order to avoid political backlash (Pierson 1994). This does not, however, necessarily imply stability. Policy change is an inherent outcome of the policy process enacted in the four countries studied, and different outcomes were obtained.

The chief factors are the nature of the state and the institutionalization of relationships among the various political actors such as parties, bureaucrats and interest groups. It is argued that these two variables are crucial aspects that explain divergence in the type and scope of reforms. As these relationships have been structured over time, the construction of the welfare state becomes a central element because it establishes, to use March and Olsen's (1989) terminology, the 'appropriate relationships' among the various political actors. This section discusses the principal elements of current theoretical debates and introduces the theoretical framework used in this research, as well as the methodology employed to evaluate the framework's utility.

Current theoretical debates: the challenges to welfare states

The re-emergence of institutions as an important consideration within the field of political science (March and Olsen 1989; Peters 1999) applies also to studies related to the retrenchment of the welfare state (for a review, see Green-Pedersen and Haverland 2002). For the most part, institutions have been considered a hindrance to politicians seeking to reform the welfare state, first because of their ability to veto suggested reforms (Immergut 1992; Bonoli 2000) and, second, because of what is referred to as 'institutional stickiness' (Pierson 1994, 1998). It is rare to find cases where a simple majority in a national parliament is sufficient to carry out welfare reforms. Even though this assertion has been widely supported in the literature, there have been few studies where institutions supported retrenchment (King 1995; Ross 2000b). For example, King (1995) demonstrates that the reintroduction of 'workfare' in both the United States and the United Kingdom was facilitated by the pre-existing institutional structure.

Pierson's work delineating the difficulties commonly associated with retrenchment politics (Pierson 1993, 1994, 1996, 1998, 2000; Pierson and Weaver 1993) generated an important debate within academic circles on the merits of the 'new' politics of the welfare state. It is thus logical to begin our theoretical discussion of pension reform by reviewing his body of work and the criticisms levelled against it.

Strongly rooted within the neo-institutionalist literature, his main contribution is that welfare retrenchment is quite different from welfare expansion. Pierson (1994) argues that retrenchment is a difficult and costly political undertaking: it is much easier to expand benefits than it is to reduce or eliminate them; the latter generates an avoidance of blame rather than a taking of credit. Moreover, the electorate tends to have a negative bias; it is more cognizant of losses than equivalent gains (Weaver 1986). As a result, Pierson claims that the welfare state resembles nothing so much as an immovable elephant.

Pierson outlines three focal elements that contribute to the stability of the welfare state: its popularity, its path dependency and its institutional stickiness. Each is discussed in depth in the following pages. The first factor is the popularity of the welfare state. Social programmes, and public pensions as a prime exemplar of these, enjoy broad support among the electorate owing to the direct benefit received from them. This rests on the argument that 'policies produce politics' (Pierson 1994: 39). For example, it is very difficult for a politician or a political party to get elected on a platform where cuts to pension benefits are a central feature. This is exacerbated by the fact that older citizens also tend to participate more in elections than do the young. Further, pension recipients currently belong to interest groups that promote their concerns. Pierson claims that the welfare state was actually instrumental in generating the creation of interest groups seeking to protect their benefits (Pierson 1994: 30). For example, no American politician can afford to ignore the AARP, with its 30 million members (and votes) (Pierson 1994).

The rising political power of the elderly has been challenged both empirically and theoretically, however, by the realization that they, despite their shared concern about pension benefits, nonetheless do not comprise a single, unified interest group. In the four countries studied in this book, associations representing retirees tend to be divided along ideological

(Sweden), occupational (France) and religious (Belgium) lines. Pierson himself acknowledges that Thatcher was able to push her 1986 reform through because the British pensioners' groups were divided amongst themselves (Pierson 1994: 71). Another critique made against the utility of the 'grey-power' thesis is the existing amount of variation that Lynch, for example, notes with respect to the percentage of various states' budgets that are apportioned to the elderly, with the United States and Italy significantly favouring the elderly. She states that 'younger age groups enjoy significant benefits in many countries' (Lynch 2001: 433). This challenges the generalized applicability of the so-called grey-power thesis.

Another problematic assertion is the assumed link between public opinion and election results. Thatcher introduced what are considered very 'unpopular' reforms, yet was elected and re-elected to office for over 10 years. This apparent anomaly is even more puzzling when we consider the fact that the British political system offers little opportunity for blame-avoidance tactics. Contrary to the position in the United States, for example, in the UK a policy cannot be blamed on another political institution like the Congress. In the same vein, Ross (2000a) challenges the power of opinion polls in sustaining the welfare state. She does not dispute this support, but she also directs our attention to other polls suggesting that retrenchment measures such as the Personal Responsibility and Work Opportunity Reconciliation Act (associated with the phrase 'ending welfare as we know it') became a very popular initiative under the Democratic Clinton administration in the United States (Ross 2000a: 19).

The cases reviewed in this study support the assertion that it is difficult to retrench the welfare state. Despite that acknowledged difficulty, however, there is widespread consensus among politicians in industrialized countries that the current generous pension plans must be reformed.[1] The main conflicts engendered by pension reform are related to the extent of the reforms and the way they are enacted. Swedish politicians from all major parties went out of their way to ensure that pensions were kept off the electoral agenda, and in this they succeeded. The 2002 French election, however, resulted in both political camps proposing a similar reform to the public sector despite the strength of the opposition such attempts had faced in 1995 from public unions and a large segment of the population. Public-sector reform was implemented soon after the elections by Raffarin's right-wing government in 2003. The Socialists were deeply divided in their response, and they chose to criticize the process by which the reform occurred, rather than its content (Béland and Marier 2006). Thus, the electorate was faced with a choice between two main parties that were both advocating and endorsing pension reforms; it was thus not possible to link reform initiatives with a single politician or party.

The second important element stressed by the 'new' politics of the welfare state is the importance of programme structure, which creates policy paths that restrict reform options. Path dependency has been linked mostly with historical institutionalism, emphasizing the 'legacy of the past' (Peters 1999). It suggests that an institutional structure creates a path restraining the number of policy options available by increasing the costs of alternatives. David (1985) describes this phenomenon by explaining why QWERTY persists on computer keyboards despite more efficient alternatives such as the Dvorak configuration. 'QWERTY-nomics' stresses that once individuals adopt a standard and invest in it, the costs of switching to another increase over time, even though more efficient alternatives may arise. Similarly, all pension players have invested in, and are comfortable with, their original pension plans and are thus reluctant to change them substantially, despite the fact that the plans may not any longer be workable owing to ongoing demographic change and new socio-economic realities.

Historical institutionalists claim that institutions also delimit the power and even the formation of political preferences at the same time as they emphasize the strength of specific political actors. Even if those actors act rationally, institutional structures generate unintended consequences, thus creating policy outcomes divergent from the original policy preferences. For example, Steinmo concludes *Taxation and Democracy* with a chapter stressing the close relationship between tax revenues and expansion of the welfare state. He stresses that Sweden has a more comprehensive welfare state than the United States, not because Swedes have a stronger desire for a safety net, but because the American tax system does not raise as much revenue as its Swedish counterpart. The Americans have been unable to create a national sales tax or to hide taxes the way most European nations could (Steinmo 1993: 196). For reasons beyond the scope of this book, American institutions prevented the creation of a national tax, a feature which generates more income with which to fund the subsequent and more generous expansion of the welfare state and its benefits.

Pierson (1994) also argues that previous choices constrain the range of options available to policy-makers who wish to introduce a reform. Pensions are considered to be a clear example of a path-dependent policy, since a move away from pay-as-you-go (payg) to a fully funded system would result in a double payment problem for the first generation, who would have to finance their own pensions in addition to continuing to fund the benefits owed to their elders' generation. This is one of the chief reasons why such pension reforms are implemented over a long period of time. Individuals must have a lengthy period of time to adjust their savings and careers in accordance with any new reform. People near retirement would have a very difficult time if they had to increase their personal savings by whatever percentage the pension amount they expected to receive upon retirement was unexpectedly reduced. This reality is, at the very least, as much a reflection of these practical problems as it is a strategy to avoid blame on the part of governments, and it offers insights and understanding regarding why substantive reforms have not taken place in many countries; it does not, however, heuristically explain how it is that many countries have successfully introduced substantive pension reforms despite sharing this same logistic limitation. Pierson acknowledges that his theoretical framework cannot really account for the drastic changes to the British public pension scheme, other than to state that Britain is the 'exception rather than the rule' (Pierson 1996: 161).

To their credit, Myles and Pierson account for the apparent British anomaly by incorporating another variable; the maturity of the existing programme.[2] In their view, countries that reformed their pension plans by adding a new funding component began with relatively recently developed pension plan systems (Myles and Pierson 2001: 8). On the other hand, they claim that countries such as Italy and France have had major difficulties in introducing these kinds of reforms because of the high level of maturity of their public pension schemes (Myles and Pierson 2001: 30). Though this explanation goes some way towards explaining the relative degree of difficulty associated with pension reforms, Sweden's allmän tilläggspension (ATP) programme again presents an anomaly, as it was completely mature when it was transformed in the 1990s.

A common criticism is that historical institutionalists emphasize (if not actually inflate) the stability of institutions and policies. Not surprisingly, Pierson (1994), whose theoretical framework is inspired by this school, stresses the static 'nature' of welfare programmes. The strong reliance on path dependency, a core tool employed by Pierson, reinforces this scenario. As Peters states:

> the entire analytical framework [historical institutionalism] appears premised upon the enduring effects of institutional and policy choices made at the initiation of a structure. Thus, the approach appears much better suited to explain the persistence of patterns than to explain how those patterns might change. ... [T]here appears to be little or no capacity to predict change.
>
> (Peters 1999: 68; see also Pierre *et al.* 2005)

Thus, given this 'persistence of patterns', what constitutes a move away from the status quo? There is still no clear definition of the null hypothesis of Pierson's static elephant. The term 'path breaking' is now surfacing within this style of literature, implying that certain actions are designed to favour retrenchment at a later date. For example, Bonoli and Palier (2000) argue that the inaction of the government with respect to pension reforms in France increased uncertainty among the population, thereby reducing their faith in public pensions and leading them to pursue private pension plan options. Nonetheless, there is nothing to identify clearly when or where a path is actually broken.

Another difficulty lies with the meaning of retrenchment. Parametric reforms are much easier to implement than programmatic reforms.[3] Thus, it is not surprising that parametric strategies have been adopted in most countries because they require far less analysis and debate. However, the cumulative effect of parametric reforms can, in the end, have a similar impact to that of sweeping programmatic reform. Within the realm of pension reforms, Hinrichs and Kangas (2003) have recently demonstrated that a series of minimalist changes can produce substantial changes that, when all is said and done, diverge significantly from the original structure. This outcome has also been noted when analysing the rise of the welfare state. The evolution of the welfare state is the result of slow *incremental* improvements in social policies occurring over the last 100 years. As stated by the late Ashford, 'there was never an historical turning point where leaders sat around the table and said to each other that we must now devise a welfare state' (Ashford 1986: 4). Thus, Ross argues that 'welfare states were not built over a decade or two, so why would we expect them to be dismantled over a decade or two?' (Ross 2000a: 16; see also Clayton and Pontusson 1998). Even though such criticism strikes a chord, it does not resolve the problem of measuring change, as stated on pp. 17–19. Rather than arguing about whether or not the welfare state has moved away from the status quo, the contention involves incremental changes. Similar discussions occurred in budgetary politics, resulting in a debate over the size of an increment (see Dempster and Wildavsky 1980). A move away from stability towards a more dynamic, transformative configuration still requires a solution for this measurement problem.

Pierson's partial attribution of policy stability to path dependency is also questionable. Baldwin (1990) demonstrates that path dependency restricted the opportunities available to reformers, but it did not halt the development of public pensions in the five European countries he studied (Denmark, Sweden, the UK, France and Germany). The fact that major changes occurred despite the difficulties associated with path dependence is notable. Governments have historically acknowledged these difficulties, but have also used them to their advantage. In the case of the Swedish mandatory supplementary pension reform (ATP), the Social Democrats provided very generous benefits to white-collar workers to ensure they would support their reforms to the public system even though they were themselves already covered by private alternatives. The leaders of the Landsorganisationen (LO, the Swedish blue-collar union) accepted the fact that the compromise formula led to better benefits for white-collar workers, but they understood that it was the price they had to pay for the creation of the ATP. This major shift in pension policy was part of a Social Democratic strategy that resulted in a significant increase in popular support for the party in subsequent elections (Svensson 1994). Had there not been extensive private alternatives for white-collar workers, it would have been very difficult for the Social Democrats to defend their ATP position with the LO. Thus, their efforts to replace the private path resulted in political benefits.

Even if we accept that retrenchment is very different from expansion, the association of policy stability with path dependency does not always hold.

This is clearly demonstrated by King (1995) in his study of the politics of unemployment in the United States and the United Kingdom. Part of his argument is that the institutional arrangements of both countries facilitated the reintroduction of welfare-to-work programmes because they were originally designed with these policy preferences in mind. The four cases studied in this book emphasize the fact that path dependency does not mean 'frozen' dependency. Two of the four countries studied (Sweden and the UK) introduced significant changes to their pension system, and, despite their adopting less drastic measures, some substantial changes were also enacted in Belgium and France.

Pierson's third focus is institutional stickiness. Many countries have formal rules requiring a majority well above 50 per cent for the removal or alteration of a law. The United States, with its Congress, Senate and Presidency, is a case in point (Pierson and Weaver 1993). Many authors refer often to the concept of veto points (Immergut 1992), and, from a rational choice perspective, veto players (Tsebelis 1995; 1999), to analyse the impact of institutional stickiness. Pierson focuses instead on formal institutions. His discussion of the subject emphasizes the centrality of power in the hands of the British government and the opposite situation adhering in the United States. Based on these characteristics, he builds a framework stressing the advantages and disadvantages of such institutional structures. For example, he underlines that the British political system makes it easier for a government to introduce retrenchment measures because it does not have to deal with other chambers or federal actors as is the case in the United States. However, this concentration of power also makes retrenchment actions more visible, and the party enacting such measures may be punished for it by the electorate at the polls (Pierson 1994: 31–6). This assumption is empirically and theoretically challenged by the research presented here (see the next section (pp. 19–32) and Chapter 6).

Pierson's characterization of institutions conforms to what Peters (1999) refers to as 'empirical institutionalism'. Institutions are taken as a given, and they are not expected to change. The principal variable in analyses emphasizing empirical institutionalism is the design of the institution (Peters 1999: ch. 4), but such a framework does not account for the role of the state, how governmental structures were established or the governmental institutions' day-to-day operation. As demonstrated by the current study, institutional stickiness can be avoided when actors embedded within such systems use their previous experience to work around them. This conclusion is supported by research in other policy areas. For example, challenging previous literature that posited a significant correlation between coalition governments and public deficits, Hallerberg and von Hagen (1999) refuted these findings in their analysis of budgetary politics. They emphasized the role of fiscal pacts when coalition governments took power, which reduced the importance of numerous parties within a coalition government and produced solid fiscal performance. With respect to pensions, Sweden has been able to reform its pension system extensively relative to France, despite the larger number of veto players. As is discussed later in this chapter (see pp. 20–2), it is neither the number of opportunities for a veto or the number of players holding that power that matters. What counts most is the *nature of the veto.*

Ideology and party politics

Ross (2000b) points out that the 'new politics' of welfare seriously under-estimated the importance of ideology and party politics. In one of the first studies on the retrenchment of the welfare state, Mishra (1990) presents a dichotomy in the approaches made to the welfare state by stating that a social democratic world, including Sweden and Germany, seeks to maintain the current structure of the welfare state, while a conservative world, exem-plified by the United States and the United Kingdom, attempts to alter it significantly.

Levy supports Garrett's 1998 contention regarding the importance of the difference between the Left and the Right. He claims that within con-tinental Europe, which includes many inequities in its welfare systems, par-ties from the Left adopted a strategy that turned 'vices into virtues' by altering ineffective policies favouring the most needy society members. Comparing the French governments throughout the 1990s, he concludes that partisan politics is an important source of differentiation, in terms of both approach and policies (Levy 2001: 281). An important missing ele-ment, however, is the failure to acknowledge that the Jospin government (1997–2002) did not alter previous retrenchment measures implemented by the right-wing governments of Balladur and Juppé (see Chapter 2).

Advocating a style of logic based on the public endorsement of Nixon's visit to China, Ross argues that left-wing parties are more likely to be trus-ted with welfare reforms since they have been associated with the promotion of social programmes. Voters are less likely to believe reforms are required if they originate from right-wing parties; they are not usually considered to be supportive of extensive social programmes regardless of the state of public finance. Thus, voters are more likely to believe that the welfare state needs to be reformed if the message comes from a left-wing party. A foremost reason for this argument is the long-lasting relationship between parties and issues 'leading voters to develop deep-seated, partisan-issue associations' (Ross 2000b: 163).[4] Thus, the degree of political risk associated with welfare reform varies between the Right and the Left, with the former more vul-nerable than the latter, thus emphasizing the importance of the source's credibility. In the case of pensions, Hinrichs supports this thesis when he claims that vast efforts to reform pensions were undertaken by political parties, and that these efforts helped rather than hindered their electoral fortunes: 'Retrenchments are not punished by voters if their identity is based on a reputation for pursuing foresighted, purposeful policies, which they try to utilize for increasing their appeal to the electorate' (Hinrichs 2000: 371). His concluding logic with respect to this point echoes Pierson's, however, since Hinrichs advocates a long-term perspective to diffuse immediate costs and depoliticize the implementation process while stressing the lack of transparency as an element helping the instauration of large-scale pension reforms.

Of course, political parties are influenced by factors other than ideology, such as seeking opportunities to seize or secure power (Mayhew 1974). Some courses of action are 'vote grabbers' and can thus be adopted by political parties despite their deviation from traditional ideological representations. A clear example would be Clinton's 'ending welfare as we know it' initiative, something that would be expected from the Republican Party, not from the Democrats. Given that it is thereby possible for retrenchments to be vote winners, parties can sometimes seek to introduce retrenchment measures because they expect electoral benefits.[5]

The impact of ideology has been deliberately omitted from this study because interviews conducted in the countries examined revealed a consensus among political elites about reforming pension systems. Differences persist between the mainstream right- and left-wing parties, with right-wing parties being more inclined to favour a larger role for the private sector. Even if one acknowledges these differences, it still does not help us explain why certain right-wing parties are more successful than others in their reform endeavours. For example, the British Conservatives have had more 'successes' than their French counterparts.

What is a pension reform?

Prior to developing the theoretical framework that informs the remainder of this study, we must define pension reform. Public pensions are very complex systems influenced by a multitude of factors, many of which are not directly related to pension plans (e.g. fertility rates, labour-force participation, growth and immigration). As demonstrated by the numerous projections made for the four countries, the alteration of these parameters can yield very different results. However, the central difficulty in assessing pension reform remains the fact that its effects are far from immediate. Most measures are implemented over a long period of time, with new rules targeted at younger generations. For example, the Swedish pension reform involved a 20-year transition period. Thus, it can take 30 to 40 years before the full impact of a reform can be assessed. Moreover, due to the degree of variation in all the factors affecting pension systems across Europe, it is extremely difficult to generate systematic comparisons. The figures obtained by the European Union represent an amalgamation of various econometric models where each 'external' variable (growth, unemployment, immigration, etc.) was agreed upon and then directly applied to each national model.

These difficulties should not prevent us from attempting to rank or classify pension reforms, yet few frameworks have been proposed to deal with this issue. Two pieces are particularly useful. First, Pierson notes three factors that any such framework must include: spending, programme structure and systemic retrenchment. Retrenchment implies changes that significantly affect the outcome of reforms, despite being only indirectly related to the programme; for example: constraining the sources of revenues, lessening popular attachment to a programme, altering the institutional structure of a programme and weakening pro-welfare groups (Pierson 1994: 14–17). Second, Bonoli's 2000 work *The Politics of Pensions Reform* compares and analyses pension reforms in the United Kingdom, France and Switzerland. However, the four pension reforms covered in his book are never actually ranked, and pension reform is not really defined.[6] Nonetheless, his conclusion provides an important element to consider: the difference between reforms that seek only a reduction in expenditure and reforms that seek to alter the political players and policies resulting from a particular programme change.[7] For example, he argues that the 1986 reform in the United Kingdom created a new breed of private pension holders who are likely politically to oppose changes related to capital gains (Bonoli 2000: 167).

This research seeks to build on the strength of these past works and improve the indicators used to study pension reforms by focusing on three broad aspects. First, the financial impact of a reform is scrutinized from two different vantage points: the expected reduction of governmental expenditure and the expected costs to groups of individuals. Regardless of the fact that spending does not tell us a great deal about social programmes (Esping-Andersen 1990), it is the deep-seated concern regarding the projected financial effect that current pension plans will have on the public purse, or budget, that convinces politicians that reforms are necessary. Despite a variety of changes enacted with respect to taxation and benefits levels, all four countries studied required still more changes in order to avoid even larger increases in public expenditures because of reduced economic growth combined with increased numbers of workers eligible to receive pension benefits. Thus, a chief goal of pension reform is to reduce or limit future pension expenses. Another interesting way to study the effect of a pension reform is to analyse its impact on groups of individuals. This is very interesting for political scientists, since it tells us who shoulders the burden of these reforms.

The programme structure is then analysed, and an important distinction is made between *parametric* versus *programmatic* reforms. A parametric reform occurs when a government alters only certain parameters of a specific programme without challenging or changing its basic principles. For example, an increase in the length of the required contribution period does not change the plan's overarching purpose or philosophy, or the basics of how the plan operates. A programmatic reform, on the other hand, entails a significant departure from an existing system. In such instances, all parameters are likely to be changed, and new principles are likely to be added. The difference between the two types of reform can be compared to the distinction between buying a whole new house and fixing the roof of the existing structure. A programmatic reform is more encompassing and seeks to resolve the changing demographic and labour-market realities with one major overhaul of the pension system. It is therefore far more extensive than a parametric reform.

Finally, the political implications of the reform are studied; for example, it is very important to understand how a specific reform affects the relationship between the social partners and the state. Do social partners gain new powers in exchange for their co-operation? What benefits are the social partners able to obtain, and which are excluded? Is the government seeking to marginalize them by reducing their institutional role? Does the reform introduce new divisions among future groups of pensioners? Answers to these questions have significant implications for the way pensions will be reformed in the future and are thus important considerations.

Towards a new theoretical focus: administrative structure and electoral systems

Bringing institutions in line with the state

By stressing that the 'new' politics of welfare was sharply different from theories related to the development of the welfare state, the historical features of the welfare state were put aside. Not only does this framework neglect the political aspects (Ross 2000b), but nothing is said about the nature of the state or about the historical relationships among its political actors. The generally strong reliance on the *Three Worlds of Welfare Capitalism* (Esping-Andersen 1990) and numerous other typologies emerging in the 1990s (for a review, see Abrahamson 1999) as the basis for comparison of retrenchment measures tends to further undermine the importance of the state and its relationship with political actors (politicians, unions and employers) in studies of welfare retrenchment. The result of this concentration of research resources is a high number of studies comparing 'similar' cases within the Bismarckian family without giving any real consideration to the nature of the state. Thus, France is judged as being similar to Italy, Belgium, the Netherlands, Germany and Spain because they belong to the corporatist welfare regime. The policy structure may be similar, resulting in a somewhat similar set of available policy options, but it is an unjustified leap of faith to assume that the political constellation is also similar. Belgium and France may have the same style of welfare state and pension system, but they originated from very diverse conditions, and the extant political relationships that accompanied their development are vastly different. In France, unions and employers first built friendly societies to keep social affairs separate from the state. When the French state began to institutionalize the fragmented social security system after World War II, 'the distrust of the state meant that major groups successfully insisted that they have legally defined roles in the new structures' (Ashford 1986: 298). While similar action was taken in Belgium, it was for a very different reason: the state was too weak to assume this responsibility (see Chapters 2 and 3).

Hinrichs (2000) also criticizes the use of Esping-Andersen's typology when analysing pension reforms, but he does it on the grounds that it fails to take timing into consideration as an important variable for the creation of pension systems. He stresses that the latecomers (Netherlands, Australia, Denmark, Switzerland and the United Kingdom) have all established a strong private component within their pension systems even though they come from three different welfare regimes (liberal, corporatist and social democratic). The generally heavy reliance on the private sector makes the reduction of public benefits more acceptable because citizens expect less from the public pension programme (Hinrichs 2000; Myles and Pierson 2001).

The point of departure for the following analysis is underlined in a comparative study of employment policies in the United States and the United Kingdom (King 1995). As emphasized in recent studies, early policy decisions limit the future options available to policy-makers, thereby rendering them path dependent (Pierson 2000). Path dependency does not only have an impact on policies and the options for reform; it also locks in political relationships. 'The compromises and interests influencing institutional arrangements do not necessarily evaporate or dissipate over time. Institutionalists are in danger of neglecting the politics and history of institutions' (King 1995: 212). Even though there are some valid reasons to justify a theoretical break between theories of welfare expansion and retrenchment, the interactions among the political actors involved in these activities remain embedded in the same institutional structure. Moreover, these interactions follow the same logic of appropriateness (March and Olsen 1989), meaning that the maturation of institutional structures involved the development of a set of informal rules of engagement and participation within the policy process that are difficult to alter. If social policy-making involves unions and employers, we should not expect this to change just because benefits are being retrenched as opposed to being improved. This study delineates the fact that both organizational structures *and* relationships among political actors are also path dependent. The establishment of welfare institutions brought with them an institutionalization of relationships between the state (represented by civil servants and politicians) and social partners (represented by unions and employers). Any alteration to welfare programmes thus required the participation of social partners to the same extent to which they have always been historically involved with the policy area in question.

The distinction between veto points (see Immergut 1992; Huber *et al.* 1993; Bonoli 2000, 2001) and veto players (Tsebelis 1999, 2002) is an important feature of the forthcoming analysis. Veto points have been used largely to describe the institutionalization of specific groups within the policy process and/or specific institutional features, which can then be effectively used by opposing groups to prohibit political executives from unilaterally enacting policy projects. Immergut clearly demonstrates that it is not the preferences of the medical profession that have shaped health policy, but the political processes within which policy preferences are channelled (Immergut 1992). Constitutions that outline how legislation must be adopted or changed are an important generator of veto points (see Huber *et al.* 1993). For example, bicameralism, referendums and split executives all imply that executives must receive the support of at least one other institution prior to making policy changes. The higher the number of possible veto points, the more difficult it is to reform the pension system (see Bonoli 2000: 43–9; 2001).

Informal structures or relationships, although more amenable to change, can also amount to a veto point following the logic of appropriateness described on p. 9. In many countries, social partners have been granted a managerial role in the day-to-day operation of the pension system, a role which co-exists outside the state. Collectively, social partners can exercise a veto point. The use of the word 'collective' implies that a substantial number of social partners must be opposed to a governmental proposal for the veto to work. Alternatively, in the absence of a broad consensus, employers or unions must be united in their opposition to a proposal for the veto to be effective. This is the case in Belgium and France, while Sweden and the United Kingdom represent the opposite; public pension programmes there are clearly managed and operated by the state, and the social partners were not granted much of a role. This distinction represents the first ordering principle (see pp. 23–30).

Embedded within the rational-choice version of neo-institutionalism, 'veto players' refers to actors operating within formal institutional rules. In this case, a veto player is an individual or collective actor whose support is necessary to achieve the legislative votes necessary for a measure to be adopted (Tsebelis 2002: 2). Although Tsebelis distinguishes between *institutional* veto players that arise from institutions like bicameral parliaments and divided governments, and *partisan* veto players that originate from within the electoral system, I prefer to employ the latter concept. The second chamber of Parliament that is present in Belgium, France and the United Kingdom is simply not powerful enough to generate a veto. The main argument Tsebelis (1999) advances is that the higher the number of veto players and the greater the significance of ideological distances, the less likely it is that policies will be altered. This element represents the second ordering principle (see pp. 30–2).

The distinction between veto players and veto points influenced the selection of countries compared in this study. Each example represents a combination of veto players and veto points (one has veto players and veto points; one has veto players but no veto points; one has veto points but no veto players; and, finally, one has neither veto players nor veto points). One of the main arguments advanced here is that veto points trump veto players, meaning that veto points are more difficult to circumvent than are veto players. Inspired by Birnbaum (1988), who accurately stresses the importance of the relationship between social partners and the state, this study emphasizes the integration of social partners within pension policy-making. No interest group can really decide to suddenly integrate itself within the state by simply calculating the costs and benefits it may obtain from such action. The forms of integration that have been adopted are the result of long conflicts among political actors, some of which date back to the formation of the state. Thus, the introduction of one form of co-ordination over another may not be harmonious. For example, the non-cooperation of the social partners with the state in France is the result of a long history of the *État dirigiste*, where state building involved an extensive centralization of powers (Rokkan 1999). As noted on pp. 19–20, the state sought to integrate the social partners according to its own set of rules and did not seek to co-operate with them. 'The working class has always been excluded from the state; it always had to act con-flictively' (Birnbaum 1988: 123). Thus, French interest groups sought to maintain social policies away from the state's influence because they feared a loss of control from that interaction. As a result, most strikes are very political, and unions seek to protect themselves via the introduc-tion of laws rather than through negotiation (Birnbaum 1988: 124). This is the foremost reason unions sought to build social insurance '*outside the state*' (Ashford 1986). It is worth pointing out that the institutiona-lization of unions in France has not diminished their propensity for mobilization.

Sweden represents a totally different situation. The central reason unions did not oppose the integration of unions with the state was because their power was '*lagom*', a Swedish term meaning 'just about right' (Rothstein 1991). The unions were not threatened by the state. On the contrary, unions and social activists sought to introduce their policy choices in conjunction with the state, given that they felt they could effectively control the bureaucracy in a policy sector they deemed essential (Lindqvist 1990; Rothstein 1996). Therefore, there were no objections to the institutionaliza-tion of social programmes with the state in Sweden. On the contrary, unions continued to insist on granting the state even more responsibilities. The ATP struggle is a clear illustration of this strategy. The main union con-federation, the LO, did not consider shared management with employers but rather sought (and obtained) a pension programme in co-operation with the state (see Chapter 4). The contrast between Sweden and France is even more noticeable when the evolution of the civil service is considered. While union members and social activists enthusiastically joined the civil service in order to help shape social policy in Sweden, France's social ministries were being staffed by *énarques*[8] who received the lowest exam results and who marked social affairs as their last position of choice (see Jobert 1981).

Belgium represents another form of institutionalization. The state was not perceived as a threat, and it 'could not permit itself social and political conflict to the breaking point' (Rokkan 1999: 336) owing to its fragile international situation and its dependence on international commerce. The state was also weakened from within because the bourgeoisie, dominated by French merchants, sought only a minimal state. The presence of multiple cleavages provided another significant obstacle to the extension of state power. Unions were thus in a good position to further their interests. With union membership rising because of the Ghent system, unions did not want an interventionist state, and the state could not, and did not, try to alter this choice (a position which sets Belgium apart from France). The Belgian pension system followed similar lines and was thus based on a compromise reached by the social partners during World War II, confining its management to social partners. Albeit for reasons very different from France, social partners in Belgium have also built social insurance independently of the state (see Chapter 3).

Britain represents a difficult case to categorize. The state has never been considered strong; rather, it reflected a *laissez-faire* philosophy. A Bismarckian-styled pension solution was originally rejected because state intervention was such an alien concept (Ogus 1982). For the most part, unions and employers attempted to resolve their conflicts among themselves, and unions sought to increase their representation via the parliamentary process (Birnbaum 1988: 121). The main union confederation, the Trades Union Congress (TUC), tried to obtain more power via the state, but the British Labour Party was never as successful as its Swedish counterpart. The predominance of the Conservatives, who entrenched their choice of pension system following a lengthy back-and-forth struggle with the Labour Party (Fawcett 1995), combined with the lack of will on the part of employers and unions to co-manage pension provisions, resulted in public pensions falling within the exclusive purview of the state.

First ordering principle: Parliamentary Integration vs Social Partnership

Social Partnership

Based on the previous discussion and analysis of our four cases, we could classify social insurance programmes resulting from *the way social conflicts were institutionalized* into two relational structures: Parliamentary Integration and Social Partnership. This distinction represents our first ordering principle. Found in both Belgium and France, albeit for different reasons, Social Partnership indicates that social partners are highly involved in the administration of pensions, resulting in a collective veto point. This is usually the case in 'Bismarckian' countries,[9] where benefits are granted mostly on the basis of occupational status, but also in the case of unemployment and disability insurance in Scandinavian countries. In this case, the state attenuated social conflict by including social partners in affairs related to public pensions, such as management. This institution is legitimized by the predominant reliance on contributions, rather than general revenues from the state, to finance pension benefits. Thus, pensions can be viewed as a salary because of the contributions made by the employers to the employee for this purpose (Friot 1998). Public employees are the exception to this rule, as their social security is financed mainly by the state via the Ministry of Finance. Public servants have been able to secure their future with the inclusion of a generous pension within their job description. This results in the maintenance of their civil servant status even beyond the age of retirement.

This structure gives social partners a formal role in the pension policy process,[10] resulting in a genuine veto point (Immergut 1992). It is in this context that Béland (2001) claims that French unions have an 'ideological' veto point because of their managerial role and property claims over pension policies. As a result, governments are very likely to consult social partners *a priori* before tabling a reform proposal. A reform proposal is unlikely to become public unless it is supported by the social partners. As demonstrated by the numerous committees in both France and Belgium, social partners play an important role in the development of pension reforms that are politically acceptable, and they cannot really be excluded from the process (see Chapters 2 and 3). These institutional features are quite difficult to alter or bypass. For example, France's Juppé government in late 1995 unilaterally enacted a decree to force change. Because he sought to alter a previous social arrangement without first consulting the social partners, Juppé was forced to retract his attempt to reform pensions for public employees due to the massive protest movement they organized and which paralysed France in December of that year.

In countries with a Social Partnership, the government's financial and supervisory roles in social programmes tend to be limited. As demonstrated in Table 1.1, the financial burden of social programmes is clearly assumed by the social partners. In most 'Bismarckian' countries, social partners contribute twice as much as states to pensions. When asked why social partners had so much influence over pension plans, the vast majority of union and employer representatives answered simply, 'because we pay for it'. The state legislates in concert with social partners, and its role has traditionally been confined to supervision. In France, for example, the financial aspects of social security are found in *le jaune*[11] and are entitled *l'éffort social de la nation*. They are a non-budget item, indicative of the independence of social security from the state. This is a common situation for many continental countries (von Hagen 1992; Hallerberg 2004). In France, however, prior to 1996 Parliament was only informed *post priori* of social

security's financial situation and could not comment on the budgets administered by the social partners (Mekhantar 1996: 37–8).[12]

Social partnership thus consists of an extensive dialogue between trade
unions, employers' associations and the government,[13] and the government
still needs a majority in Parliament to enact reform. Any reform proposals
must also include the social partners, who have a collective veto point
because of the legitimacy gained via their high contribution levels and their
management of pension schemes or because pensions form part of their
employment agreements.

Reform difficulties are accentuated by the fragmentation of these schemes
into three broad occupational statuses: private-sector workers, civil servants
and the self-employed. Since these pension plans have different rules and
benefits, a reform that may be considered fair for one group may not meet
the needs of another, thus causing resentment. As well, some groups tend to
be more vulnerable than others. This results in targeted reforms where certain
aspects of pension plans are revised and others remain unchanged. For example, the public pension plan for public-sector employees was not reformed in
continental countries where the lack of financial involvement was compensated for by the following: a strong unionization of the workforce, the conception of deferred wages and a lower cost associated with strikes.[14]

One of the principal contentions of this study is that veto points are more
difficult to overcome than veto players. Social Partnership leads to an institutionalized relationship structure where unions are virtually locked into the
policy process and where the union's behaviour is distinctly different than

Table 1.1 Comparative figures by country for employers' and employees' contributions
in the financing of public pensions relative to the government: aggregate
figures (average 1990–7)

Country	Employers' and employees' contributions/state contributions
France	3.82
Netherlands	3.27
Belgium	2.97
Spain	2.46
Germany	2.44
Italy	2.18
Greece	1.97
Austria	1.77
Portugal	1.30
Luxembourg	1.18
Finland	1.08
Sweden	0.88
United Kingdom	0.85
Ireland	0.61
Denmark	0.24

Source: Eurostat 1999, author calculations.

that of the political party whose support is necessary to adopt legislation. Without going into all the possible implications of integrated participation in the governance of public pensions, unions employ a very different cost/benefit calculation than do political parties. Compared to politicians, they have very specific clients, and they do not face elections (or, more importantly, re-elections). Their purpose is to protect the *droits acquis* (earned rights) of their members, and the impact of this protection on elections ranks very low on the membership's scale of concerns. Unions represent, therefore, a genuine veto point. In the Social Partnership model it is nearly impossible for the government to ignore them as a group.

This particular institutional constellation can impel the government to adopt what Bonoli calls a *quid pro quo* strategy. It seeks to gather union support (or their silence) by granting them specific requests (Bonoli 2000: 49). Thus, logrolling may be employed to gain the acceptance of the unions. As unions tend to be established and conservative institutions, they will even be less inclined to enter into negotiations involving a lot of risk, preferring to exploit 'acquired advantages and the profits accruing from the status quo than [to adjust] to new circumstances [and grasp] new opportunities or [innovate]' (Olsen 1983: 159).

Finally, it is worth stressing that the role of employers in opposing reforms with respect to France, Belgium and other Bismarckian countries has been somewhat limited for two main reasons. First, employers are more likely to lead the groups opposing reforms if they believe those revisions will result in increased labour costs, which is an unlikely scenario in continental countries where labour costs are already substantial (which is not really a problem in the UK). Countries relying heavily on contributions have had a very difficult time reducing their unemployment levels. Thus, raising contribution rates results in higher labour costs and accentuates labour-market rigidities that are arguably responsible for high unemployment rates. Second, employers share with government the aim of reducing the size of their long-term fiscal commitments.

Parliamentary Integration

In the case of Parliamentary Integration, unions sought influence over, or control of, pension programmes by capturing office and/or the state bureaucracy, as opposed to distancing themselves from the state. In effect, they join the state, which is the main financial contributor to (see Table 1.1), and manager of, social programmes. The Parliamentary Integration model corresponds to countries influenced by 'Beveridge' (such as Canada and the United Kingdom) and/or that have universal programmes (Scandinavian countries). Although this categorization includes both liberal and social democratic welfare regimes (Esping-Andersen 1990), it is worth stressing that the difference between these two lies in the generosity and coverage offered rather than in how programmes are administered.[15]

Sweden represents a case where the unions' influence was expanded successfully within the state (Korpi 1983; Esping-Andersen 1985), while the United Kingdom illustrates an incidence of limited success owing to the Labour Party's electoral difficulties (Fawcett 1995). The prime factor is that unions sought to achieve their policy objectives primarily via their link to the Social Democratic/Labour Party in Parliament. It is important to reiterate that this situation applies specifically to pensions. For example, unemployment insurance has been under the control of unions in Sweden and is organized more in keeping with the Social Partnership model. Therefore, in order to achieve generalizability, one must focus on the two underlying characteristics of the classification: the administration of the policy programmes and the electoral system of the country studied.

In the case of relationships characterized by Parliamentary Integration, governments have a great deal of influence, given that they do not have to achieve broad consensus outside the executive as do countries organized according to a Social Partnership model. They thus include more formalized veto points (see p. 21). This does not imply that actors other than political parties cannot influence and shape the pension debate. However, their access to the policy-making process is constrained by this structure. One example is the lack of involvement as a matter of principle and practice in the formal process of pension reform. For example, Thatcher's reforms were adopted without any consideration of the unions' positions, while Könberg (the former Swedish Minister of Health and Social Insurance) was able to institute a Working Group on Pensions without the formal involvement of unions and employers. Basically, the influence of the social partners is largely filtered through political parties rather than the state.

Unions and employers' associations are therefore more likely to seek support from political parties to advance their agenda. This is best exemplified by the passage of the mandatory supplementary pension (ATP) in Sweden in the late 1950s, which was established as a result of a conflict between a social democratic proposal (put forward and supported by the LO, the most influential trade union), a Centre Party proposal and one emanating from a bourgeoisie coalition (backed by employers' associations). After an intense struggle, the social democratic proposal was adopted (see Chapter 4).

The government's financial contributions are much more substantive when Parliamentary Integration is the norm. As Table 1.1 illustrates, Anglo-Saxon and Scandinavian countries are ranked at the bottom with a ratio of less than 1, meaning that the government contributes more to public pension schemes than both employers and employees combined. This leads to the government and the Parliament having more influence in the budgetary process for public pension schemes. In contrast to the situation prevailing in Bismarckian countries, both of these actors are actively involved in the preparation of the budget for this social item.[16]

Before raising the ire of Swedish political scientists with this categorization of the integration of unions and employers, let me summarize briefly my reasons for it.[17] Olsen clearly links this style of coordination (where interest groups and the state share similar goals) with Scandinavian countries. The principal argument is their strong presence within parliamentary committees and independent agencies (the so-called *verket* or *styrelse*); they have many opportunities to influence the policy process because of their active participation within it. On this basis, Olsen concludes that 'organizations have legitimate and institutionalized rights to participate in all phases of governmental policy making as representatives of specific interests' (Olsen 1983: 166).

This situation has been modified significantly over the past 15 years. The participation of unions and employers was appreciably reduced within both parliamentary committees and independent agencies (Hermansson *et al.* 1997). Their scattered presence entailed a loss of legitimacy as employers withdrew from the boards of independent agencies in the early 1990s. Thus, they now tend to focus more on labour-market issues. In contrast to both disability and unemployment insurance, pensions fall closer to being a state responsibility because the ATP reform assigned them to the state. Like the new pension system, the ATP pension system was administered by a state agency and was independent from social partners. This is evident in the lack of formal participation within the pension reform process versus the continuous presence of both unions and employers within the realm of sickness and unemployment insurance. Könberg, who was the Swedish Minister of Health and Social Insurance at the time, attempted to create another small group of politicians that excluded unions and employers (similar to the Working Group on Pensions) in order to reform sickness insurance, but he failed as a result of their strong objections. In the early 1990s, the composition of bureaucrats within the Ministry of Social Affairs also changed with the arrival of new recruits who came from a more diverse background and from other ministries like finance (Marier 2005; ch. 4).

The first ordering principle, the structural distinction between Parliamentary Integration and Social Partnership, allows us to introduce the first major hypothesis tested by this study:

Hypothesis 1: Parliamentary Integration structures are more conducive to programmatic pension reforms than Social Partnership structures, because the latter have more built-in veto points.

Ensuring a majority in Parliament is the foremost factor required to enact successful reforms within a Parliamentary Integration structure. Social partners may be involved, but their support is not as crucial as it is in countries with a Social Partnership model, because their influence is filtered through the political parties. In order to maximize preferences for reforms that are not too punitive for its members, unions depend on the strength of the party they are associated with. Therefore, we can expect *programmatic* changes in pensions with the Parliamentary Integration structure. A programmatic reform encompasses any significant change in a programme that results in a different structure. These changes may include items like new sets of rules, benefits and coverage styles and periods once a pension plan is fully implemented.

Pension reforms within a Social Partnership structure are more conducive to *parametric* reforms (or 'tweaking') since it is extremely difficult to arrive at a consensus to introduce a major pension reform when social partners have an institutionalized veto point. Tweaking implies that a government seeks only to alter the parameters of an existing scheme, items such as the contribution period, the pension's indexation or other rules within the scheme. The philosophy and the basic organizational structure of the system are not threatened by the changes. This argument is supported by Bonoli's analysis of pension reforms in France, the United Kingdom and Switzerland, wherein he states that only non-concerted efforts successfully affected the politics of the pension system, while concerted efforts 'did not significantly alter the political equilibria' (Bonoli 2000: 168).

This hypothesis also contributes to the 'veto debate'. Rational-choice theorists are proponents of a rigid conception of political parties as veto players (Tsebelis 2002) within parliaments. Empirical institutionalists (see Peters 1999) advocate the use of veto points that focus on the formalized relationships between the government and outside interest groups. The government must be able to pass this hurdle in order to implement a policy (Immergut 1992). Hypothesis 1 clearly endorses the latter.

Because four countries are compared here, two other related hypotheses can be tested, thus improving our understanding of the formalized relationship (or lack thereof) between government and social partners:

Hypothesis 1a: Reforms are most likely to occur when unions have historically had a co-operative relationship with the state (e.g. Belgium) compared to a confrontational one (e.g. France).

This hypothesis refers to two formalized relationships (Social Partnership). Even though both France and Belgium have very similar pension institutions, the relationship between the social partners and the state differs significantly. Consistent with recent work on pension reform, consensual approaches (including social partners) have proven the most effective (see, for example, Reynaud 1998). Thus, given the animosity and multiple confrontations between the state and the social partners in France (see pp. 44–7), Belgium is expected to fare better owing to its more harmonious relations with social partners.

Hypothesis 1b: Assuming that Rothstein (1996) is correct about unions controlling the state with respect to issues that unions consider salient such as pensions, and given the social democratic predilection in Sweden, then the state's expertise is more likely to be accepted and trusted by unions in Sweden than it is in France, where the state has a confrontational relationship with unions.

This hypothesis also speaks to the relationship between the state and the social actors, thereby testing Rothstein's (1996) work on the subject. Social Democrats needed to control the state bureaucracy to advance their ideological pension plan goals. With clear goals and objectives for active labour-market policies, unions successfully recruited sympathizers with the support of the Sveriges Socialdemokratiska Arbetareparti (SAP), thus prompting the implementation of social democratic measures. However, the SAP was controlled by the state when it came to education policies, as ambiguous goals and objectives were combined with a more traditional Weberian system of recruitment and promotion that was not challenged by the unions.

Swedish pension policies mirror the example of a case with active labour-market policies. The main union confederation (LO) was a strong advocate of earnings-related pensions (ATP). These were obtained only after a long political battle and represent the golden trophy of Sweden's Social Democrats (Pontusson 1993). Those involved with the implementation of this policy were sympathetic to its goals and remained committed to the programme when pension reform first appeared on the political agenda (Marier 2005). France represents a direct contrast, given its highly independent, centralized and elitist bureaucracy. The control of the state by social democratic interests ought to be considered a near impossibility. As a result, Swedish unions are more likely to argue and engage with a sympathetic bureaucracy comprised of individuals devoted to a programme they support than French unions are to accept the expertise of its public bureaucracy and engage in fruitful discussions.

Second ordering principle: proportional vs majoritarian visions

Electoral systems tend to produce different styles of government and add to the complexity of reforming pension schemes. It is actually more appropriate to refer to majoritarian and proportional-influential visions owing to the broader implications generated by the electoral rules. As Powell Jr stated:

> In the majoritarian vision citizens use elections to choose decisively between two competing teams of policy-makers, providing the winner with the concentrated power to make public policy, allowing the loser only to continue to challenge in future elections. In the proportional influence vision, citizens use elections to choose political agents to represent their diverse views continuously in post-election bargaining

that will influence policy-making. The predominant constitutional arrangements in these countries can be interpreted as designs intended to realize these visions.

(Powell 2000: 233)

As a result of extremely divergent groups, many states (especially in what Rokkan (1999) calls the *city belt*)[18] adopted the proportional-influence vision to ensure the inclusion of the various cleavages present within a society. This vision tended to freeze cleavages and generated 'consensual' democracies. Belgium is a typical example of a consensual democracy (Lijphart 1984), while Sweden, though it has experienced few coalition governments, has had many minority governments led by the Social Democrats. In order to enact most policies, the executive has had to rely on the support of at least one other political party. Contrasting the proportional system is the majoritarian system with first-past-the-post elections. A majoritarian vision provides a winner-take-all status for the winning political party and results in a strong concentration of power. The United Kingdom is the example *par excellence* of this system. France is included in this category for two reasons. First, the powers of the president are not substantial during cohabitation, at least when it comes to pensions, and mirror those of a prime minister when the same coalition controls both the presidency and the Parliament. Second, the governing coalitions do not change; the right-wing parties (Union pour la Démocratie Française, UDR; and Rassemblement pour la République, RPR) never co-operate with the left (Parti Socialiste, PS; and Parti Communiste Francais, PCF), and vice versa. It is argued here that the majoritarian/proportional distinction is very important when introducing policy reforms.[19]

On the one hand, a proportional vision results in a high number of actors conducting government business, thus increasing the number of players with veto power. Any reforms must be negotiated among the coalition partners, or, in the case of a minority government, with other parties in Parliament. This kind of government makes significant change extremely difficult to achieve and tends to favour the status quo because of the number of actors with influence and the polarization of their preferences. On the other hand, single-party governments face fewer hurdles when introducing significant changes since they do not need the support of other political parties and have to answer only to their own party members. Therefore, single-party governments tend to produce more significant laws than do coalition governments (Tsebelis 1999).

If Tsebelis is correct, a systematic bias towards parametric reforms rather than programmatic reforms should result from having a large coalition of political actors. This is why institutions with collective interest representation – social corporatism and inclusive electoral institutions – are more resistant to the neo-liberalization of the economy (Swank 2002). Thus, coalition governments might be stuck in a 'parametric trap'. This is very interesting given that most studies of the retrenchment of the welfare state emphasize the need for a large coalition behind a reform in order to avoid a concentration of blame, which can have negative electoral consequences in the future (Pierson 1994; Bonoli 2000; Green-Pedersen 2001; Schludi 2002). This occurs because the majoritarian vision concentrates responsibilities in the hands of a single party, which is then held accountable during elections for the public policies it implemented (Powell 2000). The result is that governments try to avoid blame when introducing retrenchment measures because it is easy for the electorate to trace those responsible (Pierson 1994).

Based on the previous discussion, two null hypotheses can be presented. They are considered null because the main argument presented is that the interaction between electoral systems and the institutionalized structure of relationships matters most; it is not the number of vetoes present but the nature of these vetoes (see the next section – pp. 32–7).

Null Hypothesis 1: The higher the number of political parties within a government, the less likely it is that a programmatic pension reform will occur.

Null Hypothesis 2: Based on Tsebelis (1999), a broad political coalition that includes ideologically polarized political parties is unlikely to yield a (major) pension reform.

A model of pension reform: types of pension reforms

A more theoretically interesting use of both electoral systems and the structure of relationships between the state and social partners is their amalgamation into one of four separate types that are generated by different combinations and that yield different kinds and 'levels' of pension reforms: committee, cabinet, consensual and social conflict. This "typology of pension reforms" is presented in Table 1.2. Prior to discussing each of these categories in depth, it should be noted that these types are based on the current analysis of four countries. However, the theory's preliminary extrapolation to other countries is promising, as Chapter 6 demonstrates.

Social conflict: a winner-take-all system constrained by social partners (Chapter 2)

The merging of a majoritarian system with Social Partnership is labelled social conflict because there is virtually no threshold for co-operation when these factors are combined. The powers of the executive are highly concentrated, making it prone to a winner-take-all attitude in a highly fragmented society. At the same time, however, the inclusion of social partners within the institutional structure should be more conducive to a social dialogue,

Table 1.2 Types of pension reforms

Democratic visions	Institutionalized structure of relationship	
	Parliamentary Integration *'in the state'*	Social Partnership *'out of the state'*
Proportional influence visions	committee • Sweden	consensual • Belgium
Majoritarian visions	cabinet • United Kingdom	social conflict • France

though this is clearly not the case in France. The antagonistic nature of unions comes from a continuous struggle to remain independent from states seeking to preserve a dominant role in most aspects of the society. Even employers often complain about the interference of the state in their affairs, such as the management of social security. As a result of this context of opposition to the state and the consequent absence of consensus building, France has been labelled a '*société bloquée*' (paralysed society) (Crozier 1970).

With regards to retrenchment, this case is very enlightening because accountability is definitively not an issue here: the executive is strong, visible and highly centralized (Vail 1999). Most constraints actually exist outside the legislative arena. Social partners have an important role within the management of social security, and they are included in any discussions about reforming pension plans. At the very least, they need to be consulted about any proposed changes. Even though they are weaker than is the case in Belgium, they are more likely to mobilize and have a history of striking for political reasons rather than for better working conditions (Birnbaum 1988).

The 'new' politics of welfare literature stresses that this institutional situation is very difficult for reformers, since a government cannot escape blame and can therefore be punished at a subsequent election (Pierson and Weaver 1993; Pierson 1994). However, this argument has a flip side: pension plan reform can be easier because social partners are not able to disturb the policy direction or the kind of reform a government seeks. In contrast to Belgium, unions cannot disrupt multi-party agreements by playing one political party against another. The government is in a stronger bargaining situation since it does not have to consider other parties, and it is well placed to adopt a strategy of 'divide and conquer' compared to the fragmented French unions.

Consensus: easier to achieve in times of expansion (Chapter 3)

The consensual cell originates from Social Partnership combined with a proportional-influence vision. Potential conflicts resulting from the various cleavages are attenuated by coalescent elites and the integration of minorities and social partners within the decision-making structure. Belgium represents the prototype of this cell.

Belgium is considered to be one of the exemplars of consociational democracy (alongside the Netherlands). Not only is it fragmented along class and religious lines, but, unlike its Dutch counterpart, it is also divided along language lines. Reinforcing the power of the elites is the lack of interaction among the three pillars (Catholic, Socialist and Liberal). Belgians simply live in different sociological worlds, even though the importance of those separate worlds has been decreasing over the past decade (see Chapter 3).

With regard to pension reform, an optimal retrenchment strategy in this situation would be the introduction of a grand social agreement. Traceability to a specific political party would be nearly impossible for the voters (Pierson 1994) or the unions (Schludi 2002). In the countdown towards Economic and Monetary Union (EMU), the Belgian coalition government actually sought such a strategy with its 'Plan Global', which aimed to redefine the welfare state as was done in the so-called 'Social Pact' after World War II. But the Plan Global failed because the unions did not co-operate.

As stated earlier, the creation of a broad coalition among the governing parties is simplified by creating binding agreements (usually found within the governmental declaration) and through continuous co-operation. However, these are less likely to be stable in the Belgian case since unions are able to disrupt these agreements. For example, unions can publicly stress the failure of the Socialist Party to address workers' demands, thus ensuring that it maintains a more leftist profile.

Under these conditions, government strategies tend to evolve slowly and steadily on the basis of proposals that seek to avoid hostile reactions from actors involved in the policy process. Proposals are rarely debated in public for fear they could accentuate rather than decrease the differences between the cleavages. A reform proposal is unlikely to be introduced if it is clear that unions are strongly opposed to it. The consensual type is marked by what a cabinet member refers to as '*petits pas*' (small steps). Therefore, this is the case where the least amount of 'reform action' is expected.

Committee: an expert-led democracy (Chapter 4)?

The committee example represents a situation where a coalition of political parties is required to enact a reform, but where the government does not have to deal with unions having an institutionalized role in the management of pensions, as does the Social Partnership structure. Instead, union influence tends to be expressed through the Social Democratic Party. Using Sweden as an example might seem questionable to some, but despite Sweden's proportional representation system the Social Democrats have historically dominated governments. Less well known, however, is that they often had to rely on other parties to maintain a parliamentary majority.

Further, the early 1990s marked a period when Social Democratic support was quite low, and losing the election seemed a genuine possibility. After all, the bourgeois parties were able to hold office for a similar length of time during the period from 1976 to 1994. The support of the Left could also no longer be taken for granted, as was the case for most of the 1980s. In conclusion, a single party cannot push a new pension reform through on its own in Sweden; it needs, at the very least, the support of one other party.

The other contentious issue is the role and influence of unions, both of which have been in constant decline since the end of the 1970s, prompting vigorous debate regarding the end of corporatism in Sweden. Briefly, the argument presented in Chapter 4 stresses that the adoption of the supplementary schemes in the late 1950s confined the managerial responsibility to the state, a position that the LO favoured and promoted. However, when it came time to reform the system in the 1990s, it was difficult for unions to advance the claim that they were deserving of representation because they were not as involved in this programme as they were in health and unemployment insurance. Therefore, politicians were able to create a very small reform committee without including any interest groups. In contrast to most other European countries, parliamentary committees in Sweden exert a great deal of influence in the policy process (Arter 1990). Numerous multiparty agreements originate within the committees. The various pension committees have conducted thorough investigations involving many experts.

Based on the pension reform types presented in Table 1.2, the main stumbling block is reaching an agreement among political parties. Because such negotiations are made among veto players and do not require negotiations with another kind of political actor (due to the absence of additional veto points), it should be easier to generate a substantive pension reform in Sweden than in France. In contrast to Belgium, a negotiated agreement among political parties in a coalition government should be more resistant to change because of the exclusion of unions in the formal proceedings. It is far easier to influence an agreement while it is being designed than it is to revise a final accord.

Cabinet: unlimited powers (Chapter 5)?

The cabinet example consists of a majoritarian vision and parliamentary integration. Here the government faces no veto, as it does not have to negotiate with either social partners or other political parties. This results in a significant concentration of decision-making power. It must still earn the approval of the cabinet and the Parliament, but formal opposition is minimal. The strongest capacity for a pension reform should be this type, represented here by the United Kingdom.

Pierson (1994) challenges this conclusion on the grounds that actions from this kind of government are highly visible and can therefore be readily punished by the electorate. Interestingly, this type represents a situation where the government really has no way to avoid accountability. In contrast to the three other cases, the government cannot blame any other actor for its actions. It is worse than the situation in France because it cannot blame unions for lacking true leadership in managing pensions, for example. It can still create expert commissions, attempt to sell expertise drawn from a think-tank or blame external events or actors such as the European Union, but ultimately the responsibility for reform rests with the government.

These four types of pension reform provide us with another set of hypotheses:

Hypothesis 2: The level of difficulty related to enacting pension reform should be relatively low in the consensual type of reform making, and the cabinet type should entail the most difficulty. The overall reform difficulty ranking should be ordered as follows: cabinet > committee > social conflict > consensual.

Application: Belgium should be the case closest to the status quo, and the most extensive reform(s) should have occurred in the United Kingdom. Overall, the difficulty ranking of the four pension reforms should be ordered as follows: United Kingdom > Sweden > France > Belgium.

Hypothesis 2a: Unions will be better equipped to block drastic reforms when they are institutionalized within a Social Partnership, regardless of union density.

Application: Unions are more likely to have a disruptive role in Belgium than in Sweden, despite a similar level of unionization.

Hypothesis 2b: Regardless of the number of veto players (Tsebelis 1999), it is more difficult to generate pension reform with the social conflict type than with the committee type.

Application: France is expected to have greater difficulty generating reforms than Sweden, even though it has fewer veto players.

Hypothesis 2c: The cabinet type generates more extensive reforms than the social conflict type because the latter faces veto points.

Application: The United Kingdom should be able to generate more extensive reforms than France because it does not have a structured relationship based on Social Partnership.

Hypothesis 2d: The consensual type leads to more reform difficulties than the social conflict type because it has more veto players in a similarly structured relationship (Social Partnership).

Application: Belgium is expected to have more difficulty generating reforms than is France.

Hypothesis 2e: The committee type leads to more reform difficulties than the cabinet type because it has more veto players in a similarly structured relationship (i.e. Parliamentary Integration).

Application: Sweden is expected to experience more difficulty generating reforms than will the United Kingdom.

Methodology and case selection

This section discusses the method chosen for this study and the basis for the selection of the four cases (Belgium, France, the United Kingdom and Sweden). First, with respect to methodology, Scharpf's (1997) discussion of the backward-looking bias evident in policy research is quite enlightening. He criticized King *et al.*'s (1994) decision to search for the effects of specific variables rather than for the causes of specific outcomes. Scharpf (1997) skilfully demonstrates that in policy research the chain of causation must be long enough to also explain why independent variables behave in a certain way. It is not sufficient to argue that the presence of unions compelled country X to act in manner Y; we need to know the mechanism by which the actions of the unions influence the outcome because the presence of unions elsewhere does not necessarily generate a similar result. A qualitative framework helps delineate the steps of the process that lead to the enactment of reforms, an important consideration when attempting to explain this differential outcome as it may be related to union influence.

An in-depth analysis of four countries (each representative of one of the types of pension system noted on pp. 32–6) was carried out, a strategy offering some clear advantages. First, the variance noted is likely to be larger than in a comparative study of two or three countries (or a case study), which tends to be the norm for many qualitative publications. This reduces the possibility of inadvertently choosing countries that operate outside the usual norm. Second, studying four cases allows various comparative combinations, resulting in a clearer picture of the source or cause of any variations noted. This is important because, for example, we can compare the actions taken by single-party governments (France and the United Kingdom) or multi-party coalitions (Sweden and Belgium), even as we also compare single- and multi-party systems. A similar logic can be applied to comparing the actions of Bismarckian countries (France and Belgium), where reforms are considered more problematic, both with each other and also with two other examples of different 'welfare regimes' (Sweden and the United Kingdom) (Esping-Andersen 1990). A total of nine separate comparative combinations is possible.

The four countries analysed here (Belgium, France, Sweden and the United Kingdom) were selected on the basis of both institutional structure and electoral system (see pp. 32–6). Three important considerations were taken into account while selecting the four cases. First, the European Union is often mentioned as a source of pressure to reform national pension systems via the Open Method of Co-ordination (OMC) and the impact of the Euro. Therefore, all four cases selected were members of the European Union, thus effectively removing this cause as an important alternative explanation, even though the empirical evidence suggesting that the OMC affected the outcomes is very weak. Further, there was broad consensus among those interviewed in all four cases that the European Union did not have any affect on the planning and implementation of their pension reforms. Even though Sweden and the United Kingdom are not members of EMU, both governments have attempted throughout the period studied to ensure that membership remained a political rather than an economic decision. Thus, their governments have pursued monetary policies consistent with those of other members of EMU.

Second, the four countries were also chosen because they do not represent exceptional cases for the study of pension reforms. For example, the selection of Ireland would be problematic because of its very high birth rate, which has pushed the consideration of ageing issues much further into the future and thus introduced a new variable. Norway was also dismissed owing to the large financial resources derived from its oil revenues. These more than offset the expected increase in pension benefits; thus, Norway can delay making difficult decisions and is, again, not comparable.

Third, the four cases were also selected on the basis that they complement each other well with respect to both testing the hypotheses presented and rejecting alternative theories. The impact of these decisions becomes obvious in the conclusion. For example, both France and Belgium are considered prototypes of the Bismarckian social insurance system present throughout continental Europe. Ghent is the source of the so-called Ghent system, and Bismarck was inspired by Napoleon III when he created the first social insurance schemes in the late 1800s (Esping-Andersen 1990: 40). If France and Belgium adopt different methods to deal with this pension problem, the decision cannot be attributed to the Bismarckian nature of their systems. Belgium and Sweden are also highly unionized and are both considered highly decommodified (Esping-Andersen 1990). The comparison of the different approaches taken by these two examples eliminates claims that an overly generous government is causative.

In order to trace the steps leading to the decision to reform (or not to reform) public pension schemes in Belgium, France, Sweden and the United Kingdom, three categories of materials were utilized. In all cases, substantial efforts were made to gather evidence that both supported and undermined the hypotheses listed earlier in this chapter (see pp. 28–32; 36, 37). First, all official reports and publications concerning public pensions from each of the four countries were obtained and analysed. Divergent and critical analyses generated by the interest groups involved were also collected, as well as commissioned research and academic articles in various social science journals. In addition to the analyses of pension systems presented, these reports provide interesting data on the individuals involved and the principal actors' policy positions.

Second, for many reasons, in-depth reviews of newspaper articles and editorials about pension reform were conducted in all four countries.[20] In Sweden, newspapers are an important medium for politicians and interest groups to convey and defend their positions; discussion of this topic dominated the debate sections of the papers for lengthy periods. Because the five political parties reached a consensus, there was little parliamentary debate; thus, these newspaper sections outlined the policy preferences and plans in addition to the counter-arguments of the various parties and pension groups. Similar detailed discussions also occurred, albeit far less frequently, in Belgian, French and British dailies.

The search for compromises also resulted in many private negotiations that were described in the newspapers, providing another reason to include them among the documents studied. This is particularly the case for Belgium, France and the United Kingdom. Belgium is known for ensuring that it has the support of substantial groups prior to suggesting or even examining certain policies. Thus, on the basis of interviews and official documents alone, one risks discussing only the successes and overlooking the failed reform attempts. Further, those interviewed tended to minimize the conflict encountered when they reflected on their experience within the policy-setting process (with the exception of those not involved, such as opposition parties and interest groups who were dissatisfied with the final reforms). Newspaper accounts allow a broader discussion of the reform process and provide important additional information that differs from the interpretations supplied by the individuals interviewed.

Third, with the aim of testing the hypotheses presented, in-depth face-to-face interviews with the major players involved in the pension reform process were conducted in all four countries. The individuals were selected on the basis of the documents gathered, newspaper contributions and referrals from other informants. Various ministers and their political advisors, Members of Parliament, union members, employers, representatives of the elderly and senior civil servants in the relevant departments (social affairs, pensions, finance, the Prime Minister's Office, pension agencies and the central bank) were also interviewed during the course of this research. Similar informants were chosen in all four countries to ensure balanced representation and equitable treatment of the hypotheses tested. The focus on unions and employers, for example, was as strong in the United Kingdom, where they are not expected to play a large role, as in Belgium. In each of the four cases, dissident voices were also interviewed, even when their role in the reform process was minimal and sometimes even non-existent. For example, the representative of the Left Party in Sweden was interviewed even though she opposed the compromise crafted by the five political parties and as a result did not really contribute to developing the new pension scheme (see Chapter 4). These individuals provided a wealth of divergent information that was very useful with respect to capturing the overall political processes.

The interviews were semi-structured and included 15 to 20 questions. The introductory questions were exactly the same in all four sets of interviews. Each informant was asked to describe their role within the pension reform process, the reason they were chosen to represent their faction (whether it be a political party, interest group, department, etc.), the agenda promulgated by that faction, their relationship with the other groups, any major stumbling blocks encountered and the resources and expertise they employed during the process. In order to account for any noticeable differences in the enactment of the institutional and political contexts of the reforms, some questions were altered so as to strengthen their reliability. In addition to the standardized questions asked of each informant, there were additional questions that were specific to each country. For example, French informants were questioned about whether those involved in the 1993 reform process also participated in the 1995 reform attempt.

It should also be noted in this discussion of methodology that the researcher is fluent in English, French and Swedish, a factor that strengthens the study's reliability by enabling the subtleties present in the language of origin and in the reform process to be captured.[21]

2 France

Still a 'société bloquée'?

Introduction

This chapter discusses the institutionalization of pensions and its impact on pension reform in France. The management of public pensions today is quite similar to the way it was designed at the end of World War II. Social partners were very much involved in the development of pension policies and played a central role in their implementation. This involvement, however, did not happen overnight, but was the result of a long series of conflicts and policy failures that led the state and social partners to co-operate to establish the foundation of a viable pension policy, in terms of both generosity and how it would be financed. Fifty years later, this trend is changing as the state plays a stronger, but challenged role.

The French pension system is fragmented along socio-occupational lines and includes numerous schemes (see Table 2.1). Despite this plethora of schemes, there is a convergence towards the rules and benefits granted by the largest pension scheme for private-sector workers (*régime général*), a plan that operates on an insurance basis that ties, albeit loosely, benefits to contributions. Civil servants also have various schemes, often referred to as *régimes spéciaux*, where retirement is perceived as a continuation of working life. Most civil servants are enrolled in the *régime des fonctionnaires*. They are itemized as such in the state budget and are granted benefits based on the civil servant's professional status and length of service prior to retirement, even though some contributions are made.

France introduced two main reforms affecting both types of schemes during the period studied. Balladur reformed the private-sector scheme in 1993, while the Rafarrin government introduced something similar for the *régime des fonctionnaires* in 2003. Juppé made an unsuccessful attempt in 1995 to reform the latter. In light of Chapter 1, pension reforms are analysed by examining the institutionalization of this policy area and the presence of majoritarian governments. The current chapter first outlines the type of management systems extant in France, before analysing the role of each actor within those systems during both successful and failed reform attempts.

Table 2.1 Overview of the French pension system[1]

Wage earners	Basic régime	Mandatory supplementary régime[2]
Private-sector workers	Régime général – general scheme (divided into various schemes: CNAV, CRAM, CRAV, CGSS)	One or a combination of the following: ARRCO, ARRCO AGIRC, Ircantec, CNRCC (CCI), CREPA, CRPCCMPA, CRPNPAC
Civil servants and workers from government organizations	Special regimes for civil servants	
Agricultural workers	MSA	One of a combination of ARRCO, AGIRC and non-mandatory schemes (for farm-owners/workers)
Artists	CANCAVA	
Trade and industry	Organic	Non-mandatory schemes
Liberal professions	CNAPVL CNBF (lawyers)	

Source: Adapted from ARRCO (found at the CNAV web site: http://www.cnav.fr, site accessed 17 October 2001).

Notes:
[1] A means-tested pension is also available for those earning below a specific amount.
[2] The benefits and contributions are set and managed exclusively by social partners, but they are mandated to be so legislatively.

Theorizing pension reform within the French context

The importance of the state in France

In discussing the concept of policy style, Richardson *et al.* summarize the system in France as being 'characterized by secrecy, limited consultation, immobilization, and stagnation most of the time, and an assertive government and abrupt and radical change some of the time' (Richardson *et al.* 1982: 1). Affecting this process is a powerful state considered strong enough to overrule interest groups in pursuit of its national interest (Krasner 1976; Wilson 1987). As Merrien emphasizes, interest groups like unions are only admitted into the policy-making process to the extent that they fit into the state's plan, in which case they become a representative segment of the national interest. The state decides which members are representative, and it has actively sought to defend its interests against private ones (Merrien 1991: 283).

Pension politics do not escape this strong centralization of power for many reasons. First, numerous elements related to public pensions can only be changed by an executive decree signed by the prime minister and endorsed by the president. These powers are established in the Constitution of the Fifth Republic as a means to reduce the legislatures' power. Second, public pensions are politically very sensitive matters. In the early 1990s, then prime minister Michel Rocard stated that attempting to reform public pensions could lead to the resignation of any government, and he opted to centralize this policy area at Matignon. The failure of core pension elements in the Juppé plan in 1995 accentuated the centralization of pension policy-making. Finally, many analyses related to pension reform were performed by the Commissariat Général au Plan (CGP), an institution in charge of French planning that was overseen by the prime minister. Prior to its elimination in 2006, the CGP played a leading role in gathering expertise on the public pension system.

The influence of the Minister of Social Affairs, the minister officially responsible for pensions, is not considered substantial. A minister must first obtain permission from Matignon prior to any discussion with the social partners; these social partners are then required to inform Matignon that the discussion has taken place. Thus, the role of any individual minister (and even the ministry itself) is extremely constrained (Quermonne 1991: 44).

France has often been referred to as a semi-presidential or semi-parliamentary system (Duverger 1980), owing to its mixture of parliamentary and presidential features; France has a split executive with both a prime minister and a president. When both come from the same party or a similar coalition the latter exercises a dominant role. On the other hand, when they come from different parties or coalitions the prime minister governs domestically, while the president's influence is confined largely to foreign issues. This formal distinction plays an important role for anyone studying 'grey areas', such as the EU, because it is difficult to define them as strictly a domestic or an external issue. The president can play a substantial informal role criticizing the actions of the government in many areas, but this requires a policy to have been either strongly associated with the presidency and/or extremely unpopular. The public pension system is very much considered a domestic issue; thus, the president has not had much impact in this debate. For example, in the last such period, Chirac was unable to do much more than criticize the socialist government's lack of progress. Mitterrand was silent when Balladur introduced the 1993 reforms. Nonetheless, a co-governing administration can impact the debate in instances where the prime minister is seeking election as president.

In his article on social policy reforms, Vail (1999) uses the example of France as a strong state to emphasize the complexity of activating a retrenchment policy because it is very difficult to avoid blame. The executive is strong, visible and highly centralized. It is, therefore, difficult to diffuse blame as can be done in the United States, where the president can blame the legislature, and vice versa, because both have a legitimate and powerful influence in the decision-making apparatus (Pierson and Weaver 1993). When examining the case of old-age pensions, it is difficult to support the position of a strong state. By advocating the virtue of private savings and supporting the *mutualités* (friendly societies) for a longer period than most democracies, the state never successfully exercised the kind of powers described above by Krasner (1976) and by Merrien (1991). Its attempt to universalize social security under one scheme failed in 1945, partly because of its earlier attempts. The fact that the first mandatory pension scheme occurred in 1930 and excluded those earning more than 3,000 francs resulted in a much longer timeframe during which private alternatives could become well established.

The social partners

France does not have a consensual history among its social partners that can be compared to that of Belgium or Sweden (see Chapters 3 and 4). The stance towards employers was quite antagonistic after World War II, in part due to their collaboration with the occupier. Class and religion were two major cleavages leading to the division of the Confédération Générale du Travail (CGT) and the Confédération Française des Travailleurs Chrétiens (CFTC), resulting in the creation of two additional unions (FO[1] and CFDT,[2] respectively). Management (*cadres*) formed its own unions in the late 1940s in the CFE–CGC.[3] Prior to their elimination, these five unions competed for members and social elections over a period of 50 years and were considered to be representative by the state. They are consulted regularly with respect to many policy issues, pensions being but one example. These consultations tend to be formalized via the Conseil Économique et Social, which is also used by governments to test the political waters of various proposals. This institution can also be used by a social partner to push its policy ideas to the forefront of political debates.

The CGT was previously the largest union in France, but it split in two at the onset of the cold war over the type of communism it would support. The CGT supported the Soviet regime, while the runaway group CGT–FO backed the democratic Communist parties. The CFTC also experienced a split regarding the role of religion within the union. Today, the CFTC is a christian democratic union which advocates and promotes traditional values. Its runaway counterpart, the CFDT, is a non-religious union that puts much emphasis on seeking agreements with employers and the government. Finally, the CFE–CGC represents predominantly white-collar workers. None of the French unions are linked to political parties, at least not in the same way that the LO supports the Swedish democrats. However, they do have informal links with political elites. For example, many members of the CGT are also members of the Communist Party. Not only do unions have ideological and professional differences, they are also distinguished along public/private lines. Most FO and CGT members work in the public sector, while the others are more representative of the private sector. This division is important given the French pension system's distinct private/public-sector schemes. Somewhat akin to the situation in Italy, many unions also include a large number of retired members.

In contrast to Sweden, the French unions are significantly decentralized, to the extent that sectors and/or branches sometimes disobey the positions advanced by the executive office. For example, the railway workers of the CFDT were clearly at odds with the executive following the introduction of the Juppé plan in 1995. Despite the support granted to the plan by Notat, the union's president, they were quick to join other unions to protest the new measures. Further, the actions of sectoral branches may vary greatly from the central positions. This was clearly demonstrated by the creation of a capitalized pillar to complement the *régime général* and the mandatory supplementary pension schemes (Association Générale des Institutions de Retraite des Cadres, AGIRC; and Association pour le Régime de Retraite Complémentaire des Salariés, ARRCO) in the insurance sector, which was supported by the CFDT, the CFTC and even the strongest opponent to funded options, the Communist CGT (*Le Monde*, 3 February 1995).

The main employer association, the Mouvement des Entreprises de France (MEDEF, previously the Conseil National du Patronat Français, CNPF), became increasingly vocal regarding the issue of reforming the public pension system. Owing to the history mentioned on pp. 46–7, employers had not traditionally had a strong and/or confrontational public profile. They sought compromises with the unions on most questions. This philosophy was significantly altered when the new leadership was instated in 1997. The MEDEF's approach is now a good deal more confrontational. Indicative of this change is the fact that its members went out on the street protesting the enactment of the 35-hour work week in October 1999 (*Economist*, 22 January 2000), and it pulled out of the social security administrative councils because it claimed to have no real power.

If one were to base the analysis of the relationships among the social partners solely on public speeches and press releases, one would be baffled. In many instances, the tone is uncompromising and clearly antagonistic. One can be left with the impression that the social partners are preparing to face off in a boxing ring rather than attempting to work together. Because of the competitive nature of the union organization in France, one cannot appear to be 'soft' on social issues that are closely related to workers' rights. When it comes to reforming the public pension system, this often takes the form of refuting the analysis of experts and denouncing the remedy as too extreme, and therefore as undermining the memberships' earned social rights. Despite this competitive environment, social partners found a 'para-doxical' way to co-exist by denouncing and sometimes even boycotting agreements, even as they participated in their implementation (Ashford 1991: 35–6). For example, despite the FO's refusal to accept and support the new '*convention d'objectifs et de gestion*' (the five-year plan negotiated between the social partners and government concerning management objectives) because it was part of the Juppé plan, it nonetheless participated in its implementation. These trends were also quite obvious during the negotiations related to the mandatory supplementary schemes (AGIRC and ARRCO). The CGT virtually never gave its support at the national level, with the FO, the CFDT, the CFTC and the CGC negotiating with the employers. Recently, the FO has been more reticent than the other three to sign on with the employers. Compared with the FO and the CGT, the CFDT took a more conciliatory tone, and was more willing to negotiate with employers. This position was somewhat difficult to maintain in the face of the CGT and the FO's less compromising stance.

The (uneasy) relationship between the state and the social partners

The interaction between the unions, the employers and the state is quite distinctive in France in comparison with other European nations. On most indices of corporatism, France ranks at the bottom. The mutualist tradition resulted in the trade unions and employers not being completely integrated within the state apparatus, and this led to a peculiar relationship between the state and the social partners (especially in the case of old-age insurance and the institutions associated with social security). Indicative of this strange relationship is the fact that the various *caisses* cannot be clearly defined as either private or public; their top management usually consists of state employees, while most of the staff are private-sector workers. These responsibilities were clearly defined in 1945, and they favoured the social partners. As underlined by Ashford (1986), social security was built 'outside the state'. The unions' power reached a peak following World War II, and it has been diminishing ever since (Guillemard 1986), even as the state took on more responsibilities as the need to reform the system grew. Starting with intense conflict within the unions, the rebirth of employers as legitimate actors and the arrival of de Gaulle, the state has gradually established itself as an important actor, setting out legislation for the various schemes to follow. However, this intrusion into the mutualist tradition, where workers (and employers) are expected to run their own schemes, has been contested constantly by social partners.

The state cannot ignore the social partners since they formally manage the various *caisses,* such as the Caisse Nationale de l'Assurance Vieillesse (CNAV). Social partners, in particular the CGT, were the focal actors who established and implemented the new system after the war, thus legitimizing it. They also identified strongly with social insurance schemes (Béland 2001). The debate between insurance and solidarity has raged on ever since the creation of the Sécu (social security). On one hand, the social partners assume that it is their responsibility to provide old-age pensions to workers on the basis of the contributions they have made in a way akin to an insurance company. On the other hand, the solidarity aspect implies that the state should ensure the well-being of the elderly, who have been poorly covered or unable to receive sufficient pensions. This debate reappears whenever pension reform is on the political agenda. To a significant extent, the social partners would like full managerial influence over old-age insurance, as they have with the supplementary pension schemes ARRCO and AGIRC. Despite all reports stating that a division between solidarity and insurance cannot actually materialize, it has consistently caused discussion and conflict between the government and the social partners. The profound attachment to managerial powers, even though they grant little opportunity to make decisions that have policy implications, underlines the legitimacy of social partners within social policy (Rosanvallon 1995: 81).

Interestingly, even the population is split on the subject. During a last-ditch effort to reform pensions by Bérégovoy's socialist government (1992–3), the Minister of Social Affairs (Teulade) commissioned a survey that included two questions on the management of public pensions. The public was clearly split between the social partners and the state. A question asking who they trusted to manage the pension system was almost evenly divided: 35 per cent indicated they trusted the state; 34 per cent chose the social partners; and 23 per cent preferred private insurance companies.

Bureaucracy

The institutionalization of public pensions is clearly another challenge to the thesis of the strong state. The French bureaucracy never had a solid foothold in this policy domain. It also lacked the prestige and the means to attract good graduates. Actually, many of the comments related to the French bureaucracy on this subject echo the critiques Heclo made of the British bureaucracy in his seminal 1974 book *Modern Social Policies in Britain and Sweden*, where he attributes the minimalist pension system operating in the United Kingdom to the lack of bureaucratic expertise and resources (Heclo 1974).

First, the traditional arena of strength for pension policies has usually been the Ministry of Social Affairs or an (independent) agency attached to it. In the French case, the ministry usually acts as a representative on various public boards related to pensions such as the CNRACL.[4] It is also responsible for the preparation and implementation of social policies. This is in contrast to its Swedish counterpart, which gives the latter responsibilities to independent governmental agencies, specifically the Riksförsäkringsverket (RFV) for pensions (see Chapter 4). However, the ministry seems to lack the resources to properly perform its mandate, which is much more complex than in many industrialized countries because of the fragmented nature of the pension system. As Bichot indicated, the statistical office of the Social Affairs Ministry lacks the resources to analyse most aspects of social insurance programmes. Further, impact studies are distinctly substandard, and feasibility analyses are conspicuous by their absence (Bichot 1999: 18). The reasons for this situation are many and diverse; they include a bureaucratic tradition that emphasized legal aspects and a reliance on the *caisses* for the implementation of its policies. The latter are managed by the social partners and are semi-private entities; they are not controlled by the government to the same extent as the RFV, for example. CNAV's employees are private-sector workers, except for top management, positions which are filled by *énarques*.

As a result, various governments have relied on a multitude of experts to write their reports. None of them has been as active as the CGP. The plan has produced four critical reports since the mid-1980s and has been the locus of pension expertise for the publication of other reports as well.[5] There has also been a heavy reliance on the Direction de la Prévision, a department within the Finance Ministry that specializes in forecasting, and the Institut National de la Statistique et des Études Économiques (INSEE). As Guillemard underlined so clearly in his 1980 study, 'external' reliance can produce dubious information with which to understand the situation of the elderly (Guillemard 1980). For example, the INSEE systematically stopped categorizing individuals according to their professional status once they reached retirement age. This was extremely misleading, given the disparities among pension schemes based on their occupational orientation. This was highlighted by a journalist at *Le Monde* who expressed his amazement that no expert really knew what the average pension of a blue-collar worker was. Indeed, up until 1988, no one even *tried* to know it (*Le Monde*, 16 March 1993). The creation of the Conseil d'Orientation des Retraites (COR) in 2000 remedied that situation.

Prior to the work done by the COR, relatively little was known about the *régimes spéciaux* (civil servants; Société Nationale des Chemins de Fer Français, SNCF; Régie Autonome des Transports Parisiens, RATP). Most reports had suggested vague measures without proper analysis, making it difficult for politicians to take a stand on or try to improve these schemes. The Balladur cabinet finally opted to tackle the subject, and it took a year to launch a series of studies on the public-sector *régimes*. It is extremely difficult to advocate a reform when no one can produce an analysis of the situation or demonstrate a deficit. The deficit of the private-sector regimes, on the other hand, was well documented and had been published many times by the newspapers.

Second, France's track record is also quite disappointing when it comes to hiring and developing experts. The *grande école* devoted to social security (the Centre National d'Études Supérieures de Sécurité Sociale) lacks research centres (Bichot 1999). Even more worrisome is the fact that the Ministry of Social Affairs fails to attract good *énarques*. As underlined by Jobert (1981), social ministries represent the last choices among graduates and are comprised of the highest number of employees without graduate degrees. With bonuses in the Ministry of Finance being two to three times more generous than in the Ministry of Social Affairs, the best *énarques* continue to seek posts in the former ministry (Marier 2005).

Despite these critiques, it would be wrong to conclude that France lacks experts to guide its government. Generally, experts from the various organizations (ministries, departments and other governmental organizations) know each other very well and end up working together on virtually every report that is produced. Their co-operation was enhanced by the creation of the COR.

Theoretical expectations: a case of social conflict

Consistent with the theoretical framework outlined in Chapter 1, France represents a case where social partners collectively constitute a veto point (first ordering principle) yet no veto players exist within the legislature (second ordering principle). The first ordering principle states that the management of pensions outside the state does not allow the government to act unilaterally in this policy domain, producing a Social Partnership model (see Chapter 1). Social partners, particularly the unions, are deeply attached to their social responsibilities. This goes far beyond the managerial role they occupy. Based on prior discussions, there are at least four elements worth examining. First, unions link the creation and/or expansion of social programmes with their participation based on the history of their earlier struggles (see Béland 2001). Second, those participating in the managerial boards of social programmes are recognized by the state. This enhances their legitimacy in the eyes of the public since they enjoy privileged access to the state, thus reinforcing their formal role in policy-making. Third, their representation on the boards results in members receiving detailed information on the programmes they formally supervised. This grants social partners a semi-expert status that they have used on numerous occasions to counter-attack the content of the plans prepared by the government. Fourth, most of the revenues generated to finance the insurance-based programmes come from contributions collected from employees and employers. As a result of these four elements, the government must ensure substantial support from the social partners, especially unions, in order to enact a reform proposal.

In terms of opposing retrenchment measures, employers have supported the government as long as its plan has not sought to increase contribution rates. The unions have been far more vocal and active in opposing reform plans. As a single organization, none of the unions represent a veto point. They must be united to stop reform projects, meaning that their veto point is clearly a collective veto. The most important union resource to express this power remains their mobilization strength (Béland and Marier 2006). Work stoppages by the SNCF and the RATP (these unions organize 75 per cent of all strikes in France) can literally shut Paris down.

Both reform attempts succeeded in part due to the fragmentation of union positions (1993 and 2003), while the Juppé plan (1995) failed owing to a lack of consultation with social partners. Social partners are not entirely dismissive of pension reforms. When interrogated on the subject in private, few deny that pension reforms are required.[6] The fragmentation of the labour movement coupled with the fragmentation of the pension system makes retrenchment a difficult matter for politicians to pursue. As a result, governments are unlikely to pursue programmatic changes, instead confining themselves to altering the parameters of the existing pension system.

The second ordering principle does not apply in France because it features a majority party system (Powell 2000) where the powers of the executive were significantly enhanced after the collapse of the Fourth Republic. The party system is a *de facto* two-party system because of permanent coalitions among political parties. The Socialist Party and the Communist Party co-operate intensively with one another, as do the conservative RPR and the liberal UDF. The RPR was replaced by the Union pour un Mouvement Populaire (UMP), with the inclusion of other right-wing deputies, including some coming from the UDF, to bolster Jacques Chirac's re-election chances in 2002. The two-round electoral system combined with the coalition structure described on p. 31 generates majority governments. This results in a reduction of the number of veto players to the extent that non-governmental parties have no genuine influence.

Reforming pensions within the French social administration

Prior to discussing reform initiatives, it should be noted that seven important documents resulting from different types of public inquiries were published between 1985 and 1992 (see Table 2.2). Even though none led to concrete reform proposals, they were instrumental in delimiting the available alternatives. Social partners expressed clear opinions about them, which allowed executives to adjust their reform strategies. However, the short tenure of socialist prime ministers in the early 1990s compromised the elaboration and negotiation of genuine reform proposals.

Balladur does the unthinkable: he introduces a pension reform ... and survives

The Right won an overwhelming victory in April 1993, obtaining 82 per cent of all seats in the National Assembly. Fearful of suffering the same fate as he had in the presidential election of 1988, Chirac opted not to put himself forward as a candidate for the office of prime minister, hence this responsibility was granted to Édouard Balladur. His government wasted no time in addressing the issue of pension reform. Most social security accounts continued to incur large deficits, and there was a strong sense of urgency that something be done to stop this trend. Vail (1999) argues that Balladur was trying to give the illusion of seeking consensus, but that

Table 2.2 Official French reports on the future of public pensions and proposals

Report (date of publication)	> age	> 10 to best 20–25	Price indexation	> contributions?	Funded part?	Others (i.e. harmonization)
1985 – *Vieillir Solidaire*	Yes, but conditioned by employment	Nothing but open because support point system		Yes, but limited-risk generational conflict	No, only solution is voluntary options	• Better sharing between non-contributory and contributory aspects and between regimes. Strengthen contributory aspects • System by points would help • Financing must be enlarged (especially for non-contributory) • Reforms must be progressive
1986 – Commission d'Évaluation et de Sauvegarde de l'Assurance Vieillesse	More progressive, but keep a minimum age		Mixed system based on price and salaries			• Strengthen rules for non-contributory advantages and increase the sources of financing (also in general) • Strengthen the contributory aspects
1987 – Rapport du Comité des sages	Yes, inevitable	Yes, 10 to 20 or 25	Must seek to link with net salaries		No, payg still best	• Strengthen the contributory aspects of the system • Instauration of system by points would be good and could favour harmonization – should still remain neutral on the architecture of the system • Harmonization of the regimes
1988 – Commission Protection Sociale, presided over by Teulade, Xth Plan		10 to 25 progressively in 15 years	Link with net salaries; Liquidation based on net salary	Increase periods from 150 to 165 quarters for full pension		• Simulation of transfer to point system – similar effects can be reached with both systems • Rejection (on philosophical and practical grounds) of separating contributory and non-contributory aspects of pensions

(*continued on next page*)

Report (date of publication)	> age	> 10 to best 20–25	Price indexation	> contributions?	Funded part?	Others (i.e. harmonization)
1991 – *Livre blanc des retraites*, with preface by Michel Rocard, prime minister		10 to 25 progressively (1 year by generation)	Price with special point linking it with growth	Increase periods from 150 to 168 quarters (1 quarter per generation)	Rejection	• Reject shift to system by points • Reject construction of a single pension regime • Reject separation between contributory and non-contributory aspects • Claim need to promote employment of elderly workers • Improve other social needs
1992 – Mission Retraites, presided over by Cottave		Reject move from 10 to 25	On net salary index to be negotiated between state and social partners	Increase period from 150 to 160 starting in 1996		• Financing via income tax of non-contributory advantages • Propose the creation of l'Observatoire des Retraites • Divided on granting strong managerial powers to the social partners
1992 – Mission Bruhnes		Reject move from 10 to 25		Increase period from 150 to 160 quarters starting in 1993		• Increase in managerial power for social partners. Social partners would fix contributions and indexations • Non-contributory aspects financed by the CSG • Widows' pensions to increase from 52% to 60% of deceased's pensions • Creation of l'Observatoire des Retraites

unions were not duped by this. Blondel, leader of the FO, stated that 'in a soft, mild way, the prime minister is trying to impose an austerity plan on us' (*Le Monde*, 8 May 1993, cited in Vail 1999: 321).

Balladur presented his proposals in mid-May 1993. He announced that all measures would apply strictly to the *régime général* and would be based on the *Livre blanc* generated by the socialist Rocard government in 1991, thus silencing the Left (Vail 1999), which was in complete disarray following the 1993 election. The Socialists were, therefore, unable to muster much opposition.

The measures consisted of increasing the CSG[7] instituted by Rocard to finance a *fonds de solidarité* (set up to finance the non-contributory portion of social security, *la solidarité*, and to service the accumulated debt of the *régime général*). Balladur also indicated that he would enter into negotiations with the unions concerning an increase in the length of the contribution period to extend pensionable years from 37.5 years to 40, and an increase in the calculation of the base pension rate from the best 10 to the best 25 years. Based on these negotiations, decrees would then be executed (*Le Monde*, 12 May 1993).

The *fonds de solidarité vieillesse* (FSV) were implemented early in June in order to finance solidarity measures for the *régime général*, which would be financed by the increase in the CSG (from 1.1 per cent to 2.4 per cent) and a new tax on both alcoholic and non-alcoholic beverages. A fraction of existing contributions would also be redirected to this fund (Ruellan 1993: 917). This plan had long been supported by the unions, who demanded a clearer separation between contributory and non-contributory aspects of the *régime général*. This strategy recognized the role of social partners in the management of social security, and could be considered part of a non-confrontational stance *vis-à-vis* the unions (Bonoli 2000: 138). Although the measure did nothing to reduce the costs of pensions, it did provide new sources of funding. A few days later, in June, the social partners were convened and met with the Minister of Social Affairs Simone Veil. They were then received individually by Balladur at the end of the month. The three main unions (FO, CGT, CFDT) afterwards claimed publicly and vociferously that these meetings did not constitute adequate consultation (Vail 1999: 321).

The government went ahead with other aspects of its plan and introduced the first pension retrenchment measures. Along with the legislation creating the FSV, other legislation indexed pensions according to prices, a measure that would have to be renewed by decree every five years. This legally formalized a practice that had been occurring since 1987 (Ruellan 1993: 919). A decree (no. 93–1023) adopted on 27 August would set an increase in the amount granted to pensioners based on the expected inflation rate (determined to be the average yearly price increase, excluding tobacco products). Any discrepancy between the expected rate of inflation and the actual rate would be corrected the following year.

Second, two other measures would be instituted via Decree no. 93–1024. The length of the contribution period required to obtain a full pension was increased from 150 progressive quarters (37.5 years) to 160 progressive quarters (40 years), starting in 1994. The reform was to be implemented over a period of 10 years by adding one quarter every year until 2003. The other measure addressed the period by which the pension amount is calculated, which was based on employees' 10 best earning years. The number of years was increased to 25 very slowly, by adding one year for the next 15 years starting in 1994, finally reaching its goal in 2008.

Contrary to many expectations, the reform did not generate a significant backlash against the government or a strong negative reaction from the social partners, aside from the CGT, who, it turned out, could not mobilize its members. Thus, the much-feared pension reform passed without much opposition, a far cry from Rocard's 1991 claim that this issue could break a government.

Explaining the reform

Various explanations have been offered to explain the relatively painless passing of this reform (Ruellan 1993; Vail 1999; Bonoli 2000). Vail pointed out that obfuscation strategies can be difficult to achieve in a strong state like France, owing to the high concentration of power its executive enjoys. He claims that Balladur sought to give the illusion of a consultation effort among the unions, but the illusion failed. Nonetheless, his reform succeeded because he was able to split the unions (public/private split) and grant them at least one concession (FSV). The split within the unions ensured that the mobilization failed as public-sector employees had no real reason to protest (Vail 1999: 321), and could represent a strategy of division on the part of the government (Pierson 1994: 22–3). Bonoli noted that the government opted for a tit-for-tat strategy by granting a longstanding request in return for imposing retrenchment measures. He also states that the co-operation of the president and the prime minister helped to reduce the executive's visibility on this front (Bonoli 2000: 147–8).

Three points should be emphasized. First, the most popular theory regarding the exclusion of the public sector is that this strategy would split the unions and ensure that the more unionized public-sector workers would not be provoked (Vail 1999: 321). This argument is, however, far too simple, and it does not take into account the knowledge available at that time. Yes, part of the government's strategy was to reform the *régime général* first, which would then create pressure to reform other schemes and minimize union resistance. However, this decision was also dictated by the expertise available at that time. As is clearly demonstrated by the numerous commissions on the subject, relatively little was known about the *régimes spéciaux* (including the basic public-sector scheme). None of the commissions went beyond advocating measures similar to those promulgated in the private sector. The *Livre blanc* represented a possible exception, but it actually specified that increasing the contribution period in the public sector would have a negligible impact owing to the rigidity of the wages paid to those employees. These conclusions were based on extending the contribution period only from 6 to 18 months, and no analysis was required to make this sort of statement owing to the wage structure.[8]

Benefits granted to those covered by the *régimes spéciaux* are more generous than those received by members of the *régime général*. Members have a younger retirement age, a more generous rate of indexation, and a lower contribution period, plus these schemes are very different in terms of rules and benefits. Nonetheless, it was not known how they would fare in the future, how much pensioners in these schemes were earning and, more importantly, what kind of measures would ease the financial pressures in the upcoming years. It took a member of the Balladur cabinet over a year just to gather the proper data and obtain reports on the subject.[9] Creating a new commission or study group to consider these aspects would only have further delayed the reform's introduction. It was in this context that the decision was made to go ahead with the reform proposed for the *régime général*.

With respect to the position of unions and the failed mobilization, a caveat is in order. Vail's reliance on these public statements obscures the other side of the coin. As stated earlier, there can be a significant difference between the public statement put forth by unions and what really happens. This particular case is a prime example, and there is good reason to question Vail's argument that the government sought to give the impression of consultations without really conducting any. First, Bonoli clearly states that the government engaged in serious negotiations with the social partners and that they were involved in the process. An interview he conducted with an official within the Ministry of Social Affairs confirms his statement (Bonoli 2000: 138). Second, an ex-member of the Balladur cabinet noted that all social partners agreed that something needed to be done and thus supported the proposed reform. The FO did not protest, while the CFDT and CGC encouraged the reforms, though price indexation was still a contentious issue.[10] Finally, *Le Monde* repeated on several occasions that all social partners privately acknowledged the need for reform.[11] The political costs associated with a possible reform had been exaggerated (Ruellan 1993: 915). Nonetheless, it is clear that the negotiations cannot be considered a concerted effort or a social pact. It should also be noted again that such agreements are rare in France (Bonoli 2000: 148).

The support of the CFDT, in concert with the CGC, was essential to nullify the possibility of a broad union movement against the reform. The CFDT represented the largest number of private-sector workers. With their membership confined mostly to the public sector, the CGT and the FO had difficulty stimulating their members to oppose a reform: it did not affect most of them, and it was supported by the union representing most private-sector workers. Balladur was thus able to circumvent this particular collective veto.

The second main argument claims that co-governance with a socialist president forced the Balladur government to negotiate with the unions (Bonoli 2000: 147). The only visible way a president can influence the debate is by publicly criticizing the actions of the government on this subject in the hope of steering a strong opposition movement. This would have been a difficult task for Mitterrand, given that he had already endorsed the *Livre blanc* written by the former socialist prime minister Rocard. His approval ratings were also mediocre at best at the time.

The third issue was the progressiveness of the decrees. Adding one quarter per year over a period of 10 years and adding one year per year to the period under which the average salary is calculated gave the appearance of a small sacrifice. One of Balladur's former cabinet members stated that 'one quarter per year – that does not upset people'.[12] These measures could be considered part of a strategy of 'diminishing traceability', as they postponed the burden of cutbacks over a very long period of time (Pierson 1994: 21–2).

Impact of the reform

More than 10 years later, it is much easier to assess the impact of the Balladur reform. Interestingly, it is possible to compare the expected impact of the measures adopted with the actual effect by using either of two methods. The first is to measure how much they reduced the regime's financial burden; in other words, how much they reduced the expected increase in the contribution rate that would have been necessary to maintain the system as it was. The second calculation involves analysing what is happening to the pensioners; that is, how much their pension was reduced.

Despite their efficiency in resolving financial needs up to the year 2010, the Balladur measures are not sufficient in the long run. This has been clearly conveyed by recent reports on the subject. According to the COR, by 2040 the regime's deficit could be as high as 325.5 billion francs (49.6 billion euros) in a worst-case scenario; and 260.6 billion francs (39.7 billion euros) in the best-case scenario (COR 2001: Annex 8).[13] The measure having the most impact in this example is indexing the pensions to the cost of living rather than according to the gross salaries of current wage earners. Using a study from the CNAV, Ruellan (1993: 921) explains the financial effect of this measure. Price indexation is the equivalent of reducing the contribution rate by five points in both favourable and unfavourable economic scenarios compared to if the system had continued to be indexed according to gross salaries.

None of these numbers, however, indicates what the impact of the Balladur reforms on current and future pensioners was. The increase in the length of the contribution period from 37.5 years to 40 years was negligible in the short term, partly because at the time the reform was introduced it was estimated that more than 60 per cent of the new pensioners had already contributed 40 years;[14] those pensioners would not be affected by this change.

This reform has long-term consequences for those who experienced the turbulent economic period following the oil crises. France previously had one of the lowest employment rates among those over the age of 55. As of 1990, 65 per cent of pension requests for the *régime général* came from individuals who were not employed (Ruellan 1993: 924). The long-term consequences of this measure are likely to encourage citizens in upcoming generations to work past the age of 60 in order to receive a full pension, otherwise an individual would have to enter the labour market at age 20 and work without interruption until age 60 or so.[15] Considering the low employment rate of many youth and the duration of current educational requirements, the likelihood of having to choose between a reduced pension or a longer career will be much more common in the years to come. Retiring prior to having worked for 40 years can be quite unattractive, as individuals are penalized by *both* the rate (which slips by 1.25 per cent for every quarter below, with a minimum rate of 25 per cent) and the duration (calculated as a fraction of the total period).[16]

The effect of the second measure seeks to decrease the salary level upon which pension amounts are based from 10 to 25 years. Even though it should have a bigger impact on those with precarious jobs, it also affects those with stable careers, as more of the earlier, less-well-paid years of pensioners' careers would now be included in the calculations. With the contribution ceiling also being a factor (it has not been indexed properly over the years), Ruellan demonstrated that both white-collar and blue-collar workers faced a proportional reduction in their income replacement rate (Ruellan 1993: 922).[17] Thus, this measure is more likely to affect those with either an ascending or an interrupted career.

The measure having the greatest impact, and the one most criticized by unions, is switching from an indexation based on gross salaries to a price indexation. As seen earlier, this switch results in a sharp reduction in old-age pension expenses, but it also has the same effect on pensioners. It has a strong cumulative effect because pension contributions made early in someone's career are price indexed for the remainder of the career, instead of following the evolution of wages. The latest figures provided by the COR underline this point clearly. Assuming 2000 to be the year of reference, the relative amount of the average pension is expected to decline by 26 per cent *vis-à-vis* the average gross salary (COR 2001: Annex 8). These figures do not even take into account the period 1987–2000, which was also price indexed.

Juppé enters slowly, awakens the sleeping giant and hits a train

Following Chirac's election to the office of president in May 1995, Alain Juppé was appointed to the position of prime minister. He was a former

Foreign Affairs Minister and one of Chirac's staunchest supporters. Some ministers of the UDF–RPR coalition returned, but Matignon's entire cabinet was replaced.

During his presidential campaign, Chirac's main election promise was to repair the 'social fracture' in France. His campaign was surprisingly geared towards the Left, partly as a result of Balladur's presence in the campaign, as he was advocating austerity measures to restore growth. Chirac claimed the opposite, that economic growth would generate enough revenues to allow the government to avoid cutting the welfare budget (Bonoli 2000: 142). Juppé's nomination was actually quite welcome at the time; he had a reputation as being highly appreciated by the civil servants of the Ministry of Foreign Affairs, where he served under Balladur, and of being a fine diplomat (*Le Monde*, 14 December 1995).

More than seven months after the presidential election, however, the economic situation worsened, creating further public deficits. France was forced out of the European Monetary System in September, and its currency faced attacks from speculators, while the financial markets replaced their francs with more stable currencies. During the month of October, there were serious doubts that France would be able to join the EMU, and concerns to that effect were voiced publicly by German policy-makers (Pitruzzello 1997).

Pension reforms returned to the forefront of the political debate at the end of August 1995. Juppé announced that the government was again considering a major reform of the social security system. He claimed, however, that the consultation would be broader and more intricate than the one Balladur and Rocard had performed, and, further, that decisions would be made quickly. Juppé also stated that the French did not currently receive equitable retirement benefits (*Le Monde*, 31 August 1995) and he met with the social partners soon afterwards.

A report Balladur requested from the CGP updating the forecast in the *Livre blanc* and taking into account the 1993 reforms was published at the end of the month (*Report Briet*). It claimed that the situation was worse than that outlined in the *Livre blanc*. For example, it stated that the equivalent of 2.4 contribution points would be required to maintain the financial equilibrium of the *régime général*, while the *Livre blanc* claimed that there was no deficit at all. It was also quite critical of the disparities between the *régime général* and the *régimes spéciaux* (including the *régime des fonctionnaires*), which was probably what prompted Juppé's statements on fairness. The report had been ready since May, but the government opted to delay its official publication.

In contrast to the *Livre blanc*, much attention was devoted to analysing the *régimes spéciaux*. The report included various simulations assuming that these *régimes* functioned on the same contribution base as the *régime général*. These simulations showed that reforms were still required in the private sector, but that the financial situation of the *régime spéciaux* was more critical, leading to the conclusion that more than 20 contribution points (or 80 billion francs) would be necessary to achieve the same balance that existed in 1993.[18]

In the meantime, the seven major public-sector unions (CFDT, CGT, FO, CGC, UNSA,[19] CFTC, FSU)[20] were able to organize a common front against the freezing of their salaries for the next year and the threats made to their social benefits. The 10 October strike was a success. All seven union leaders marched together for a common cause, something that had not happened since 1978. The unions proclaimed war on the government (Pitruzzello 1997)!

The upcoming events produced the largest public manifesto since 1968, paralysing Paris for weeks. On 12 November, the government announced that the *régimes spéciaux* were unique, and that these must be examined prior to implementing reforms. Following a meeting with Chirac, Blondel (FO) stated that the momentum to reform pensions in the public sector was coming to a halt. The government was expected to make a formal announcement that it would be consulting the social partners in the upcoming three to six months in an effort to find a solution (*Le Monde*, 13 November 1995). According to Bonoli, unions were informed on a non-official basis that pension reform had been left off the agenda (Bonoli 2000: 143).

On 15 November, Juppé presented his reform plan to the Assemblée Nationale. In terms of scale, it represented the most drastic agenda since the creation of social security in 1945. It tackled health, family and pension; addressed the system's financial needs and increased the role of the state in the system. The health sector was drastically reformed, and a new tax was levied to finance the still-growing debt of 250 billion francs from the social security system (RDS).[21] Family benefits were to be frozen in 1996 and they would at least partially be included as income for taxation purposes. Finally, the plan proposed the introduction of a constitutional change permitting parliament to vote on the social security budget.

With regard to pensions, the Juppé plan advocated pension reforms for the *régimes spéciaux* by extending the length of required contributions for a full pension from 37.5 years to 40 years and by creating a *caisse* (much like the one currently in place for local civil employees and hospital workers – CNRACL) for civil servants as well (modelled on the *régime général*), in order to increase the transparency of the system. The exact measures necessary to implement these objectives were left to a special commission that was expected to submit its final report within four months.

The whole process was extremely secretive. According to Bouget, several ministers were not even informed of the Juppé plan. He claims that only four social advisors and high-level civil servants were involved with the prime minister and the president in its preparation (Bouget 1998: 168). Ministers within his government would later complain about the secretive tendencies of the prime minister and his advisors. Several ministers considered resigning, complaining that their role was so limited that they could only 'explain the decisions taken without them' (*Le Monde*, 14 December 1995). The CFDT was the only union really consulted, and even that was only a few days prior to the announcement in parliament. Nicole Notat, its leader, was not told about the pension reforms, nor about the introduction of the new tax to finance the social security system's deficit (Vail 1999: 323).

The common front that was present in October collapsed soon after the announcement of the Juppé plan. The CFDT broke ranks by officially supporting the plan's general guidelines. Unions like the FO and the CGT were very critical of this stance. Blondel (FO) proposed that Notat (CFDT) should change jobs as she 'seems to be talking like a Minister' (*Le Monde*, 17 November 1995). The critiques of the CFDT were not limited to other unions, however. Many members and regional representatives within the CFDT protested vehemently, especially railway workers. The FO, which served as president of the main health insurance scheme and had a membership comprised largely of civil servants, was very opposed to the plan and asked for its immediate removal. The CGT expressed a similar attitude. Strikes by civil servants were scheduled for 24 November,[22] but they eventually found common ground regarding pension reform, and the CFDT still favoured the health insurance reform.

On 23 November, the railway workers went on strike. In addition to their opposition to the Juppé plan, unions were also opposed to any plan advocating an internal reorganization of local transportation to improve the finances of the SNCF. The following day, Paris subway workers joined them. The strike soon spread to other civil servants, and even to students. By 5 December, hundreds of thousands of people marched in Paris against the measures. That day featured a handshake between Blondel (FO) and Viannet (CGT), representing unions that had split over their Communist allegiance. Such close co-operation had not existed since the FO left the CGT. Both maintained that the Juppé plan had to be abandoned and called on all workers (public and private) to join the movement.

On 5 December, Juppé defended his government against a vote of no confidence in parliament and made a televised address underlining his willingness to meet and consult the social partners on the subject of pension reform. The Minister of Labour and Social Affairs, Barrot, met with the social partners over the next few days to study the implementation of the reforms and the forms of consultation that should be adopted. He also stated that the existence of the *régimes spéciaux* was not in question, but that reforms were necessary for the economic health of the country. Finally, Juppé announced the creation of the Commission Le Vert to study the *régimes spéciaux* and to open discussions with the social partners (*Le Monde*, 7 December 1995).

This intervention did not appease the unions. The FO and the CGT emphasized that the word 'consultation' was carefully substituted for the term 'negotiation'. They also claimed that the government had not made any progress. The teachers' unions (the FEN[23] and the FSU) refused to support any increase in the length of contributions for a full pension and remained opposed to the plan. They joined the movement on 7 December. On the other hand, the CFDT, the CFTC and the CFE–CGC stated that Juppé's speech represented a beginning and that discussions with social partners should take place immediately. The employers' association supported the government's efforts and the decision to tackle social security and the *régimes spéciaux* separately, with its leader claiming that the Juppé plan was 'fundamental for the country' (*Le Monde*, 8 December 1995).

The social movement continued to progress, and it remained strong even in the local communities. Juppé proposed a social summit during another public address on 10 December. With respect to the reform of the *régimes spéciaux*, Juppé surrendered by taking public-sector reform off the reform agenda (*Le Monde*, 12 December 1995). He followed that up with a statement that the aims of the Commission Le Vert were 'not well understood', and he opted to suspend it. The commission's work lasted but five days! Few unions were consulted, but it was boycotted by the core unions backing the protest movement: CGT, FO and FSU.

Explaining the failure of the Juppé plan

The reforms to the *régimes spéciaux* proposed by Juppé failed; however, it is important to stress that other points were adopted. Reforms to the health system were considered the most urgent, as it had a deficit nearly double the pension system's deficit. The reforms to family benefits were maintained. Further, the new sources of revenues were all adopted (RDS, increase in the CSG, increase in health contributions for the unemployed and elderly). Finally, parliament's role increased substantially with respect to financing social security. These new powers implied a greater supervisory role for parliament, which had historically been consulted only *after* the implementation of the budget by the social partners (Mekhantar 1996: 37).

Juppé's confrontational approach marked a clear break with the strategy adopted by previous governments, whether they were from the Right or the Left. Vail presents the welfare reforms of 1995 as a case of 'welfare Bonapartism' (Vail 1999: 322)! He claimed that Balladur was able to pass his reforms because he gave at least the appearance of having consulted with the unions. This was much more effective than Juppé's confrontational approach.

Other possible explanations have been suggested regarding the role of railway workers, Chirac's promises and the strength of the unions in the public sector. First, the Juppé plan came at a time when the government was negotiating with the unions a new plan for the SNCF, which was losing a substantial amount of money every year. These negotiations were quite difficult, and the railway unions even asked that the plan proposed by the government during the strike be removed. The government eventually appointed a socialist negotiator to draw up a new plan (Pitruzzello 1997). Tackling both a restructuring of the railway company and a change to their pension plan was politically dangerous, especially when the SNCF and RATP have accounted for roughly 80 per cent of all strikes in recent years. Thus, mobilizing these workers was probably easier than it might have been with the other sectors, and they had the ability to virtually shut Paris down. Most accounts claim that it took four to five hours for the suburban population to reach Paris during the strike. Further, a comfortable retirement was one of the major benefits offered by these two enterprises. Despite their early retirement age, they tend to earn less per month than other civil servants (97,300 francs vs 130,000), and the SNCF and RATP, their structural benefits notwithstanding, do not represent a large financial commitment because they are small régimes (*Le Monde*, 12 December 1995).

Second, as Bonoli emphasized, the unions obtained the general support of the French population because many of them felt that Chirac had reneged on the most important promise of his campaign, which was to restore the 'social fracture'. An opinion poll conducted after the announcement of the Juppé plan demonstrated that 68 per cent interpreted it as a broken promise from the president (Bonoli 2000: 147). Third, it has been pointed out that the unionization rate of the public service is substantially higher than that of the private sector. However, had this element been a factor, Juppé's strategy would have been different. As Bonoli stated, 'a stronger labour movement in the public sector, if anything, should have pushed the government to seek agreement with the unions' (Bonoli 2000: 146). The government sought to create a division between the private-sector workers and public-sector workers by emphasizing the latter's unjust treatment with respect to retirement. Juppé continually insisted that the French did not enjoy equitable retirement benefits. This strategy implies that the government did not believe that the private sector was at a disadvantage when it came to seeking approval for this decision.

Based on the theoretical discussion presented in Chapter 1, I shall propose another argument. The socialists opted to rally their troops by maintaining that the government had adopted reforms without consultation. After all, few people were consulted and the plan came as a surprise even to people working for the government at the time. There was something more behind the protest movement and the fearlessness with which unions undertook their protest. They viewed themselves as legitimate actors in the process who ought to have been consulted in such an undertaking. Yet this clearly was not the case here. From the Balladur reform, we know that finding a compromise and encouraging co-operation from the CGT were nearly impossible in practice. However, it was possible to ensure that the FO would not protest too vehemently, because it had traditionally been more open towards negotiations between employees, employers and government (Bouget 1998: 169). In both cases, CFDT was on board and more or less accepted the government's measures.

Two core factors changed in the case of the Juppé plan. First, some elements of the CFDT, concentrated in the railroad industry in the public sector, openly challenged their leaders' original position, thus forcing the union's executive to adopt a new stance stressing its opposition to the process by which pensions were included in the reform package. Second, the government launched a frontal assault on the FO and challenged the legitimacy of social partners by increasing the power of the state over social security. The FO had held the presidency of health insurance for most recent years. It was clearly attached to this position, and most of its members are civil servants. Understandably, the FO was opposed to the reform and felt compelled to protest strongly. The Juppé plan generated a common front due to its 'attack' on public-sector pensions, launched without significant consultation or commissions on the subject, but also because it reversed the previous trends established between the government and the social partners on the management responsibilities of social security. Both Balladur and particularly Bérégovoy's government (1992–3) sought to increase the distinction between the solidaristic role of the state and the insurance role of the social partners. Bérégovoy was even willing to leave 'real' managerial responsibilities to them in his plan. Balladur did not go that far, but granted the unions' request by ensuring a source of financing for non-contributory aspects of the scheme. This, in turn, opened the door to a possible increase in the responsibility granted to the social partners. The Juppé plan reversed this movement by increasing the role of parliament and by entering the field of implementation (a domain reserved for the social partners) by asking them to negotiate a mission plan with the government. Thus, instead of moving towards separating or clarifying the responsibilities of both governments and the social partners, the government increased its role and expended the managerial dilemma of social security.

Impact of the Juppé reform

The adoption of an extra tax (RDS) to finance the debt incurred by social security and the introduction of parliament as a new player in the system were eventually implemented, while the reform of the *régimes spéciaux* was abandoned. The new tax added extra revenue to the system and implied that the government formally accepted financial responsibility for these *régimes*. This had already been acknowledged in practice, but it became institutionalized with the creation of the Caisse d'Amortissement de la Dette Sociale (CADES), an institution responsible for the reimbursement of social security's accumulated debt.[24] Parliament became involved with financing social security when it was asked to vote annually on the law regarding its financing. Historically, parliament's role had been very minimal, with the budget for social security simply included as an annex (known as *Les Jaunes*) to the state budget.

The implementation of pension legislation is now under the scrutiny of the state, as the CNAV must negotiate with the government regarding a four-year plan called the '*Convention d'objectifs et de gestion entre l'État et la CNAV*', a plan that includes managerial objectives related to the *régime général*. This document must be approved by both the state and the administrative council of the CNAV. The FO refused to support this undertaking, but nonetheless participates in its implementation.

Thus, the Juppé plan contributes to the ongoing dispute between the social partners and the state on the management of social security. On one hand, critics point out that the government took the lead with respect to ensuring the system's viability by paying its deficit and making unpopular decisions to save it, while social partners – unions in particular – defended the system without giving too much consideration to the financial implications of such measures. Therefore, it should come as no surprise that the government sought to expand its role in the adminis-tration of the *régime général*. On the other hand, the social partners demonstrated that they were able to be more flexible and that they could take more 'appropriate' measures than the government when it came to the mandatory supplementary *régimes* (AGIRC and ARRCO). Both of these *régimes* were reformed in 1994, 1996 and 2001. Further, with the possible exception of the CGT, unions have advocated certain measures to contain the costs of pensions and have accepted, mostly privately, the necessity for reform.

Jospin consults, but does not reform

With regard to pensions, the Jospin government's five-year administration will be remembered as one that held many consultations that resulted in no reforms. Fearful of the consequences that were so vividly demonstrated by the Juppé plan, the government reverted to a negotiated approach in the hope of achieving a compromise with the social partners.

During the early months of its mandate, it became clear that the govern-ment would continue to implement those of Juppé's measures that survived the events of November/December 1995. The CSG was raised from 3.4 to 7.5 per cent, while health insurance contributions were decreased from 5.5 to 0.75 per cent. This change in taxation and funding was adopted as part of the law on the financing of social security, one of the decrees the Juppé government adopted. The bill also included an extension of the RDS until 2004, though it was originally scheduled to end in 1999. The FO protested that decision, claiming that the government was extending the measures taken by Juppé (*Le Monde*, 28 November 1997; *Le Monde*, 2 December 1997).

Along with the financing bill, Jospin introduced the *fonds de réserve pour les retraites*, a collective, capitalized fund that was managed by the state and designed as a cushion to offset the expected financial difficulties caused by the upcoming demographic changes. First proposed by Bérégovoy in 1991, the objective of the fund was to obtain 150 billion euros by 2020. The money would be collected from privatizing national assets, the *fonds de solidarité vieillesse* excess, the sale of the so-called third generation of mobile phone licenses and other undisclosed sources. The government realized far less income than it had hoped, and the fund accumulated only 25 billion euros by 2005. Its very future is doubtful owing to continuous deficits experienced by the FSV since 2001 and because the recent privatization generated so much less income than expected. During the period 2002–4, the fund received between 4 and 5 billion euros annually. However, this amount shrank to 1.3 billion in 2005, and even among right-wing politicians few advocated using those funds to finance the FSV deficits (*Le Monde*, 1 December 2005).

The Charpin Report

In 1998, the government asked the director of the CGP (Charpin) to establish a diagnosis of the (future) financial situation of all pension *régimes*, which would be shared as much as possible with the social partners and the managers of the various *régimes*. The note written by the prime minister underlined that Rocard's 1991 *Livre blanc* was essential for the government to initiate the reform by 1993, as it underscored the necessity of making adjustments to the pension system. Charpin was well known in government circles. When the Socialists were in power in the 1980s, he had been a ministerial advisor, and he was a counsellor at the headquarters of the Socialist Party under Jospin in 1984 (*Libération*, 22 March 1999).

As required by the mission statement, Charpin established a consultation commission which included the social partners, a pensioner representative, state representatives from five ministries[25] and managers from the various pension schemes. Eleven meetings were conducted between October 1998 and March 1999.

L'Avenir de nos retraites, also known as the Charpin Report, presented a bleak future for the French pension system. First, it stated that the demographic balance of most schemes would shift dramatically; the majority would have less than one contributor paying into the scheme for every pensioner drawing benefits. Second, based on macro-economic projections made by the *Direction de la Prévision* (Ministry of Finance), the report claimed that the financial needs of the whole pension system would reach 290 billion francs in 2020, rising even further to 700 billion in 2040 if there was no change.[26] Assuming an unemployment rate of 6 per cent, an additional 255 billion francs (or an increase of 33.5 contribution points) would be required in 2040 to attain a financial equilibrium similar to that experienced in 1998 by the civil servants' scheme. The *régime général* needed 380 billion francs, or slightly less than 10 contribution points, to be financially stable.

Based on the (future) financial difficulties of the French pension system, Charpin advocated proposals similar to those unsuccessfully implemented by Juppé after concluding that 'the diagnosis found in this report demonstrates that a global reform of the retirement system is necessary' (Charpin 1999: 144). He then advocated numerous policy changes, many of them extremely controversial. First, Charpin proposed lengthening the contribution period needed to obtain a full-time pension prior to the age of 65 to 42.5 years. He emphasized that this increase should be applied universally, so that both private- and public-sector schemes would require contributions of 42.5 years before members could draw a full pension previous to reaching retirement age.

He then rejected the idea of unifying the pension schemes, though he maintained that it was imperative to adopt common principles and avoid 'unjustified' differences. Charpin was quite critical of the lack of reforms administered in the public-sector schemes, emphasizing that they also needed to be reformed (Charpin 1999: 15).

Third, the report advocated the introduction of more individual choice in the retirement phase and reducing the rigidity of the borders between different life phases. This point was later echoed in another commission report published in September, stressing the need to make retirement a more progressive process.[27] Fourth, Charpin suggested that periodic adjustments respecting the objectives of solidarity and universality be built into the pension system by negotiation between the government and the social partners. He further proposed the creation of a steering committee (to advise government, social partners, retirement associations and pension schemes) to research long-term projections every three years and suggest measures that could be adopted to ensure the future of the pension system. The government later endorsed this initiative when it became clear that its efforts to reform the civil servant pension scheme would engender strong opposition from the unions. Finally, the report promoted the creation of a collectively funded reserve to ensure a smooth passage into the demographically difficult years. Thus, it provided support for the governmental decision to create such a reserve in 1998 (*fonds de réserve pour les retraites*).

The report's conclusions pleased none of the social partners. On one hand, the MEDEF[28] claimed it did not go far enough in terms of proposed action and strongly emphasized the burden the public-sector scheme represented; the government's contributions surpassed 50 per cent in many cases, compared to an average contribution rate of 15 per cent. They noted that public-sector schemes had not yet been reformed and that it was imperative that measures similar to those adopted for the *régime général* be introduced (Charpin 1999: 256).[29] Emphasizing that the state as employer needed to introduce reforms (MEDEF, 26 July 1999), the MEDEF claimed that the deficit in the public-sector scheme was three times the size of the private-sector scheme's total. Vice-president Denis Kessler also indicated that a longer contribution period would be required and that 'we must end the illusion of retirement at 60 years old' (*Libération*, 22 March 1999). The *fonds de réserve pour les retraites* was criticized for being inadequate at a time when the government was experiencing deficits.

On the other hand, there was significant consensus among the unions that increasing the length of the contribution period was inappropriate at a time when youth were experiencing high unemployment and older workers were being pushed into early retirement. Most also criticized the alarmist tone of the report, claiming it was not conducive to a proper pedagogy and debate. These were, however, the sole points in common among them.

The CGT argued that the solutions proposed by Charpin were inappropriate and too drastic, and that the current social system should not be challenged. They advocated an increase in employment to resolve the pension difficulties and also proposed increasing the employers' contributions by including profits, other non-wage earnings and financial gains (Charpin 1999: 235–7).

The FO challenged the economic assumptions made in the report and refused to accept an increase in the length of contribution periods. It stated that promoting this sole measure as a way to save the payg system was 'pathetic' and 'provocative' (Charpin 1999: 238). It advocated a return to 37.5 years for private workers. Their main point of contention centred on increasing revenue sources by strengthening the *fonds de réserve pour les retraites* in order to finance the increasing costs of public pensions. The FO remained committed to avoiding any changes to the *régimes spéciaux*, a position shared by other public-sector unions such as the FSU, the UNSA and the CGT.

By supporting the Charpin Report's conclusions, the CFDT broke ranks with the other unions. It stressed that an improvement in employment rates would not fully address what was needed to sustain the pension system and that periodical meetings would be necessary to adjust the system's parameters based on the changing economic, social and demographic context. Nonetheless, it added that the employment situation of the youth and the tendency to exclude employees above 55 from the labour market should be addressed before serious discussion on pension reform took place. More specifically, the CFDT proposed an increase in the contribution periods for all basic pension schemes, that retirement age be based on the length of one's contribution, that all salaries should be taken into account, that a more effective indexation of pensions be developed and that the *fonds de réserve pour les retraites* be increased.

The CFTC acknowledged the challenges facing the pension system, but criticized the 'dramatization' of the debate. Like the FO and the CGT, they wanted to return to a contribution period of 37.5 years. They proposed a debate regarding a new family policy that might consider ways to modify members' professional and working lives in ways likely to increase the birth rate. Other proposals included the creation of private pension funds at the sectoral level and a certain convergence between the public- and private-sector schemes. The CGC advocated an alignment of all schemes along with more individual choices in the system. It proposed altering the employers' contributions by shifting the burden from salaries to sales. It claimed that the prices of goods would remain the same, but this option would render French companies more competitive as it would result in a relative decrease in wages while increasing the prices of foreign goods.

Following the official release of the report on 29 April, the government announced that a second round of consultation led by the Minister of Employment (Martine Aubry) would soon begin. The government prepared to focus on three central features: consolidating the payg system, reconstructing a full employment society and progressively reforming pensions. The government's strategy consisted of negotiating and consulting with the social partners (one pension scheme at a time) in order to present a plan by the end of the year (*Le Monde*, 28 and 29 April 1999). Aubry met the social partners in autumn 1999. The CFDT mentioned a meeting with her, stating that it was more a discussion than a consultation about reform proposals (CFDT 1999).

Counter-expertise challenges the conclusions of previous commissions

A few weeks after the publication of the Charpin Report, the Fondation Copernic (1999) published a volume challenging its diagnosis and proposals. The first edition was actually called *Contre-rapport Charpin*. One of many groups of this kind created in the aftermath of the social protest of December 1995, the foundation was comprised of union leaders, economists and sociologists, and supported by 600 members opposed to neo-liberalism (*Le Monde*, 24 May 1999). The group recognized that such a movement would be difficult to recreate and opted instead to 'attack' the expertise backing the proposals of governmental commissions and to contest the financial/economic implications of demographic change. They argued that more active measures such as increasing the employment rate and instituting policies promoting economic growth would be more effective than reducing the quality of pensions.

The question of old-age pensions also made its way to the *Conseil Économique et Social*. The council includes social partners and various experts and is considered to be the consultative/corporatist institution of the state. Both the government and the social partners generally test the political waters by submitting proposals to this institution. René Teulade presented a report in January 2000 on the future of pension schemes that led to a vote on its adoption. The report's main thrust had already been presented to a Socialist committee (see Taddei 2000: 77). The Teulade Report challenged the Charpin Report's conclusions and sided clearly with the unions[30] by promoting higher growth and employment as a solution to the pension crisis. The report stated that an annual growth rate of 3.5 per cent would be enough to stabilize the current pension expenditure/GDP ratio without having to increase the length of contribution. This growth rate would also allow a return to an indexation of pensions based on wages. In contrast, the Charpin Report assumed an average growth rate of 1.7 per cent annually over the long term in its forecasting models.

Thus, the report principally advocated measures that would improve the growth rate. First, it promoted a better understanding of the retirement process and an end to current practices favouring early retirement. Second, the report urged the government to actively improve the employment rate to reduce the impact of there being fewer employees below retirement age. Teulade also proposed the creation of a national 'watchdog' centre for pensions, seeking complementary financing as well as strengthening the *fonds de réserve pour les retraites*, and the guarantee of a fair replacement rate for pensions (Teulade 2000: 25).

The social partners were clearly divided on the report. The MEDEF was so outraged that it attempted to pass a motion to make changes, which according to them could have led to a consensus were it not defeated by 45 to 125. Employers questioned the methodology used by the report's authors and its lack of reform initiatives, especially for the *régimes spéciaux*. Following the final adoption of the report, the MEDEF stated that it would no longer participate in pension discussions (*Le Monde*, 12 January 2000).

The CFDT was the only union that used the strategy of opting to abstain to indicate its refusal to approve the report. It supported measures such as indexing pensions based on salaries, ensuring that enough resources were injected into the *fonds de réserve pour les retraites* and increasing the number of individual choices with regard to the length of a working career. However, the CFDT was very critical of the economic assumptions made in the report and the lack of discussions on narrowing the gap between the *régime général* and the *régimes spéciaux* (Teulade 2000: 53–5). The latter opinion is not surprising considering the relative strength of the CFDT in the private sector.

The CFTC and the CFE–CGC supported the report mainly on the basis that it did not question the payg system, and that it considered the importance of seeking a progressive transition into retirement. Both the CGT and the FO were highly supportive of the report because it closely matched their respective positions. First, it did not threaten the *régimes spéciaux*. Second, it advocated a return to indexation based on salaries rather than prices. Finally, it opposed increasing the length of the contribution period. The FO actually restated that it was still seeking to return to 37.5 years of contributions for private-sector workers.

Interestingly, the Teulade Report was also much criticized by experts working in the field. Contrary to the usual process applied when Charpin's and other studies commissioned by the government were created, in this instance none of the bureaucrats normally involved in the studies' development were so much as consulted, much less asked to participate in its production. Those interviewed were quick to point out that the projections

included very basic calculation mistakes.[31] For example, the French economist Florence Legros pointed out that Teulade ignored the fact that an
increase in salary also implies an increase in future pension payments
because workers contribute more. Thus, the higher the growth rate, the
higher the pension would be (*L'Express*, 19 April 2002).

The government continues with the consultation process

After many delays, the Jospin government announced that it wanted to
negotiate a pension pact with the social partners in March 2000. Jospin
insisted on reaching a consensus, citing the Juppé approach as one to avoid.
In terms of policy objectives, he pled for an increase in the length of the
contribution period for civil servants, but offered to consider a part or the
totality of the bonuses (*primes*) and the difficulty associated with certain
professions, such as the nursing personnel in hospitals. Jospin further reiterated that the specificities of the *régimes spéciaux* would not be questioned
(*Le Monde*, 22 March 2000).

Despite the government's willingness to negotiate, the FO, the CGT and
the FSU were quick to condemn its position. The FO and the FSU refused
to make any concessions on the pension code, and the CGT stated that
negotiation could not occur if unions had first to accept a lengthening of
the contribution period. As a result, all three called a strike for the end of
March. The CFDT, the CFE–CGC and the CFTC, on the other hand,
supported the gesture made by the government.

One month later, the Jospin government altered its approach. The implementation of the *Conseil d'Orientation des Retraite* (COR) supported
Charpin and Teulade's suggestion regarding the need to create a steering
institution for pensions. Three main objectives were granted to Yannick
Moreau, COR's president. First, the COR had to delineate the actual
financial situation of the various pension schemes, taking the evolution of
social, demographic and economic conditions into consideration. Second, it
was mandated to propose a series of measures to ensure the financial viability of the pension system in the long run. Finally, the COR was asked to
look for solutions that maintained the coherence of the payg system while
ensuring both solidarity between the schemes and equity between the generations. It was mandated to submit a report every two years analysing the
current pension scheme situation while proposing measures to ensure their
long-term financial equilibrium. Thirty-three members were appointed to
the commission; close to half (16) came from social partners. Indicative of
the increasing role of parliament in pensions, three senators and three parliamentarians were also selected. The remaining seats were granted to public
officials (4), experts (4), pensioners (1) and the national family association
(1). The MEDEF refused to participate, claiming that Charpin had already
accomplished this task, and said it would take part only when the government was ready to develop reforms (*Le Monde*, 29 May 2000). The creation

of the COR prior to the presidential and legislative elections of 2002 moved the issue of pension reform down on the list of priorities.

In early December 2001, Moreau presented the first COR report. The future state of affairs painted by the report closely matched Charpin's conclusions. According to most experts, COR's main contribution was to dismiss the Teulade Report.[32] With respect to policy action, the report emphasized three principal points. It first noted that a change was necessary in how older workers were perceived in order to keep them in the workforce longer. Second, the population needed reassurance that there would be enough employees paying into the pension schemes to fund their future pensions. It underlined that the replacement rate was about to decrease from an average of 78 per cent to 64 per cent in 2040, but proposed no solutions. Third, it advocated increasing the length of the contribution period for civil servants in exchange for including bonuses (*primes*) and more flexibility regarding the age at retirement. It did not tackle other *régimes spéciaux* such as the SNCF and the RATP. Overall, the report suggested that the government should adopt multiple measures to respond to the upcoming social, economic and demographic changes (COR 2001).

Despite its challenge to the public sector, the publication of the report was welcomed by most social partners, who were quick to point out that a return to 37.5 years of contribution in the private sector would only cost 0.3 per cent of GDP. Further, it addressed the decrease in the relative amount received by pensioners *vis-à-vis* workers. Despite projections similar to Charpin's, its tone was much less alarmist, and this contributed to its broader acceptance.

The Fillon reform

Already in the 2002 electoral campaign, political parties stated that pensions needed to be reformed, but they refused to be too specific regarding the details. Early in 2003, the new right-wing government of Jean-Pierre Raffarin began analysing reform scenarios. The civil service and social affairs ministers (Jean-Paul Delevoye and François Fillon, respectively) invited social partners to discuss pension reform. During this meeting, the government presented a well-crafted draft. Interestingly, the *régimes spéciaux*, with the exception of the scheme for civil servants, were absent from the discussions. Six principal propositions were introduced. First, an increase in the length of contribution required for the public-sector scheme was scheduled to ensure that both public- and private-sector schemes would require 40 years worth of contributions for a full pension by the year 2008. Second, the government proposed the abolition of full pension rights with a contributory period of only 15 years for women with three children working in the civil service. Third, the government planned to introduce a 3 per cent penalty per non-contributed year and add up to 2–3 per cent for every additional year worked after the age of 60. To harmonize the penalties between the private-sector and public-sector schemes, penalties for pre-retirement were reduced by 10 per cent in the public sector. Fourth, the government sought to introduce measures to increase individual savings. Fifth, it planned to raise the level of the minimal pension available to those with a low wage who have nonetheless contributed consistently. Finally, the proposal granted full pensions to individuals who met the contribution requirement prior to age 60 under specific conditions (workers with careers that began at age 14 or 15) in order to obtain the support of the CFDT, since it had been one of their foremost demands over the previous 15 years. The two ministers also argued that these propositions could still be altered *in theory* prior to their presentation to the ministerial cabinet at the end of May.

Unions responded rapidly. Not surprisingly, more radical unions such as the FO, the CGT, the UNSA, and the FSU emphasized these measures as retrenchment with only financial objectives in mind. The CGT claimed that retirement income would decrease by 20 per cent while the FO's leader immediately called for a strike to denounce the proposal. More surprising, however, was the opposition of the CFDT, which had approved the orientations of the governmental policy on retirement in March. It argued that the counter-measures were insufficient and represented short-term solutions. Its leader stated that 'the total does not add up' (*Le Monde*, 18 April 2003). The MEDEF supported the government's plan since it avoided contribution hikes (*Le Monde*, 23 April 2003).

Despite united opposition to the reform among the unions, the organization of a common front proved difficult. The more radical FO and, to a lesser extent, the CGT both presented a hard line by requesting the withdrawal of the reform, while the CFDT and the white-collar union CFE–CGC remained optimistic that a compromise could be worked out with the government. As such, the unions agreed to strike on 13 May and presented a common text that included a line on the need to reform pensions at the request of the CFDT (*Le Monde*, 24 April 2003).

The government received a clear message on 13 May. With more than 60 per cent of workers on strike (compared to 30 per cent in 1995) and one to two million citizens in the street, the opposition to the reform proposals gathered strength (*Le Monde*, 14 May 2003).[33] Soon thereafter, Fillon entered into a long, 10-hour negotiating session with the CFDT and the CFE–CGE to resolve the crisis (*Le Monde*, 14 May 2003). To obtain their support, Fillon promised to increase minimal pensions for low-wage earners (raising them to 85 per cent of the minimum wage instead of 75), increase pensions beyond the rate of inflation, increase pensions for individuals belonging to multiple pension schemes and grant full pensions to those who began contributing at the age of 14, 15 or 16 with a full career. Further, the 10 per cent penalty for pre-retirement would be reduced to 5 per cent and the CFDT received assurances that civil servants' bonus pay (*primes*) would be included as pensionable earnings. On 15 May, the CFDT and the CFE–CGE ended their protest to support the new plan. The CFTC unofficially gave its support as well (*Le Monde*, 23 July 2003).

Other unions (FO, CGT, UNSA, FSU) advocated new demonstrations against the proposal. Despite pressure from within, the CGT did not advise its members to imitate FO and organize a general strike. At the end of May, however, teachers launched a general strike. The most significant movement occurred on 3 June when between 450,000 and 1.5 million citizens were in the streets. However, the number of striking members was only half as many as had participated in the previous strike on 13 May. Subways and trains continued to operate as a result. Another important strike occurred on 19 June, when between 116,000 and 320,900 demonstrators had only a minimal effect on services like public transportation. This was the union members' last significant protest against the reform (*Le Monde*, 19 June 2003).

In the meantime, opposition members of parliament sought to disturb the legislative process by introducing amendments. During the proceedings from 10 June to 24 July, the Communists presented nearly 7,000 amendments, while the deeply divided Socialists introduced 2,900 (*Le Monde*, 23 July 2003). Despite these actions, the bill was adopted on 24 July. A few days later, however, a group of socialist deputies and senators challenged the validity of the reform and sent the bill to the Constitutional Counsel for further examination, claiming that it violated the principles of equality enshrined in the Constitution. The counsel validated the reform on 14 August 2003, and the bill became law on 22 August.

Conclusion

The example of France fits neatly into the typology presented in Chapter 1. As expected with a Social Partnership relationship, the presence of social partners within this policy domain is the main obstacle to pension reform, and this constitutes the first ordering principle. In fact, responsibility for public pensions is actually a source of contention between the state and the social partners. The state enacts the laws and parameters of the pension system, with the possible exception of the mandatory supplementary regimes (ARRCO and AGIRC). However, this mandate is not fully accepted by the social partners who retain control of the administrative councils of the various pension *régimes*. As a result, the social partners simply do not trust the state, albeit for different reasons. Unions view any attempt to institute a committee or commission as a way to secure retrenchment, while employers interpret the same action as a means to further delay reforms. By conducting their own independent reviews and analyses, social partners also successfully challenged the expert authority usually granted to the state. Not surprisingly, this troubled relationship is not conducive to programmatic reforms, thus convincing the government's executive to focus solely on parametric reforms.

Balladur succeeded in reforming pensions in the private sector, and Raffarin was able to do the same, albeit 10 years later, with the civil servants' scheme. Even though the centralization of political power increases the visibility and ensures the traceability of the source of reforms (thus, according to Pierson (1994), accentuating the difficulties of retrenching the welfare state), this feature of the French political system has proven to be the most effective way to divide the unions. When unions spoke with one voice, which was the case in the aftermath of the Juppé plan in December 1995, they prevented the implementation of substantive measures reducing public pensions. However, Balladur was able to divide unions by targeting the private-sector scheme first. Due to weak unionization as well as the predominance of the CFDT within the private sector, the pension system was modified without much resistance. The implementation of this reform facilitated Raffarin's task in 2003. It was easier to obtain the co-operation of the CFDT, the CFTC and the CFE–CGC once two longstanding requests with limited financial consequences were granted. Most of their workers were unaffected by the reform and sensed that they had already secured that compromise during the 1993 reform. Moreover, Raffarin opted not to reform the *régimes spéciaux* of the RATP and the SNCF, whose highly mobilized workers formed the nucleus of the 1995 protest. This sequence of events thus broke the unions' collective stance and allowed the unpopular measures to be implemented.

The second ordering principle specifies that a broad political coalition including ideologically polarized political parties is unlikely to yield a (major) pension reform. The centralization of political authority in France implies that the government does not have to negotiate with other political parties to execute a successful reform. However, in this case the first ordering principle significantly limits the scope of possible reforms a government can propose. Thus, for example, French executives have been more constrained than have the British (see Chapter 5).

3 Belgium

Seeking to adapt in a crumbling consensual world, one small step at a time

Introduction

Because Belgium's pension system is so similar to both France's (Chapter 2) and Sweden's (Chapter 4), its study contributes an interesting dimension to this volume. Owing to its proximity to, and a brief occupation by, France prior to its independence, Belgium has been heavily influenced by France's system. As such, it is not surprising that the historical development of these pension systems shares many attributes. Unlike in France, the difficulties of reforming numerous Belgian schemes at once are accentuated owing to the fact that Belgium has large governmental coalitions that minimize the executive's effectiveness. Belgium also has much in common with Sweden with respect to the generosity of its welfare state; it is often favourably compared with its Nordic counterpart. Esping-Andersen's pension decommodification index ranked Belgium second among industrialized countries, directly after Sweden and ahead of other Scandinavian countries (Esping-Andersen 1990: 50). Like Sweden, Belgium is considered a highly corporatist country with a small economy vulnerable to world markets (Katzenstein 1985).

Belgium's public pension system underwent many changes prior to the major 1968 reforms that form the basis of the current pension system. Owing to the above mentioned period of French occupation, civil servants were granted special status prior to Belgium's independence, a status they retain. In the case of private-sector employees, the Belgian pension system experimented with voluntary organizations for a trial period, and later subsidized pension schemes that were managed by voluntary organizations. These arrangements were then replaced by mandatory occupational schemes for specific groups of workers. Following the Social Pact of 1944, the level of benefits and the administrative structure for each occupational plan improved significantly. Intense debates on the structure of the new public pension system led to the adoption of a pay-as-you-go (payg) funding mechanism in 1953 for private-sector workers. These changes were part of an ongoing battle between the Socialists, who viewed social protection as a 'public service', and the Christian Democrats, who sought to minimize government's role. The difference between the platforms of the two parties narrowed as pensions became an electoral issue. Both sought to demonstrate leadership by reforming pension plans, a competition that led to 16 consecutive increases in benefits from 1945 to 1962 (Vanthemsche 1994: 166)! In 1968, a major reform merged previously disparate occupational schemes for private-sector workers into one all-encompassing system managed by the social partners.

Having briefly outlined the historical background of Belgium's pension system, two main issues are addressed in this chapter. The principal theoretical elements used to evaluate the Belgian case according to the framework presented in Chapter 1 is followed by a review of the reforms, both successful and ineffective, enacted during the 20-year period from 1985 to 2005. A theoretical discussion of that process concludes the chapter.

Theorizing pension reform within the Belgian context

A 'pillarized' world?

At first glance, Lijphart's (1968) typology of political systems seems to apply very well to Belgium. The consociational democracy category, originally conceived as a Dutch peculiarity, fits Belgium well. However, the political culture and society are fragmented not only along religious and class lines, but also by language. Moreover, language divisions are defined both territorially and politically (e.g. between Flanders and Wallonia). Following the events at Leuven, parties running in 'federal' elections since the late 1960s have sought to earn seats exclusively within Flanders or Wallonia. There are no federal parties that present candidates throughout the entire country.

According to Lijphart's typology, Belgium's political stability results from 'coalescent' elites who represent groups hierarchically and suppress the creation of popular movements against their leadership. The lack of interaction among the different groups in the populace further strengthened the power of the political elites. This is a consequence of 'pillarization', a cradle-to-grave, socio-economic division of the country into different sociological groups. Individuals socialize within each pillar, granting benefits and privileges to their own members, thus pillars significantly influence political and electoral support (Swyngedouw 1998: 53; see also Seiler 1999: 44–51).

Belgium's consensual democracy has been called an 'armed peace' owing to the difficulties that arise for any single political group that tries to circumvent the country's pillarization. The French Socialists and the Flemish Christian Democrats have such important and deep roots in their respective regions that it is very difficult to govern against their interests (Swyngedouw 1998: 54). Partly as a result of such pillarization, the political system maintains a high level of secrecy. Major decisions are negotiated among political leaders behind closed doors.

These political arrangements have been challenged often since the mid-1970s, particularly at the grassroots level; new parties successfully entered the political arena and voters began switching parties between elections (Swyngedouw 1998: 54–5). Despite a level of corruption similar to that extant in Italy, Belgium did not experience a 'clean hands' movement, as judges depend on political parties for their promotion. Thus, it would take something as extreme as the murder of children and excessively poor handling of the 'Dutroux affair' to provoke a strong public reaction against the pillar system (Seiler 1999). As stated by Delwit *et al.*, what were common transactions between the political and industrial world only 10 years ago are now considered acts of corruption (Delwit *et al.* 1999: 10–11). Other events – 'chickengate' (a scandal related to contaminated chicken), for example – resulted in a backlash against the Christian Democrats during the 1999 election, banishing them to the opposition bench for the first time since World War I.

Van den Brande (1987) contests this view of Belgium's political system. He claims that the political stability of the country has nothing to do with the special skills of its elites, but is rather the result of an equilibrium generated by cross-cutting ties. For example, while socialist workers from Wallonia often co-operate with socialist workers from Flanders, they also work with Catholic workers from Wallonia. This prevents the formation of distinct cleavages, which could accentuate the levels of conflict (van den Bulck 1992: 35).

The state with a small 's'

Regardless of the actual causes of Belgium's political stability, the end result contrasts drastically with France's political culture, where the state has attempted to override groups and organizations. The conception of a strong state is absent in Belgium. Due to the large number of cleavages, consensus is needed to maintain even the most basic state unity; a strong state would probably be a recipe for dismantlement. The Belgian state was conceived as a minimal state with a limited public administration and a radical transformation of this arrangement was never sought. Despite strengthening the public sphere, the state was unable to displace the power of organizations and was therefore forced to act as a mediator, rather than a leader (Delwit *et al.* 1999: 7–8).

Belgium tried to import French models, but they could not be maintained in their original form. For example, it was no coincidence that the French conception of the *bureau du plan* resulted in a single plan (1971–6) when it was transferred to Belgium. Essentially, it was extremely difficult to find a compromise for long-term state planning, thus the French plan's centrifugal force did not fit well. As a result, the Belgian plan eventually became an independent office of expertise devoted to the study of major public policies. It is now a mediating device for social partners that provides external, neutral guidance. In fact, it now has much more in common with the Dutch planning agency and the *Direction de la Prévision* within the French Ministry of Finance than with the now defunct *Commissariat Général du Plan* in France.[1]

With such a conception of the state, it is not surprising that the Belgian civil service lacks the tradition and prestige of its French neighbour. The bureaucratic elites are not trained and formed at a Belgian École Nationale d'Administration (ENA), but, rather, are from disparate institutions strongly anchored in regional and/or religious settings (Delwit *et al.* 1999: 9). This outcome goes hand in hand with the notion of pillarization.

The fact that it is not possible to apply the concept of 'majority rule' in Belgium offers another contrast to the French system. This political acknowledgement is clearly expressed by Huyse (1980): 'If in a country like ours one political family imposes its will unilaterally, the result is a serious crisis putting the system itself in jeopardy' (quoted in van den Bulck 1992: 36). Belgium's decentralization and the split of its political parties in the late 1960s further reduced the likelihood of majority rule. Since the strength of political parties varies within each region, and given that a coalition can only be formed when parties share at least a somewhat similar platform,[2] it would be unlikely to have a government with fewer than four parties. The current 'rainbow' coalition consists of six parties, two from each of the Greens, Socialists and Liberals.

Radical policy options tend to be eliminated rapidly since they require broad support among coalition partners. Belgium's most important guideline is the *déclaration gouvernementale*, which traces the objectives and aims of the coalition government. Specifically, it is negotiated among the coalition partners prior to the formation of the government. As it can take several months to agree on the content of the agreement, any significant deviation tends to present problems, as it requires a new round of negotiations within the coalition.

Another important aspect tends to further reduce the possibility of swift changes in Belgium. Unlike his French counterpart, the prime minister must work with representatives of the other political parties holding key ministries (*kerncabinet*) when having serious discussions with social partners. Moreover, coalition partners traditionally guarded their territories and protected them by securing the ministerial position attached to them. The current government is very transparent in this respect. Broadly speaking, the Liberals are in charge of finances; the Socialists, of social affairs; and the Greens, of environment and transport. The Socialists (Parti Socialiste, PS; and Socialistische Partij Anders, SP) have in fact had control over the Ministry of Pensions and the Ministry of Social Affairs continuously since 1988 (see Table 3.1). Any pension reform is therefore unlikely to succeed without a strong endorsement from the Socialists.

Table 3.1 Political control over the Belgian Ministry of Social Affairs and Pensions

Government coalition	Position	Name	Political party
Martens V 1981–5 (CVP, PSC, PRL, PVV)	Minister of Social Affairs	Jean-Luc Dehaene	CVP
	State Secretary for Pensions	Pierre Mainil	PSC
Martens VI 1985–7 (CVP, PSC, PRL, PVV)	Minister of Social Affairs	Jean-Luc Dehaene	CVP
	State Secretary for Pensions	Pierre Mainil	PSC
Martens VII 1987 (CVP, PSC, PRL, PVV)	Minister of Social Affairs	Jean-Luc Dehaene	CVP
	State Secretary for Pensions	Pierre Mainil	PSC
Martens VIII 1988–91 (CVP, PSC, PS, SP, VU)	Minister of Social Affairs	Philippe Busquin	PS
	Minister of Pensions	Alain van der Biest	PS
Martens IX 1991–2 (CVP, PSC, PS, SP)	Minister of Social Affairs	Philippe Busquin	PS
	Minister of Pensions	Gilbert Mottard	PS
Dehaene I 1992–5 (CVP, PSC, PS, SP)	Minister of Social Affairs	Philippe Moureaux	PS
	Minister of Pensions	Freddy Willockx[a]	SP
		Marcel Colla[a]	SP
Dehaene II 1995–9 (CVP, PSC, PS, SP)	Minister of Social Affairs	Magda de Galan	PS
	Minister of Public Health and Pensions	Marcel Colla[b]	SP
Verhofstadt I 1999–2003	Minister of Pensions and Social Affairs	Frank Vandenbroucke	SP
Verhofstadt II 2003–2007	Minister of Social Affairs	Rudy Demotte	PS
	Minister of Pensions	Frank Vandenbroucke[c]	SP
		Bruno Tobback[c]	SP

Source: CRISP (www.crisp.be).

Notes:
[a] Colla replaced Willockx on 18 July 1994.
[b] Colla was forced to resign in the spring of 1999, less than two weeks prior to the election.
[c] Vandenbroucke resigned on 20 July 2004 and was replaced by Bruno Tobback. Political parties are identified in the following manner: CVP = Christelijke Volkspartij; PRL = Parti Réformateur Libéral; PS = Parti Socialiste; PSC = Parti Social Chrétien; PVV = Partij voor Vrijheid en Vooruitgang; SP = Socialistische Partij; VU = Volksunie.

It is important to note that the governmental coalition does not operate as a unified team. The executive of each ministry is filled with numerous experts and political attachés that are intimately associated with the party in charge. For example, the vast majority of individuals serving in the executive of the pension ministry are closely associated with the Flemish Socialist Party. Non-political civil servants focus strictly on policy implementation and are rarely consulted to develop new policies (Dierickx 2003; Marier 2006). Thus, the party in charge of an individual ministry has a great deal of influence in the design and elaboration of projects as long as it falls within the guidelines of the *déclaration gouvernementale*. The other parties are kept abreast of the evolution of projects and have a final say when a proposal is presented to the ministerial cabinet. This style of policy-making reinforces the importance of coalition agreements and the role of the *kerncabinet*.

Social partners

The point of departure in establishing a constructive social dialogue is the so-called Social Pact of 1944, which was secretly negotiated among the moderate wings of both employers and employees during the German occupation. Its purpose was to harmonize the relationship between both parties while extending social insurance benefits. Ironically, once the war was over the Social Pact was ratified by neither unions nor employers. It was nothing more than a declaration of principle. Nonetheless, social scientists generally agree that the main objectives of the Social Pact were implemented after the war without much further discussion (Pasture 1993: 695–6; see also Vanthemsche 1994: 43–74). This basic compromise was similar to other post-war settlements reached throughout western Europe and covered three main aspects. First, unions and employers agreed on what was negotiable (wages, working conditions, etc.) and what was not (the overall operation of the business, such as investment and rationalization of production). Second, growth was to be shared between capitalists and labour. Third, there was an explicit agreement to favour consensual decisions and strategies (Hancke 1991).

In Belgium, union membership is relatively high at roughly 60 per cent of the labour force.[3] Interestingly, union membership did not evolve as a result of the pillar, but rather because of the social benefits unions offered their members (Pasture 1993: 709). In contrast to the political parties, the three major unions and the main employer association remained under federal jurisdiction and have thus far resisted pressure to decentralize the way the political parties have.

The Algemeen Belgisch Vakverbond/Fédération Générale des Travailleurs Belges (ABVV/FGTB) is the socialist union, and it has a membership of 1.2 million. A significant portion of its membership, 22.3 per cent, comes from the public sector. Similar to the way the PS in Wallonia is dominant politically, it has stronger roots there than in Flanders. It has close ties with both socialist parties (PS and SP), although it is officially run independently of political parties. This is the union that is most likely to strike for political gain.

The Algemeen Christelijk Vakverbond/Confédération des Syndicats Chrétiens (ACV/CSC) is the largest union in Belgium, with a membership of more than 1.5 million. It is stronger in Flanders than in Wallonia and has had a close relationship with the Christian Democratic Party (Parti Social Chrétien, PSC; and Christelijke Volkspartij, CVP), although this relationship has not historically been as close or as formalized as the one between the socialist union and socialist parties. Like the Confédération Française Démocratique du Travail and the Confédération Française des Travailleurs Chrétiens in France (see Chapter 2), this union is more likely to co-operate with the government in its efforts to reform social policies. Despite strong historical differences with the ABVV/FGTB, their present relationship is much more co-operative. Their common front began to develop in the 1960s, and it eventually resulted in an attempt to merge (Pasture 1993: 709). They differ substantially from the French arrangement, as they do not tend to compete with one another.

The Algemene Centrale der Liberale Vakbonden/Centrale Générale des Syndicats Libéraux de Belgique (ACLV/CGSLB) consists of 220,000 members, and 25 per cent of them work in the public sector. It has traditionally had a more limited role than the other two unions. It was some time before the ACLV/CGSLB was officially accepted as a genuine partner. This union has no link with political parties comparable to those established by the other two unions. The main employer association is the Verbond van Belgische Ondernemingen/Fédération des Entreprises de Belgique (VOB/FEB), which represents more than 30,000 small, medium-sized and large enterprises. Like unions, it is divided into various federations. It is worth noting that the VOB/FEB has maintained a dialogue with the unions. Thus, it has neither adopted the French MEDEF's antagonistic tone nor threatened to leave the social institutions it manages jointly with the unions, such as the *Rijksdienst voor Pensioenen/Office National des Pensions* (RVP/ONP).

The relationship between social partners and the state

Despite a formal institutionalization that is similar to that in France, where benefits are divided along the lines of wage earners, civil servants and the self-employed, the relationship between the state and the social partners is more harmonious than in France. The evolution of the state accounts for that situation. The concept of the state was never strongly developed, and unions have not historically been threatened by it. On the contrary, unions turned to the state to expand their members' power and social benefits. Alaluf explains that social protection began to take shape progressively with a minimum level of intervention from the state (Alaluf 1999: 219), leaving a strong policy role for social partners and other private organizations, such as the friendly societies (*mutualités*) that still manage health insurance. The historian Vanthemsche reaches similar conclusions in his study of the evolution of social security in Belgium:

> We have seen that in Belgium (maybe more than anywhere else in Europe) private organizations have played a crucial role not only in the creation, but also in the functioning of the *current* social security system. Trade unions, friendly societies of all kinds, employers' *caisses*, etc. have created the various social insurances and have been integrated within a general system of protection established in 1944. Of course, these private initiatives have slowly changed form and, as a consequence, nature: they have been transformed in semi-public organizations. ... The semi-officialization of the private initiatives (for example those taken by unions or employers) ... reduce[d] the likelihood of conflict ... the co-management takes here all of its importance: it implied this 'ceasefire' between workers and employers, which we just mentioned. This co-management also had the effect of keeping the state at bay since the majority of social partners at the time continued to have doubts about it. Despite the semi-officialization of private initiatives, Belgian social security never became *étatiste*.
>
> (Vanthemsche 1994: 192–3, emphasis added; author translation)

This self-found peace is one of the reasons the government did not look for alternatives to the Social Pact of 1944. It must be noted that the war depleted the unemployment insurance funds accumulated by the unions and the instauration of a single union (UTMI)[4] by the occupier eroded the strength of both Catholic and Socialist unions. While the Social Pact can be seen as a way to re-establish the state's power, it also resulted in an opportunity to increase its powers with respect to social security.

In an earlier section of his book, Vanthemsche discusses the doubts that social partners had about the state following World War II. Both employers and Catholics sought to limit the political authority's role within the system. For the employers, co-management ensured that it would have a strong voice in social security. For the Catholics, an increased role on the part of the state might have marginalized Catholic organizations, an important tool to maintain the place of religion within the society. The Socialists were divided into two broad camps. The first faction, which had strong support within the socialist union, favoured co-managing social security, which would have given workers a voice in how their social programmes were managed. This group would have preferred to manage without the employers, but including them could result in the extension of other benefits. The second group was mostly a political wing that hoped to establish the notion of 'public services' where rights would be universal and not related to income, class, gender or race. The Socialist Minister of Labour and Social Affairs, Léon-Eli Troclet, strongly defended this notion of public service within the government (Vanthemsche 1994: 93–9), but it never became prominent in the rest of the country.

It is also important to emphasize that no one feared that a state *à la française* could develop and control social security on its own. The major opponents of the state's increased role were the employers. This can be attributed partly to the inclusion of the Socialist Party within the government in the early 1920s, which resulted in measures benefiting unions and promoting collective agreements.[5] This line of reasoning implies that the employers considered the state a weak actor easily controlled by parties with hostile interests, such as the Socialists. The fact that some socialist politicians tried to implement the notion of public service reinforced this hypothesis. As in Sweden, the Socialists seemed to believe that controlling the state was feasible (see Chapter 4 and Rothstein 1996). The union's pragmatic view, combined with the near impossibility of achieving political control without the Christian pillar, made this an unworkable option.

The state tended to stay out of areas that were negotiated by the social partners (i.e. the labour market and social security) until 1981, when a Christian–Liberal coalition entered fields traditionally run by the social partners (such as altering labour-market rules and unemployment insurance). The social partners' role has diminished somewhat since then, but they were not replaced by the state. Rather, the state has become another partner in a new social relationship (Hancke 1991).

Even today, the government must act with caution when seeking to reform pensions; it must consult regularly with social partners to secure their endorsement. As was stated on numerous occasions in interviews, acting *à la* Juppé, or even *à la* Balladur, is simply not an option for the Belgian government. Government proposals in the social field require lengthy consultations with social partners and can only be implemented one small step at a time. A more pessimistic view claims that the state acts more like a referee than as an independent actor, and that Belgian policy-making is actually more about containing conflict than solving any problems (van den Bulck 1992: 52).

In addition to the co-management of social security, unions discovered another route to enter the political arena: the pillars. Although the importance of the pillars has been decreasing, they nonetheless remain an important point of entry into the business of government. As is demonstrated on p. 95, when divergences occur among unions, they do not hesitate to use the political party of the same pillar to increase their political strength. However, unions have rather successfully maintained a common front during the past 40 years, and such tactics usually occur early in the negotiation process in order to test the political pulse of a proposal and promote it.

Bureaucracy

In addition to the cabinet of the pension ministry, three important bureaucratic actors are involved in the pension reform process: The RVP/ONP, the Federal Planning Bureau (FPB) and, to a lesser extent, the Belgian Central Bank (BNB).

The RVP/ONP is more similar to the French CNAV (see Chapter 2) than to the Swedish RFV (see Chapter 4). It administers the public pension system for salaried workers, as well as the guaranteed minimum pension. The management board consists of 14 social representatives,[6] one government official and one delegate from the Ministry of Finance (ONP 1999: 4). The role of the government on this board is quite limited owing to the fact that contributions are paid predominantly by employers and employees, thus legitimizing their participation in decisions regarding pensions. The administration of the pension fund is consensual as the board implements existing legislation. The RVP/ONP is not officially involved in the political process of reforming pension schemes but nevertheless exercises an advisory role, given that it administers the public pension scheme. As in France, its director-general (DG) is neutral. It would be difficult for a DG to enter the political arena, given the inherent potential to interfere with the board's views and jeopardize its role as an impartial representative of the organization. Finally, the Ministry of Finance oversees the pension scheme for public servants.

The second core actor is the FPB. As mentioned on p. 88, the FPB is mostly confined to the production of expert analysis and does not share many characteristics with its French counterpart. Nonetheless, its role in Belgian pension reform is quite important since the government has mandated that the bureau be the main public office for producing the figures and statistics related to the pension system. Interestingly, its figures have been criticized, not for being too pessimistic, but for the opposite. It has tried to reassure the public that the Belgian pension system will be viable in the future, suggesting debt reduction as a means to generate new revenues for the system.

The Central Bank is the third bureaucratic actor with a limited and indirect role in pension reform. It has acted as an institutional balance to the plan, a function filled by finance ministries in most industrialized countries. It should be noted that, because of the market's possible reaction, the Central Bank is not a strong public actor. Most of its influence is channelled behind closed doors through the budget and finance ministries. It gained 'official' recognition and was involved with the plan as a junior partner in the creation of Belgian experts to work with the EU's Working Group on Ageing within Ecofin.[7] The bank pointed out that some of the plan's assumptions are quite optimistic and that the maintenance of the current system will need to address the relative decline of pensions *vis-à-vis* wage earners resulting from price indexation.

Federalism

Before outlining the Belgian case, it is necessary to discuss whether or not federalism has had an impact on discussions of pension reform. The main theoretical framework could be dismissed on the basis that Belgium is a biased example and that its relative inactivity with respect to pension reform has more to do with a federal structure leading to a decision trap (Scharpf 1988) than with different types of veto players.

Prior to 1988, Belgium was a unitary state. For most of its period of independence, it was culturally and economically dominated by the French part of the country. However, the combined effect of a strong industrial decline in the French region and a sharp increase in economic growth in Flanders undermined French dominance within Belgium. Support for decentralization gained momentum in both regions during the 1960s and 1970s, paving the way for a federal state (see Witte 1992; Lentzen 1998).

Social security has been disputed between both regions. Flanders transfers sums as large as 2.5 billion euros to Wallonia every year, resulting in north–south tensions. Based on these numbers, a Flemish regional newspaper might run the following headline: 'Every year a Flemish family buys the equivalent of a car for a French family'. Despite these contentious titles and perceptions, studies demonstrate that the differences are the result of socio-economic conditions rather than culture or ethnicity (Vaes 1998: 174).

Obviously, the French political parties are unanimous in their desire to maintain the federal nature of social security, with the Socialists being the least intransigent. A key argument put forward by these parties is that social security is one of the only remaining programmes holding the country together. The situation is slightly more complex and nuanced in Flanders, even though all parties support the idea of regionalizing at least one branch of social security. The Flemish Liberals (VLD) proposed increased reliance on the private sector, a policy that would benefit the Flemish region since it would result in lower financial transfers to the French regions. This party tends to be the most nationalistic of the three 'democratic' parties, which is not surprising because it sought to merge with the nationalistic Volksunie (VU) in an attempt to break the electoral dominance of the Christian Democrats (CVP).[8] The CVP supported the creation of a new system splitting social security into a contribution-based system for pensions and unemployment insurance and a tax-based system for family allocations and health insurance. This proposal was severely criticized by the French parties, especially the Socialists. They viewed the proposal as a way to favour splitting social security because it would be easier to transfer health and family allocations once they were based on income tax. The SP was the least vocal about this issue, but it favoured certain capitalized options to complement existing programmes. Because they seek to sever most, if not all, ties with the south, the extreme right Vlaams Blok Party and the VU favour a Flemish-only social security plan.

Despite these tensions, there are also many reasons to believe that regional differences do not matter with respect to pensions. First, social security is exclusively a federal jurisdiction, leaving the regions with no role to play. For example, pensions in the private sector are administered by the RVP/

ONP, which has its central office in Brussels and regional offices throughout the country.

Second, pensions are simply not mentioned as a policy sector that could be divided regionally by the main political actors. The reasons are quite simple and are related to the fact that pensions are linked to contributions,[9] thus higher wages result in higher pensions. Wages have been higher in Flanders for quite some time, thus pensions there are the most expensive. Since 1985, the differences between the average French pension (which are generally higher due to the retirement of workers with long careers in the industrial sector) and Flemish pensions have been declining rapidly (*Le Soir*, 6 January 1995). Peeters (1996) confirms this trend in a study comparing this evolution in the three Belgian regions. Even if one accounts for non-contributory elements, such as the granting of pension rights based on the worker's previous salary (despite the fact that no contributions were made) during a period of unemployment, there is no clear winner or loser. The high unemployment rate in Wallonia is compensated for by the greater utilization of early-retirement schemes, considered by the Flemish people to be a mixture of unemployment insurance and employer compensation.[10] Therefore, it is not surprising that most of the pressure to decentralize social security has been largely confined to health and family allocations rather than to pensions.

Theoretical expectations: a consensual case

Belgium is expected to have the greatest difficulty implementing reforms to its public pension system due to political relationships based on Social Partnership operating within a proportional-influence vision that generates multiple veto points and veto players. Consistent with the first ordering principle regarding the generation of veto points, the significant participation of the social partners within the administration of pension policies ensures them a privileged place in reform attempts engineered by the government. As in France, the veto point is a collective one requiring substantial opposition to a governmental proposal on the part of social partners. With employers supporting retrenchment measures that do not rely on raising contributions, unions must be united in their opposition to be effective. The two main unions, the ABVV/FGTB and the ACV/CSC, are very attached to the public pension system and unlikely to support proposals that threaten key elements of the current system. Changes in the philosophy or structure of the system, such as granting a predominant role to the private sector within the public pension system, simply cannot occur without the unions' consent. And as in France, unions have not shied away from taking their opposition to the streets.

The effectiveness of the veto point held by the unions is much enhanced by a very potent second ordering principle, which states that a high number of veto players (accentuated by ideological differences) is likely to generate policies similar to the status quo. The Belgian political system generates multiple veto players, accentuated by the informal rule of having parties from both Flanders and Wallonia in the governing coalition. Therefore, if the French Socialists are needed in the governing coalition, the Flemish Socialists will also join the government. A coalition of four to six political parties is required to ensure the adoption of any reform proposal. The previous coalition of Socialists (PS and SP) and Christian Democrats (PSC and CVP) and the coalition, operational since 1999, that is comprised of Socialists (PS and SP), Greens (Vert and Agalev) and Liberals (Parti Réformateur Libéral, PRL; and VLD) makes it difficult to envision the adoption of programmatic reforms. Not only are these coalitions fairly large, but they are also ideologically diverse, resulting in two main factors that privilege policies not straying far from the status quo (Tsebelis 1999). The Liberals have promoted a stronger role for the private sector, while the Socialists have fought just as hard to increase the generosity of the current system.

What makes the Belgian political landscape more prone to inaction is the combination of veto points and veto players. Unions have different institutional avenues to influence governing coalitions such as the RVP/ONP, the National Labour Council and each of the political parties within the coalition. For example, the ABVV/FGTB can stress 'non-socialist' behaviour if it believes that the Socialist Party is leaning towards a measure opposing the interests of its workers. In contrast to France, the government is ill equipped to adopt a divide-and-conquer strategy because it faces numerous hurdles within its own executive, with each party having a different linguistic and class base.

Not surprisingly, Belgium represents the case nearest to the status quo in this research. The few attempts to seek programmatic changes to the public pension system never received much consideration and were rapidly discarded. It took a lot of pressure from the EU to introduce the only significant parametric reform, an increase in the retirement age for women. The other measures introduced consisted of utilizing multiple tools, such as correlating the indexation of pensions with inflation to contain costs.

Reforming pensions in Belgium: a long march to nowhere?

The European Court of Justice pushes and Willockx sets the table ... then leaves

With strong pressures to reform (attributed partly to high unemployment rates among older workers as well as generous benefits to public-sector employees), demands to restructure the pension system began in the early 1980s. It took close to 15 years to enact even minor adjustments improving its sustainability, and the government unexpectedly needed the help of the European Court of Justice (ECJ). At first glance, the Belgian pension system for workers in the private sector did not appear to need as drastic an amount of reform as was the case in France; for example, the number of years worked before earning a full pension was already set at 45 years for men[11] (7.5 years more than in France), pensions were indexed to prices rather than wages and the retirement age was set at 65 for men and 60 for women. However, to counteract the negative impact of requiring a lengthy contribution period for a full pension, many non-contributory features were instituted that significantly minimized the link between contributions and benefits and made the system more costly. This is one of the principal reasons why the government sought reform. Ironically, the government had to increase the generosity of non-contributory elements, such as pension points for unemployment, to ensure that women would not be penalized too much by an increase in the length of the contribution period required to draw a full pension (from 40 to 45 years).

The first genuine reform attempts occurred during the 1980s, and two are worth noting. First, the Mainil (PSC) reform of 1983 introduced limits on pension accumulation for both the private and public sectors, improved the quality of pensions for the self-employed and improved pension coverage for men and women by granting survivors' pension rights to the former and family pensions to the latter. Originally, the government's plan sought to present more drastic measures, such as reducing civil servants' pensions, but Mainil faced stiff opposition, in the face of which he withdrew those measures that the unions opposed (Anderson *et al.* 2006). The second set of reforms occurred as part of the so-called St. Anna budgetary plan, which sought to cut expenditures by 5 billion euros. To meet the EU directive regarding equal treatment of the genders (see p. 89), the government first circulated a proposal to increase the retirement age for women to 65 to correspond with the men's retirement age. This option was rejected unanimously by all social partners because it would engender deficits in other insurance schemes. Following a summer-long period of union strikes and demonstrations, the government opted to introduce modest measures such as an indexation freeze, higher contributions and a reduction in future pensions (Anderson *et al.* 2006).

During the summer of 1988, the FPB was asked by the State Secretary for Pensions to present information regarding the future of the pension system. Less than a year later, the FPB was assigned to prepare projections outlining the future expenses of the entire social security system. This was requested to provide guidance during the contemporary legislative debate over the possible introduction of a lower retirement age. An official document was presented in May 1990,[12] most of the year having been spent gathering data and creating the basis of the simulation model (MALTESE – Model for Analysis of Long-Term Evolution of Social Expenditure) to be used in future years. This preliminary document analysed the social security system and stated that pension expenditure would rise from 6.8 per cent of gross national product (GNP) in 1987 to 11.1 per cent in 2030, given an annual growth rate of 2.25 per cent. The share of pension expenditure within the social security system was expected to rise from 36 per cent to more than 50 per cent, regardless of the scenario enacted.

The timing of these projections coincided with the Belgian government seeking to adapt a 1979 European directive (CEE 79/7) on equal treatment between men and women. The European Commission (EC) began to tackle its link with pensions in the early 1990s and asked Belgium to change the discriminatory treatment in the private sector's pension system (*Le Soir*, 6 January 1995). Thus, the central question became whether men were going to be offered retirement at 60 to match the women's age limit or whether women would be forced to wait till they were 65 to receive a full pension, as men did. Thus, in 1990 Belgium instituted a flexible retirement age system. Men were granted the option to retire at 60, with no additional penalty aside from the fact that their pension would still be calculated based on 45 years of employment. Therefore, someone working 40 years and retiring at the age of 60 received a pension derived from the calculation formula of 40/45. The calculation for women's benefits was left as it was.

Belgium organized its first large public gathering to discuss the future of pensions at the so-called 'Roundtable' organized by the Minister of Pensions, Freddy Willockx (SP), in 1992–3. It included social partners, pensioners' organizations and a number of experts. Various options for the future were discussed, but the difference in treatment between men and women kept resurfacing and became a central feature of the debate when, on 1 July 1993, the ECJ ruled against the adjustments Belgium introduced in 1990. Essentially, the ECJ claimed that gender discrimination had not yet been eliminated; a man working 40 years and choosing to retire at 60 would obtain a pension based on the ratio 40:45, while a woman would obtain it on a 40:40 basis. It stated that the new measures had to go beyond granting the opportunity to retire at the same age in order to include the same method of calculating pension benefits for both genders. Further roundtable discussions followed, but no concrete compromise emerged. Nonetheless, the roundtable allowed Willockx to recognize the types of reforms likely to be supported by the social partners.

The pension roundtable occurred even as broader discussions seeking to reform the entire social security system were taking place. In July 1993, the government proposed the recreation of a new social pact that it termed the 'Plan Global'. The main objective was to negotiate an overarching agreement on employment, competitiveness and how to finance social security with the social partners (Arcq and Chatelain 1994: 57). The government intended to make substantial savings to significantly reduce the whole system's deficit in the medium term, which would facilitate its incorporation into the budget. This process was required in order to meet Maastricht's convergence criteria. A deficit of 110 billion Belgian francs (BF) (2.8 billion euros) was expected for 1996, and the goal of the new measures was to achieve a balanced budget by that year, one that did not show a deficit.

With respect to social security, the Global Pact's five objectives were: (1) to make social security financing more favourable to employment; (2) to redefine its basic principles; (3) to reform its structure; (4) to ensure the financial equilibrium of the system; and (5) to revise certain spending mechanisms (Reman 1994: 132).

A committee of experts, the Verplaetse Group, was set up in early August 1993 to prepare propositions for the end of September. On 20 October, the day after public submission of the report, Prime Minister Dehaene presented a number of issues to be negotiated, some from the report and some from the government's commitments to the social partners. The prime minister asked the social partners to offer their opinion of the whole package promptly, but ABVV/FGTB immediately refused, though the ACV/CSC agreed to participate. Four days later, Dehaene stated that the government would work alone, as the negotiations had failed. A series of strikes soon followed. Social security reforms did not occur, and the government instead opted to increase revenues by raising taxes on alcohol, tobacco and energy. A social security reconstruction plan was included, but only as a wish-list. The Global Pact presented by the government included a proposition to subsume all social security receipts and expenditures within the same department so that the excess stemming from family allocations, for example, was available to finance the deficit in health insurance. This concept of 'Global Management' (*gestion globale*) was adopted in early 1994 (Arcq and Chatelain 1994: 57–62).

As a result of the ECJ ruling, legal actions against the Belgian government became more frequent, with men demanding their pensions be counted as women's were, based on 40 years of work instead of 45.[13] Willockx decided to press on with his reform project, which circulated in January 1994. Originating from the roundtable, the reform project aimed: (1) to increase the retirement age of women (along with the period of contributions needed to earn a full pension) so that it would be the same as men's by the year 2006; (2) to eliminate the revalorization of pension contributions paid between 1955 and 1974; and (3) to reform the non-contributory elements of the pension system. The proposal was confined strictly to wage earners in the private sector and the self-employed. Twenty billion BF in savings were expected to result from these measures. Adjusting the ECJ ruling the other way, that is, reducing the retirement age and length of the contribution period for men to make it consistent with that of women, was never seriously considered because it would have cost an additional 140 billion BF (*Le Soir*, 6 January 1995).

The Willockx plan negotiations did not go smoothly, and the room available to manoeuvre was quite limited. First, various women's associations, including those from the governing parties (PS, SP, CVP, PSC), were extremely critical of the impact such a reform would have on women, given that their pensions were already much lower than men's;[14] this reform would increase the current gap by an additional 11 per cent. Most also asked Willockx to introduce the reform at the latest date possible, 2020.[15]

The French Christian Democrat women argued that due to women's precarious career paths many of them would be dependent on derived rights (such as pensions accrued by marital status), which undermined the objective of achieving more individual rights in the social security system (*Le Soir*, 19 January 1994). French Socialist women pointed out that the only women receiving pensions comparable to men were widows, regardless of whether or not they had worked (*Le Soir*, 16 February 1994). The Equal Opportunity Office between Men and Women was also critical of the reform project, suggesting that it did, however, take the realities of the labour market into consideration.[16] Statistics published in *Le Soir* in 1996 strongly support this criticism. As of 1993, only 16 per cent of women had a complete career by the time they reached retirement age, and 76 per cent did not have even 35 years of employment (*Le Soir*, 10 September 1996), never mind 45 years. The wave of protest that followed led Willockx to delay the official introduction of his plan.

Willockx's intentions were not confined to the private sector. In mid-May 1994, the media learned of a project circulating within the cabinet of various ministries to reform the civil servants' pension scheme. When France occupied Belgium in the 1800s, it instituted its pension for civil servants the same way it was done in France; generous pensions were considered a deferred wage and an integral part of the status of being a civil servant. As a way to stimulate employment, the government took over the role of the private sector by hiring many of the unemployed in the 1970s. While the wages offered were below market level, the generous pension was used to encourage individuals to work in the public sector. This strategy ensured that the employer could hire more employees at an affordable immediate price and postpone some of the costs. However, it is precisely the *en masse* retirement of those workers in the upcoming years that is now creating financial problems for the government.

As is the case in France, the conditions and benefits of the public-sector scheme in Belgium are more advantageous than those in the private sector. Each year gives the right to 1/60th (a *tantième*)[17] of the reference salary in one's career, usually the last one, with a replacement ceiling of 75 per cent. Differences exist within the civil service, but most relate to the number of *tantièmes* required to obtain a full pension. The most privileged positions with regards to these criteria are university professors and the magistracy, whose pensions are accorded on the basis of only 30 *tantièmes*.[18] The most advantageous element of the civil servant pension system remains its indexation mechanism. Contrary to the system valid in the private sector, pensioners in the public-sector scheme see their pensions indexed at the same rate as wage increases in the public sector. In Belgium this is referred to as *péréquation*. Thus, if civil servants obtained a wage increase of 3 per cent, current pensioners would see their public pension benefits increase by the same percentage. This is by far the most expensive element of the entire system and the one that governments have tried to alter. The Plan Global called for measures to reduce the financial impact of civil servant pensions, which account for 17 per cent of the state budget (excluding servicing the debt), by 750 million BF (*Le Soir*, 19 July 1994).

The end result is a stark difference between the average monthly pension received by wage earners (20,145 BF) and the self-employed (11,788 BF) and that of state employees (54,931 BF) (*Le Soir*, 4 January 1995). More importantly, as described in the chapter on France (Chapter 2), the replacement rate of private-sector pensions decreases over time relative to the average wage because it is indexed to increases in the cost of living. It is worth noting, however, that civil servants do not have access to the second pillar, comprised of pensions negotiated within a collective agreement or an enterprise. Nonetheless, these were never widespread and were not easily accessible to many workers. In the private sector, only one-third of all wage earners participated in the second pillar, and the size of that segment was limited.[19] Private pension funds represent 10 per cent of GDP, while pension rights represent more than 250 per cent (Pestieau and Stijns 1997: 6).

Willockx's proposals for the pensions of civil servants sought to alter two key elements. First, they aimed to delay the effect of *péréquation* by imposing an annual ceiling of 1 per cent. Thus, if wages were to increase by 3 per cent in year X, pensioners would receive an incremental increase of their pensions (1 per cent in years X, Y and Z), which would enter into force on 1 July rather than 1 January. The second element would eliminate the preferential *tantième* treatment received by some sectors of the civil service such that everyone would have 60 *tantièmes*. Two other elements under consideration were placing a ceiling on widows' pensions and including any years worked in the private sector (*Le Soir*, 19 May 1994).

The unions' reactions were both immediate and negative. Both representatives of the public-sector sections of the main unions (FGTB and CSC) expressed their disapproval, but maintained that consultations within their union were needed. The most optimistic reaction came from Hervé Decuyer (Centrale Chrétienne des Services Publics – Confédération des Syndicats Chrétiens, CCSP–CSC), who stated that the reform elements were less radical than those presented to unions earlier (*Le Soir*, 20 May 1994). Willockx, for his part, expressed regret that his plan was publicized so early in the process. The discussion of the proposal by cabinet members was delayed, and the project was then shelved following opposition within the government, particularly from the Minister of Justice, Melchior Wathelet (PSC).[20] Wathelet faced strong lobbying from the magistracy to reject Willockx' proposal (*Le Soir*, 5 January 1995).[21]

A month later, the entire reform process suffered a serious setback when Willockx announced that he was leaving his position to lead the Flemish Socialist Party during the upcoming European elections. He claimed, however, that he would be able to present his project to reform private-sector pensions, which had previously been announced for January. Willockx left for Strasbourg in July, leaving no reform project behind.

Colla replaces Willockx, delaying the reform further ... but experiences some 'success'

Following Willockx's departure, Colla (SP) was appointed Minister of Pensions on 18 July 1994. All projects were shelved until after the federal elections of 1995. During his first year as minister, Colla actually implemented measures to generate alternative revenues, such as a solidarity contribution of 2 per cent for high pensions (more than 40,000 BF for those living alone) and an additional 9 per cent tax on energy.

Reforming social security was a core element of the 1995 electoral campaign, largely because of the strong neo-liberal attitude adopted by the Flemish Liberals (VLD), and partially supported by the French Liberals (PRL).[22] The VLD election campaign posters featured an elderly woman beneath the slogan 'Pension Funds will Disappear in 5 Years!'[23] This new programme to reform the social security system was adopted at the March 1994 VLD congress. It became a clear focus of its electoral campaign at both the regional and federal levels. Inspired by the pension funds of its Dutch neighbour, the VLD proposed a new system that would include both funded and payg elements. Claiming that contributions for the pension system, then set at 19 per cent, would need to reach 29 per cent in the future, the Flemish Liberals advocated raising the contribution rate to 24 per cent, of which 5 per cent would be invested in pension funds. They claimed that the funded component would eventually generate enough savings to reduce the payg portion to 15 per cent within 20 years, freezing contribution rates at 20 per cent. Further, they suggested increasing the minimum pension by 6,000 BF a month and extending the second pillar via funded schemes financed by employers.

In spite of a slight improvement in electoral results from the era of Partij voor Vrijheid en Vooruitgang (PVV),[24] the liberal ancestor to the VLD, the election of 1995 was viewed as a defeat given the level of support the polls reported prior to the elections. The president of the party, Verhofstadt, resigned soon after the election. The party's social security proposal was neither accepted nor trusted by the public. As an anonymous member of the party stated, 'Guy [Verhofstadt] was considered as the one who would tear down pensions' (*Le Soir*, 28 November 1995; author translation). Ironically, the implementation of this programme would have been quite difficult given that both the Association of Insurance (UPEA) and the Belgian Association of Pension Funds (ABFP) expressed their attachment to the first pillar and restated that their role was to complement it, not replace it.[25]

The Socialists and the Christian Democrats gathered enough support to build a new government. The *déclaration gouvernementale* presented on 28 June 1995 was not clear on the subject of pensions. As in the previous coalition agreement of 1992, the government stressed the importance of drastically reducing the debt in order to be able to sustain the payment of pensions beyond 2010. In its declaration, the government further announced that the pension system would be supported and that it would be modernized in line with new familial realities and the evolution of the labour market, as well as adapted to reduce the financial consequences of population ageing. The media also stated that one of the government's objectives would be to control the increasing expenditure of the current public servants' pension scheme (*Le Soir*, 19 June 1995). Two other elements related to pensions were mentioned. First, the government promised to ensure that poor pensioners receive a fairer part of the increased standard of living. Second, it stated that it would seek to promote the second pillar of the pension system by encouraging employees and employers to reconsider its importance with a new legal framework.

A few months after the introduction of the new government it was evident that Belgium would make whatever adjustments were necessary to enter EMU. Belgium's participation, like Italy's, was accompanied by a big question mark. There was a strong commitment from the government, and existing institutional powers were reinforced (see Hallerberg 1999), but social security reform immediately came up again as a necessary element to reach the Maastricht convergence criteria.

Willockx's proposal for the private sector resurfaced and obtained the same kind of reaction as it had the previous year. The women's association within the Flemish Christian Democrat Party restated its concerns about the new reform. Specifically, it asked that if the government opted to continue with its reform project it would also work more aggressively towards equalizing professional opportunities (*Le Soir*, 23 June 1995). In November 1995, following contacts with the social partners at the top level, Colla announced that the reform for private-sector workers and the self-employed would be in place by the end of the year. He also argued for the creation of collective pension funds to create a strong second pillar.

It soon became apparent that the public-sector unions' support would be much harder to get. Rumours circulated that Colla had proposed something even more radical than Willockx had. The *péréquation* would be maintained for low salaries, and the preferential treatment received by certain groups of civil servants (i.e. lower *tantièmes*) would be abolished. He also wanted to calculate pensions according to a worker's entire career, instead of the last five years of work. These measures would have led to a certain harmonization of pensions granted in the private sector (*Le Soir*, 15 November 1995). The unions were unfazed by Colla's initiatives. It was repeated in newspapers and during interviews with both social partners and a cabinet member from the Ministry of Pensions that the only way to describe the negotiation was with the word 'blockage'. The public-service unions simply refused to negotiate a reduction in their pensions.[26] The general strike movement in France halted public discussions on this subject, resulting in the addition of the phrase 'We are not going to act *à la* Juppé' into politician's speeches.

Discussions to reform the pensions of private-sector workers resumed in May 1996. As part of the three broad conditions that would allow Belgium to enter EMU, it was announced that a pension reform would be included and that it was the action engendering the strongest reactions (*Le Soir*, 19 May 1996). The stumbling-blocks were with the ABVV/FGTB and the PS. In the ABVV/FGTB, internal conflicts over pension reform paralysed the search for consensus on this matter. Led by the Walloon regional federation,[27] women and public servants, as a group, refused to move beyond the 40-year calculations for women.[28] A more pragmatic group led by the Flemish federation supported negotiations towards lengthening the contribution period as long as the government ensured a decent pension for all women. The final compromise accepted by the ABVV/FGTB rejected any lengthening of the period of contributions for women if they were not to be compensated for the unfair treatment they received in the labour market (*Le Soir*, 30 May 1996, 8 June 1996, 18 June 1996, 19 June 1996).

The leadership of the French Socialist Party had trouble getting support from its grassroots constituents for an extension of the contribution period for women. The women's association within the party asked for the removal of all points related to the acceptance by the PS of the pension reform (*Le Soir*, 18 June 1996). To appease the critics, the party leadership promised during the congress to ensure that: (1) the transition period would be long; (2) the reform would consider the differences between men and women at the end of a career; and (3) it would seek to raise the minimum pension (*Le Soir*, 1 July 1996).

It should be noted that the protest movement was not confined to these two organizations. First, the CSC adopted a compromise line where it was willing to accept a new pension system in which a full pension would be based on 42 or 43 years. However, it also asked for improvements to the current system. It wanted an improvement in small and minimum pensions and a more favourable consideration of low-salaried and part-time wage earners. Second, the parliamentary committee dealing with the issue of equality between men and women[29] voted against any generalization of pensions based on a 40-year career, but raised serious questions about any solution that required everyone to have a 45-year career before they could collect a full pension. The committee pointed out that such amendments needed first to estimate the increased costs to other sectors of social security (such as unemployment insurance) and the negative effect they would have on women's pensions (*Le Soir*, 26 June 1996).

As a result of this opposition, Colla's official proposal was delayed further. He was so discouraged that he even presented a surprise new solution. Probably inspired by the Swedish reform, Colla suggested something similar to the life-income principle (see Chapter 4), where every year worked would earn pension points. Those working part time or unemployed would receive points equivalent to the minimum pension. The individual could then choose when to retire. He asked the FBP to study this further, stating that he would present this idea to the cabinet at its next meeting (*Le Soir*, 22 June 1996, 24 June 1996). The idea was soon discarded, as it failed to gather support – even from his own party. It was never brought up again, due to his own government's failure to support it. Whether or not it was a good idea is a moot point. The central problem was the length of time that was necessary to gather enough expertise regarding the new system and, more importantly, the time required for each political actor to study the proposal, which generally resulted in yet another round of negotiations.

The momentum associated with the introduction of the pension reforms in both the private and public sectors increased in autumn 1996. Working with the hypothesis elaborated by the FPB, a brainstorming group including experts from various ministries worked on various scenarios in September 1996. Unions continued to be consulted, but their resistance to the reforms, especially the public sector's opposition, did not seem to decline. As a precautionary measure, more than 1,500 civil servants from the three major unions gathered in front of Val Duchesne, where the Council of Ministers was meeting, and pledged to defend their pensions (*Le Soir*, 14 September 1996). Faced with continuous pressure not to alter the civil servants' pensions, the government abandoned those plans.

The government officially announced the introduction of the first reform at the end of September 1996. It had first been proposed by Willockx in late 1993 and was clearly riddled with numerous compromises. The reform included five core elements. First, women were required to have 45 years of contributions in order to collect a full pension, but this requirement would be implemented over a long transition period of 13 years.[30] Women would immediately need to contribute 41 years for a full pension, but an extra year's contribution would be added every three years until the period reached 45 in 2009. Second, the flexibility to retire between the ages of 60 and 65 retained the same 'penalty',[31] but the minimum number of years of required contributions was gradually increased from 20 to 35 (two years every year until 2005, which was when a period of 35 years would be reached). Third, pensions were revalorized during the period 1955–74 by a coefficient of 1.036 (or 3.6 per cent). This coefficient would be removed gradually, and eliminated in 2005, at the rate of 0.004 per year. Fourth, the government introduced a minimum pension right for each year of work. In order to obtain this benefit, a person had to be employed for at least 15 years in a job at least one-third of the time, which could include a period of unemployment. Thus, someone having a part-time or broken career could receive a pension based on a full-time career at the minimum wage. Finally, for non-active periods considered to be part of a redistribution of work, pension points were granted as a means of compensation. The value of the assimilated period could be doubled or even tripled for the education of a child below the age of six. The final two measures had a direct impact on women (who have more precarious positions than men) and lessened the impact of the increase in the length of their contribution period.

It is important to note what was not included in the pension reform. For example, non-contributory benefits granted for sickness and unemployment were left untouched. Willockx had earlier proposed to reduce the level of compensation so that 'fictive' points would be granted on the basis of the average wage instead of the wage of the previous year. The early-retirement scheme was also unaltered, with the exception that women would have to wait for an additional period of time before they could get it. A similar reform was introduced for the self-employed.

The overall response to the reform was quite positive, with the exception of opposition from the Liberals, who claimed that Colla's proposal was not truly a reform, but simply an adjustment to bring women's pensions in line with men's (*Le Soir*, 2 October 1996). Probably fearful of the backlash their previous position had caused within the populace, the Liberal's criticisms remained fairly moderate. Due to implementation delays, the reform would be enacted six months later (i.e. on 1 July 1997 instead of 1 January). The co-ordination of the reform with early-retirement schemes partly financed by the employers and the granting of pension rights to part-time workers were extremely problematic (*Le Soir*, 3 January 1997). A public protest against the way the government instituted the calculation of the minimum right for pensions occurred in February 1997. Other demands included a more favourable indexation of pensions and a solution for the transitional problems of early-retirement schemes caused by increasing the age of retirement for women (*Le Soir*, 7 February 1997).

Consequences of the 1996 pension reform: real savings?

Contrary to expectations, the pension reform did not engender significant changes within the system, to the extent that doubts were raised regarding whether it actually produced any savings at all. The FPB produced a special planning paper on the effects of the new reform entitled *La Réforme des pensions: Une Nouvelle Génération et un nouveau contrat* (Festjens 1997). Interestingly, the author of the report, Festjens, analysed the effects of the reform on both individuals and the state budget. The projections assumed an annual growth rate of 2.25 per cent, stable long-term interest rates of 4 per cent and an unemployment rate of 5 per cent.[32]

The individual effects of the new reform were quite negligible. Most individuals lost less than 1 per cent of the value of their pensions. The long-term effects were negligible, if not positive. Most of the negative effects of increasing the length of contributions affecting women were compensated for by granting the minimum pension right for individual career years falling below the minimum wage. In the worst-case scenario, a 1 per cent reduction in pension benefits was realized for unmarried women pensioners in 2010. The main savings measure is the elimination of the revalorization granted during the period 1955–74 rather than the increase in the length of women's contribution periods.

The 1996 reform actually introduced new expenses to other social security programmes such as unemployment, disability and early retirement. It was assumed at the time that by the year 2007 more than 20 billion BF would be required by these programmes as a result of the reform. This is a direct consequence of the fact that many women between 60 and 65 years of age will most likely end up being unemployed or in early-retirement programmes. Belgium's employment rates for older workers (55+) are the lowest in Europe, and many older workers find themselves in long-term unemployment or in early-retirement schemes. This is a practice that was considered acceptable for most of the 1970s and 1980s. Even though it was criticized heavily in the 1990s, no sharp decrease was experienced and social partners continued to reject any change. Thus, despite pension savings of 33.8 billion BF in 2007, the state budget ends up being reduced by 16.3 billion BF (approx. 6.5 billion euros) once additional expenditures from other social security programmes are taken into account. The reduction in pension expenditure for other programmes occurs because many women have mixed careers. When a career is longer in the private sector, the points from the other regimes are transferred into it (Festjens 1997: 75).

Based on her analysis, Festjens concluded that those who will suffer most from the reform are women with a stable career. They are unlikely to obtain minimum pension rights because they do not have career breaks or precarious positions; thus, they suffer the full effect of the reform without any ameliorating effects. These women are likely to lose 9 to 11 per cent of their pensions should they decide to retire at 60 (Festjens 1997: 75).

A caveat is in order as we interpret and analyse these projections. The total savings might actually be lower than the plan projected. Considering recent developments in the Belgian economy, the rates of both growth and unemployment must be considered overly optimistic. The average growth rate for the period 1990–2000 was 2 per cent owing to strong growth in the second half of the 1990s. Had the plan used the same macro-economic hypothesis as the Economic Policy Committee (where the growth rate is expected to be 2.5 per cent from 2002 to 2011, 1.8 per cent between 2011 and 2021, and 1.2 per cent thereafter), the potential savings would have been lower. Purely in terms of savings, growth is the key element in a pension system that is price indexed, as the revenues increase in real terms while expenses increase only in terms of new adherents to the system (but not as a result of the evolution of pensions, which remain frozen in real terms).

Can Belgium succeed where Juppé failed? Seeking to reform public-sector pensions

Willockx was the first minister to consider seriously reforming public pensions. However, he withdrew his proposal in the face of strong pressures from civil servants, particularly from the magistracy. Colla had high hopes early on, but the French reaction to the Juppé plan forced him to reconsider.

Unlike the situation in France, most Belgian civil servants are unionized. Introducing pension reform in the private sector reactivated discussions to do the same in the public sector. The third attempt was as successful as the previous two.

When the pension reform in the private sector became official, all the politicians stated that something must also be done about the public sector. After all, this was the sector where pensions were expected to grow most quickly due to their indexation to wages instead of prices. The retirement of the numerous agents hired in the 1970s was giving the government huge headaches. At a time when budget constraint was the norm, pension expenditures in the public sector were expected to double within 20 years.

The head of the PSC group, Jacques Lefèvre, mentioned that he regretted 'the lack of measures for public sector pensions' (*Le Soir*, 2 October 1996). The main leaders of the other three political parties in the coalition (Dehaene [CVP], Vande Lanotte [SP] and Busquin [PS]) confirmed their wish to reform the public-service pension system on numerous occasions; there was a political consensus on this issue. All parties recognized that the basic agreement of lower wages and higher pensions in principle could not be altered. This implied that current pensions and those forthcoming in the near future could not be touched. However, they argued that a reform that included a long transition period ought to be considered because of changing conditions within the civil service. State employees now earned wages similar to those working in the private sector, the value of job security was worth significantly more than it was 30 years earlier and the number of years in retirement had also increased (*Le Soir*, 8 October 1996). The main objective for the government was still delaying or reducing the effect of the so-called *péréquation*.[33]

In the discussions surrounding reform, public servants ensured that the government understood the readiness of the opposition. Sponsored by the three major unions, a strike of more than 14,000 people paralysed Brussels for a few hours at the end of January. Their main demand was respect of their status and their pensions (*Le Soir*, 30 January 1997). Pension reform discussions disappeared for about six months. Two newspapers, *L'Écho* and the *Standaard*, surprised everyone by announcing that the government was close to adopting a reform in the summer of 1997. *L'Écho* claimed that the *péréquation* would no longer be automatic and that the *tantièmes* would be increased by four for all civil servants (*Le Soir*, 7 June 1997). The *Standaard* referred to a reform project similar to the one Willockx advocated. The *péréquation* would have a ceiling of 1 per cent per year, and an increase in the number of *tantièmes* would be encouraged via the granting of bonuses (*Le Soir*, 17 June 1997).

These rumours were strongly denied by the Minister of Pensions and his cabinet. Colla even called the idea of increasing all *tantièmes* by four ridiculous, stating that such options had not even been properly studied. Cabinet members maintained that inter-ministerial discussions had not yet begun (*Le Soir*, 7 June 1997). To weather the storm, the prime minister called a press conference a few days after an inter-ministerial meeting devoted to the issue. Dehaene claimed that reforming public-sector pensions was a part of the *déclaration gouvernementale*, but that his government was strongly committed to the process of negotiation with the unions. Finally, he rejected all questions concerning the rumours initiated by the media since no precise scenario was being considered by the government (*Le Soir*, 20 June 1997).

The tone of the unions was uncompromising. First, the liberal union (Syndicat Libre de la Fonction Publique/Vrij Syndicaat voor het Openbaar Ambt, SLFP/VSOA – a branch of ACLV/CGSLB) stated that touching the *péréquation* and increasing the *tantièmes* would amount to a declaration of war (*Le Soir*, 7 June 1997), a surprising reaction for a union known for its pragmatism and conciliatory attitude. Second, the Fédération des Syndicats Chrétiens des Services Publics/Federatie van de Christelijke Syndicaten der Openbare Diensten (FSCSP, a branch of ACV/CSC) decided to adopt a 'wait and see' attitude, while the Centrale Générale des Services Publics/ Algemene Centrale der Openbare Diensten (CGSP, a branch of ABVV/ FGTB) announced warning measures.

A frustrated Colla would make a final pledge in early 1998 to convince the opposition to alter its stance:

> My file has been ready for months. I have ideas, proposals. Up to now, it has not been politically feasible to implement them. ... It is possible that those who do not want a reform could avoid it during this parliamentary mandate. Will it be a victory? No. The problem will remain on the political agenda. I ask solemnly the political leaders, my friends in the union movement, and all civil servants to reflect well on this. It is in their interest that this reform happens as soon as possible. Even if we vote in a year, I am ready to make a reform that is socially acceptable and that guarantees the uniqueness of the public servant scheme.
>
> (*Le Soir*, 7 January 1998)

Failing in his last attempt, Colla redirected his energy to his other main portfolio, Public Health. This turned out to be even more devastating than his pension work, as he ended up being one of the two main political figures implicated in the 'chickengate' scandal involving contaminated chicken, and he was forced to resign in early June 1999.

Following the June 1999 elections, Frank Vandenbroucke (SP) became the new Minister of Pensions. Having recently arrived from political exile in Oxford, where he obtained a PhD in Social Science, he opted for a successful course of action: inaction. He referred the issue to those who negotiate wages (*Le Soir*, 14 September 1999). This implied moderating the increase in public employees' salaries, which in turn moderates the increase in the pension paid by the Ministry of Finance. This 'new' strategy also received the support of the government. As a result, pension reform in the public sector was not included in the *déclaration gouvernementale* in 1999.[34]

Implications of the failure to implement reform in the public sector

The failures of previous governments to reform the civil servants' pension scheme do not imply that the current government has fully given up. In fact, crafty solutions have been devised to reduce the possible effect of a significant increase in the number of retired civil servants. First, many new employees are hired on a contractual basis, which puts them into the wage-earner pension schemes. This also has the negative effect of abandoning the tenure traditionally associated with the civil service. Second, Vandenbroucke deferred to his new solution, which was the cost-containment of wages. Lower wage increases result in lower pension increases. As with private investments, compounded wages play an important part in one's pension. Minor increases early on can result in solid savings 30 years down the road. This was in effect the aim of the Willockx proposal. Nonetheless, this tactic cannot function unilaterally, as the government must negotiate wages with the unions. When projections were released in the mid-1990s, unions were quick to point out that wages were not evolving as quickly as claimed by governmental studies. However, it must be noted that a key reason behind the wage increase of civil servants is that they are now better educated and trained. As such, they are obtaining higher wages and larger raises, which is affecting the average wage for the entire civil service. This is one of the reasons newspapers and analysts contest the validity of the claim that wages in the public service are lower than in the private service. This is a direct reversal of most of the hiring done in the 1970s, which included many blue-collar or less-skilled individuals who usually earn lower wages than those paid by the private sector. Owing to *péréquation*, these individuals end up benefiting from their children's greater skills.

A third way to minimize the size of civil servant pensions is to reduce the rate of hiring. The ultimate tool would be to replace civil servants not when they retire, but when they are deceased. Of course, this is not a strategy employed by the government, but it is now relying more on the private sector, thus reducing the state's payroll. A fourth option employed by the government is the introduction of a new pension tax referred to as a 'solidarity contribution'. Since 1 January 1995, this tax has been applied to pension income above 44,163 BF (*Le Soir*, 4 January 1995), thus affecting mostly civil servants' earnings, as their average pension is much more generous than those earned by workers in the private sector (54,931 BF vs 20,145 BF). The rates for this progressive tax vary from 0.5 per cent to 2 per cent.[35] To sell this new tax as a means to introduce intra-generational solidarity, Colla included as taxable income all pension contributions made to a second pillar and invested in collective pension funds retroactive to 1981. Following numerous court cases in which the ONP tried to stop the reimbursement of collected contributions, all amounts obtained via the second pillar were eliminated from consideration. Thus, by the end of the 1990s a large proportion of the pensions affected by the solidarity contribution were within the public sector.

These options may reduce the financial drain of the upcoming pensioners in the civil service, but they cannot genuinely alter it. Further increases in any of these options are likely to result in strong opposition from the groups affected. Thus, unions have successfully defended their core benefits.

Complements, or the future core of the pension system? The *Zilverfund* and the second pillar

Following the 1999 election, pension reforms were again on the government's agenda. However, in contrast to its predecessors, none of its measures proposed to retrench any of the pension schemes. The new government enacted three principal measures. First, it established the creation of a demographic fund, referred to as *Zilverfund* (Silver Fund). It also established a legal base alongside fiscal incentives to promote the development of the second pillar via the creation of group insurance or pension funds at the company or sectoral level. Finally, the minimum pension was increased substantially in the spring of 2000. This last section discusses the first two measures, as they are the most likely to have an impact in the future.

Following a study by the FPB claiming that public funds would be made available in the upcoming years, the Minister of the Budget, Johan Vande Lanotte (SP), proposed the creation of a *Zilverfund* designed to prepare the state for the consequences of population ageing starting in 2030. It was noted on numerous occasions that new funds would be available once the debt was reduced. With Belgium's entrance into EMU, the lower interest rate within the Euro-zone allowed Belgium to shrink its public debt and interest payments on its debt, leaving budgetary room for pensions. Vande Lanotte's plan would make use of the public funds available from reducing the public debt, starting with 25 billion BF, up to the year 2002. This figure would reach 220 billion BF annually by the year 2013, and that amount would be invested every year thereafter until 2030 (*L'Écho*, 11 May 2000).

This plan was broadly supported within and outside the government. Prime Minister Verhofstadt (VLD) stated that such projects conformed to the *déclaration gouvernementale*. The PS, the ABVV/FGTB and the Greens supported it in principle and claimed that it was a step in the right direction but requested more details. The CSC came out strongly in favour of the plan, giving a 'gold medal' to the minister (*Le Soir*, 12 May 2000). The *Zilverfund* was adopted at the end of 2001. It consists of government bonds, and the end result is no different from having the debt further reduced. As of 2004, the fund had accumulated close to 12 billion euros.

Clearly present in the *déclaration gouvernementale* was the creation of a second pillar accessible to all wage earners. Strongly endorsed by the

Liberals, who obtained an expansion of private pensions, this was the only pension measure where consensus could be reached within the coalition government (Anderson *et al.* 2006). Thus, it was not surprising that the Vandenbroucke plan was unilaterally adopted in January 2001 by the Council of Ministers. Contrary to many industrialized countries, this pillar was underdeveloped in Belgium, and was most often instituted according to the will of the employer; thus, most of the benefits accrued to management. As a result, a key objective of the reform was to 'democratize' this pillar that was currently utilized by only 30 per cent of workers. Its purpose was to ensure that it became an item of negotiation in the collective agreements of all branches at the sectoral level. To ensure the support of social partners, they were granted the responsibility of managing the funds themselves. This was an important point for the unions, since the previous system allowed employers a quasi-free hand. Sold as a means to ensure a pension that would not result in large discrepancies between the final wage and the first pension (and not a replacement of the first pillar), its importance may increase significantly in the future if proper indexation is not granted to first-pillar pensions. The WAP/LPC legislation (*Wet op Aanvullende Pensioenen/Loi sur les Pensions Complémentaires*), also known as the Vandenbroucke Law, was adopted in 2003. It promoted the establishment of defined contribution plans and introduced a minimum mandatory rate of return for employers. Further, the pension cannot be liquidated prior to age 60. All plans involving employers are subject to this new law (Vermeylen 2004: 7–9). As of 2005, second-pillar coverage increased by roughly one million workers (Anderson *et al.* 2006).

Conclusion

Consistent with the typology presented in Chapter 1, Belgium has had the most difficulty introducing pension reforms. Unlike France, it could not generate a pension reform in the public sector in spite of a similar approach contrasting the discrepancies between those working in the private sector and those employed in the public sector. Its consultation strategy with the unions did not bear fruit, and the fear of a wave of protest *à la* Juppé persuaded the government to avoid this route. In contrast to France, where both main parties announced that a pension reform within the public sector would be occurring following the election of 2002, the Belgian coalition government made the opposite promise. The Belgian government needed an ECJ directive and three years of consultation in order to comply with the court orders, and generated only very limited savings in the end. More problematic is the fact that numerous non-contributory elements remain strongly anchored in the system. Thus, the 45-year career required to obtain a full pension is more a myth than a reality. When all is said and done, the link between contributions and benefits was further weakened by the reform.

The expansion of the second pillar is becoming increasingly important to guarantee future pensioners' financial security. Belgium's pension system ranks 12th in the EU with respect to the replacement rate of its system, a direct consequence of price indexation, and the financial involvement of the state has declined continuously since the early 1980s (Montagne 2000: 2), generating even more reliance on contributions. The problem is that many periods are assimilated, meaning that benefits are granted without any contributions. Because the government is not sufficiently subsidizing these periods, contributions serve as subsidies as well. Thus, the government would have to reverse this trend to meet its obligations and face the upcoming demographic changes in a low growth environment. This is in essence the aim of the *Pacte des générations*. As a result, the expansion of the second pillar is necessary to attain high replacement rates for workers and to protect them from the uncertainties faced by the first pillar.

The political difficulties associated with the introduction of the reform are supported by the typology presented in Chapter 1. Limited policy change is expected in a consensual cell generated by Social Partnership operating within a proportional-influence vision. The combination of a large number of veto players within a governmental coalition associated with veto points in its social security structure resulted in a position very similar to the status quo. Consistent with the first ordering principal, the integration of social partners within the policy process accentuates the difficulties of pension reform. The Ministry of Pensions has acknowledged their administrative role within the process, and social partners have privileged access to the decision-making apparatus. In the case of civil servants, pensions represent an entitlement included in their job description, resulting in increased legitimacy and rights to oversee the programme.

The influence of social partners was expressed in numerous ways. First, most discussions in Belgium are conducted in private and rarely receive public attention unless a formal announcement or agreement arises. However, leaks to the media occurred when the direction of the discussions challenged the basic premise of the existing pension schemes. Regardless of the source of the leak, these news reports served as a rallying point to mobilize union membership. In a few cases, they have been enough to force the government to back down or even deny specific proposals and/or discussions. This leads us to the second way social partners can influence pension politics, namely that unions have been able to effectively mobilize and protest, thus sending warning signals to governments concerning possible reforms. Third, social partners also challenge the expertise of governmental actors, though not to the same extent as in France, owing to the existence of a more collaborative spirit that exists between the state and the social partners. Nonetheless, by virtue of their membership within the ONP, social partners have access to numerous documents to challenge the assumptions and empirical claims made by government officials concerning their pension system. Finally, and this point is closely tied to the second ordering principle (see pp. 30–2), social partners have been able to effectively use the fragmented leadership produced by broad coalition governments in Belgium. By their presence within the policy process, unions can ensure that socialist parties remain true to their values, and employers can do the same with liberal parties. For example, no socialist party wants unions to make public the extent to which Socialists are accepting proposals opposed to their ideology and electoral platform. Social partners can thus interfere with agreements and reduce (or at least stop the expansion of) the range within which proposals can be accepted by each individual party.

The second ordering principle states that a broad political coalition including ideologically polarized political parties is unlikely to yield a (major) pension reform. The Belgian case supports this hypothesis. However, evidence suggests that the major hurdle is striking an agreement with social partners and not consensus among political parties (which is achieved cyclically via the *déclaration gouvernementale*). The key exception is the 1994 election, when the Flemish Liberal Party campaigned aggressively on a platform of privatizing pensions. Those negative results sealed the extensive differentiation it had with other parties, as the Flemish Liberal Party abandoned that stance in favour of more parametric measures. In contrast to France, where a strong and unified executive can effectively split the unions, Belgium's executive can be split by social partners, making reforms far more difficult. Nonetheless, the coalition government has occasionally succeeded in dividing the unions with implicit or explicit support from the ACV/CSC for certain reform measures (Anderson *et al.* 2006). The two ordering principles developed by this research demonstrate the two core difficulties the Belgian government faced and explain why they experienced only limited success in reforming their pension schemes.

4   Sweden

Do unions still matter? Committees instil a radical pension reform

Introduction

The Swedish pension system is imbued with social democratic values reflecting the hegemonic domination of the Left in the post-World War II period. Although most observers link the pre-1998 system with the Social Democratic Party (SAP), the development of the first form of assistance for the elderly was actually introduced by the Liberals, a centre/right-wing party. The introduction of the ATP[1] pension system in the late 1950s was designed to 'equalize the pension status of all wage earners' (Esping-Andersen 1985: 108). In contrast to France and Belgium, the Swedish pension system is universal and applies equally to all workers, irrespective of employment sector. The ATP struggle was a central political issue in the late 1950s, leading to much conflict between political parties and labour-market partners. That struggle resulted in two elections and a referendum on the subject. The two main bourgeois parties (Conservative and Liberal) supported the expansion of voluntary, private occupational pensions administered by unions and employers. The Centre Party favoured a substantial increase in the basic pension while promoting a voluntary occupational pension administered by a governmental agency. The Social Democratic Party promoted a compulsory, supplementary, earnings-related pension paid by employers and administered by the government.

The Social Democratic option was eventually adopted, with full benefits determined according to the 15 highest earning years (of a minimum 30-year career). With many white-collar workers already covered by private plans, the SAP successfully instituted this rule to make the public alternative more appealing. With the complementary role of the universal basic pension, also co-financed by employers and the state since 1973, the expectation was that retirement income would equal 60 per cent of an individual's working wage. Pension benefits were adjusted for inflation, and processes were put in place to adjust pensions whenever the cost of living increased. In the 1960s, the administration enacted legislation to make those adjustments automatic (Heclo 1974: 248). As a result, the real value of the basic pension more than tripled from 1949 to 1984 (S. Olson 1988: 41). When these automatic increases were combined with the ATP's maturity, public pensions evolved into a genuine replacement wage as opposed to a subsistence benefit.

The Swedish pension system remained very stable[2] until the pension reform of 1994/1998, which was the result of a five-party agreement. An entirely new pension system and philosophy were instituted based on a notionally defined contribution model. The pension reform process survived both a change of government and internal dissent within the SAP. Consistent with the theoretical expectations outlined in Chapter 1, the predominant role of the state in governing the pension system allowed politicians to concentrate on finding a compromise, leaving unions and employers a very limited role.

Theorizing public pension reforms in the Swedish context

A social democratic state?

Any discussion on the strength of the Swedish welfare state tends to begin with the hegemonic power of the Social Democrats and their firm control of the political executive in conjunction with a co-operative bureaucracy.[3] Prior to the 2006 election, the Social Democrats had been in power for all but nine years since the end of World War II (1976–82 and 1991–4). Despite this electoral dominance, the Social Democrats have often had to rely on another coalition partner or a supporter (most often the Communist/Left Party) to maintain power, creating a political environment where compromise and negotiation are featured prominently.

The Swedish state, while influential, was not perceived as precluding private interests, as is the case in France. On the contrary, the state actively included them in the decision-making process. As was so clearly emphasized in Rothstein's (1991, 1992) work on this subject, it was the Liberals who, in the early 1900s, sought to increase the participation of both labour and employers in social affairs by encouraging them to choose their own representatives to sit on national boards addressing social issues. In contrast to the competitive and unproductive political climate of both France and Germany, the Swedish state sought the involvement of both labour and employer groups in order to 'increase that state's knowledge and information about many social problems entailed by the "labour question"' (Rothstein 1991: 162).[4] This corporatist structure is considered to be largely responsible for the generous, universal welfare system (Korpi 1983; Esping-Andersen 1985, 1990) and for the country's strong economic growth (Cameron 1984; Katzenstein 1985; Garrett and Lange 1991). The co-operation and involvement of both unions and employers in the state were considered important factors in the Swedish model's elaboration. Rothstein (1996) and Lindqvist (1990) go even further in their assessment, claiming that private interests – in this case, unions – actually 'captured' the state in certain policy sectors (see pp. 113–4).

In contrast to the way the pension system is structured in France, Swedish pensions are not centralized in the Prime Minister's Office. Commissions on pensions do not report directly to the prime minister and have not been under that office's direct supervision, owing largely to institutional factors. The power of individual ministers and ministries tends to be quite strong, especially if one compares the arrangement to those in France and the United Kingdom. When coalition governments prevail, individual ministries also tend to have a certain independence from the centre. Mattson (1996), for example, argued that negotiations within the governmental coalition allowed ministries to extend their resources beyond targets set by the Ministry of Finance. Thus, rather than relying on a cabinet member specializing in pensions, as is the case in France, a Swedish prime minister is more likely to rely on the experience and expertise of his/her minister or of a state secretary affiliated to the ministry.

One of the core aspects of Swedish governance is its reliance on expert commissions and parliamentary committees in the policy-making process. In fact, it is difficult to find a Swedish article tackling public policy with no mention of an SOU.[5] These reports tend to play a large role in the public debate on policy, and the object and the parameters of a public inquiry clearly identify a government's intentions. Thus, contrary to the situation adhering in most Western democracies, the parliamentary committees of the Riksdag have a great deal of influence (Arter, 1990; Hermansson, 1993). Parliamentarians are by no means bystanders on these committees. They tend to specialize in a few policy areas and are involved much earlier in the policy process than their European counterparts. Finally, the committee system is considered very important for a minority government, within which it can seek coalition partners for a bill and avoid a possible vote of no confidence in parliament (Arter 1990: 125–33).

As illustrated in Table 4.1, the main architects of the pension reform of 1998 – Könberg, Gennser, Petersson, Wiklund/Frebran,[6] Hedborg and Thalén – had been associated with pension committees for many years. Most members who left a committee did so for personal or electoral reasons.[7] The two committees strongly associated with the 1994/1998 pension reform and the working and implementation groups have been remarkably stable and have consistently featured the same core group of individuals.

One of the principal results of this policy structure has been strong policy coherence and vision. For example, in *Taxation and Democracy* Steinmo (1993) clearly demonstrates that Sweden has been able to avoid the constant remaking of tax policies resulting from the introduction of new governments in the United Kingdom and the complexity of the American tax system, which cannot be reformed as a whole due to the constellation of power that seeks endless additions to the tax code, thus reducing its fluidity.

Table 4.1 MP representation on Swedish pension committees (1984–2004)

Bo Könberg (FP)[a]	X	X	X
Margit Gennser (M)		X	X
Pontus Wiklund (KD)	X	X	
Anna Hedborg (S)[b]		X	X[b]
Åke Petersson (C)		X	X
Doris Håvik (S)	X		
Gösta Andersson (C)	X		
Ingegerd Troedsson (M)	X		
Ingegerd Elm (S)	X		
Karin Nordlander (V)	X		
Bertil Whinberg (S)	X		
Barbro Westerholm (FP)[a]		X	
Leif Bergdahl (ND)		X	
Ingela Thalén (S)		X	X[c]
Per Lennart Börjesson (V)		X	
Ulla Hoffman (V)		X	
Rose-Marie Frebran (KD)			X
Inger-Maj Klingvall			X[c]
Maud Björnemalm (S)			X
Arne Kjörnsberg (S)			X
Hans Svensson (S)			X[c]

Notes:

[a] He was the Minister of Social Affairs under the Carl Bildt government of 1991–4 and head of the working group (pensionsarbetsgruppen). Westerholm took his seat as representative for the Liberal Party during this period. She became the president of the second largest pensioner organization (SPF).

[b] She resigned in 1996 to become the General Director of the National Insurance Board and thus remained a key actor in the process.

[c] Rejoined the group in September 1999, replacing the tandem Klingvall/ Svensson. In order to be consistent with the Swedish acronyms, political parties are identified in the following manner: M = Moderaterna (Conservatives); FP = Folkpartiet (Liberal Party); C = Centerpartiet (Centre Party); KD = Kristdemokraterna (Christian Democrats); S = Sveriges Arbetarespartiet (Social Democratic Party); V = Vänsterpartiet (Left Party); ND = Ny Demokrati (New Democracy).

Bureaucracy

The policy-making apparatus in Sweden is formally divided into two distinct components. First, the departments are responsible for policy planning and formulation. Departments are considered relatively small, as the total number of staff for all departments was only 1,800 in 1991 (Pierre 1995: 142–7; Peters 1995). In the case of pensions, the main responsibility for policy planning and formulation rests with the Ministry of Social Affairs. The Ministry of Finance can also claim a legitimate role, since pensions represent a large part of public spending. Second, the implementation process falls within the jurisdiction of numerous agencies, such as the *Riksförsäkringsverket* (RFV – National Social Insurance Board)[8] in the case of pensions. These agencies are considered quite independent from their respective ministries, are much larger organizations (with a total of 390,000 employees) and are responsible for daily administrative work. The only contact permissible between agencies and departments is assumed to be informal (Pierre 1995). Nonetheless, final decisions regarding the implementation of laws and regulations rest with the director-general of the board (Rothstein 1996: 80).

From a comparative perspective, the RFV performs tasks that are similar to the Office National des Pensions (ONP) in Belgium and the various *caisses* administering the various pension schemes, such as the Caisse Nationale d'Assurance Vieillesse (CNAV), in France. On paper, they are relatively similar as both implement the rules and regulations determined by the government. However, there are substantial differences with respect to their independence *vis-à-vis* the government and the role of unions and employers. The RFV has more independence than its Belgian and French counterparts. In the latter two cases, the director-general cannot publicly voice his/her preferences and advocate specific social policies without reprisals from the Minister of Social Affairs and/or the social partners who control the administrative council of the pension agencies. In the Swedish case, the board is more diverse and includes other actors such as parliamentarians and experts, and it is part of the state apparatus because its employees are civil servants. When asked about the status of the RFV, both K.G. Scherman (DG 1982–96) and Anna Hedborg (DG 1996–2004) stated unequivocally that the RFV was a state agency that was not managed by unions and employers, as is the case in Belgium and France.

In practice, both Swedish agencies and departments seek to maintain informal contacts with each other, and as a result agencies play an important role in the early stages of the decision-making process. First, due to the complex nature of the issues faced by elected officials today and to the department's limited number of employees, the agencies' expertise and resources are needed to draft proposals. Second, their involvement ensures a smooth implementation process by guaranteeing that proposed policies can be carried out as planned. Finally, agencies have a strong incentive to be active in the early stages of the policy formulation process since most important decisions tend to occur at this stage.

As the evidence presented in this section suggests, pension system reform followed these practices to a large extent. First, the RFV produced sections of the main document leading to the 1994/1998 reform (SOU 1994[20]) and provided most of the data used by the Ministry of Social Affairs. This role should not be underestimated, as its projections constituted the framework and substance for debate among political actors; the negotiation of various alternatives was largely based on data presented by the RFV. Second, the RFV very actively promoted pension reforms in the 1980s and the early 1990s, in addition to devising solutions to the problems faced by the ATP. Its independence and non-political status were essential in convincing both politicians and interest groups that reform was needed, and very few dissident voices countered that claim, in stark contrast to public offices in Belgium and France.

Unions and employers' associations

For most of the twentieth century, unions and employers' associations co-operated extensively, particularly following the historic 1938 agreement of Satlsjöboden between the Landsorganisationen (LO) and the Svenska Arbetsgivareföreningen (SAF), which set the ground rules for collective bargaining and co-operation.

More than 80 per cent of workers in Sweden belong to one of the three largest union confederations: LO, Tjänstemännens Centralorganisation (TCO) and Sveriges Akademikers Centralorganisation (SACO). As compared to France and Belgium, unions do not tend to be divided into socio-professional or public/private lines, but, rather, according to economic sectors. The LO represents more than 85 per cent of blue-collar workers and has the highest membership of any union (2.1 million). It is comprised of 16 federations, the two largest being the Swedish municipal workers' union and the metal workers' union. Historically, it has had very close ties with the Social Democratic Party. On average, 70 per cent of the LO's members tend to vote SAP;[9] LO members were *de facto* SAP members until the late 1980s, when collective party membership was abandoned owing to pressure from the other political parties.[10] The TCO represents most white-collar workers and has more than 1.2 million members. Finally, the SACO represents academics and professionals, with a membership of 500,000 members.

At the end of 2001, the two largest employer associations, the SAF and the Sveriges Industriförbund, merged into a new association called the Svensk Naringsliv (SN – Confederation of Swedish Enterprise). The SN has a membership of approximately 48,000 small and medium-sized companies. The SAF and the LO originally set the standard for centralized wage bargaining until the former abandoned the process in 1990. Negotiations now occur within each economic sector.

The relationship between 'social partners' and the state

First and foremost, it is important to stress that the term 'social partners' does not exist in the Swedish language; instead the word *arbetsmarknadsparterna* (labour-market partners) is employed. The significance of this goes beyond pure semantics; it implies that unions and employers' associations do not consider themselves to be mandated beyond labour-market issues, and that the separation of responsibilities between the government and labour-market partners is much more defined than it is in Belgium and France.

In direct contrast to France, unions and employers' associations are both very centralized and very hierarchical. They also face a relatively less

competitive environment. They do not distrust the state and have participated actively in the elaboration of many policies, especially those related to
the labour market. The influence of the LO was once considered so strong that
its president was believed to be the most important political figure after the
prime minister. This role's importance has diminished since the 1970s, however,
and was further constrained by the decision of employers in 1991 to withdraw from the administrative councils of national boards such as the RFV.

Two important characteristics of the corporatist state in Sweden are crucial elements of the treatise defended in this study and should be highlighted: the first is that unions were less influential in the pension debate in
Sweden than they were in France and Belgium. The state has often been the
forgotten aspect of the triangular corporatist equation.[11] The works of
Korpi (1983) and Esping-Andersen (1985) challenge the conception of a
triangular relationship by theorizing conflicts that fall along class lines.
They envision a class power struggle where labour seeks to reduce the
power of capital by seeking democratic dominance. The social democratic
thesis clearly emphasizes the importance of achieving strong political power.
Esping-Andersen is clear on this point, stating that the differences between
liberal and social democratic regimes lie in the political power of labour:
'Where ... labor fails to realign the nation's political economy and assert
dominance, the result is continuously low, or at most, moderate de-com-
modification'. He further claims that the high decommodification scores
obtained by Austria, Belgium and the Netherlands in the 'Conservative'
regime are due to 'the strong political position of the social democratic
labor movements' (Esping-Anderson 1990: 53).[12] Thus, a core variable is the
LO–SAP association, with the latter controlling the reigns of government.
Corporatism might have been important in generating strong economic
growth, but its relationship to the expansion of the welfare state seems to
follow a different pattern.

This point was clearly demonstrated by the ATP struggle. The two poles
of the conflict centred on the mandatory option proposed by the LO–SAP
coalition and the voluntary option advocated by the bourgeois parties–
employers' coalition. As outlined on pp. 113–4, the LO successfully promoted the idea with the Social Democrats, who, though reluctant at first,
eventually endorsed it.[13] Seeing a possibility to expand its support beyond
blue-collar workers, the SAP seized the issue and was able to obtain a state-
controlled, mandatory earnings-related pension scheme by attracting
enough white-collar workers to its side. The ATP system became one of the
golden trophies of the Social Democrats.

The main point here is that this new pension scheme was to be administered by the state. The spirit of Saltsjöbaden, where both the SAF and the
LO sought to keep the government out of labour-market issues, was not
reproduced here. The LO turned to the state, which had been dominated by
social democratic rule since 1945, and actually refused the SAF's late efforts
to create a scheme outside the realm of the state, which would have resulted

in a supplementary earnings-related scheme similar to those found in France (AGIRC and ARRCO), albeit in a more comprehensive and generous form. The foremost question, then, is why did the LO opt to trust the state?

Rothstein's (1996) *Social Democratic State* provides one answer to this question, noting that control of the bureaucracy is an important variable in explaining the successes and failures of the Social Democrats. The state is not a passive entity, and it can play an important political role (Birnbaum 1988). Gaining control of political office is only one part of the equation, however. More challenging and equally important is to influence, or at the very least neutralize, the bureaucracy. While the CGT in France was able to gather enthusiastic supporters to implement the new social security system in the aftermath of World War II (see Chapter 2), it did so in a system that was built 'out of the state' (Ashford 1986). The LO did something similar, but it was part of the state, as enthusiastic recruits from the labour movement joined the civil service. Rothstein's most important contribution remains, however, his observation that the state is not a unified apparatus. He compares two institutions (labour-market and education authorities) and concludes that the Social Democrats were able to implement their objectives in the former while failing in the latter. The chief reason for the success of the active labour-market policy was the extent of dedication. More specifically, the Social Democrats obtained a significant commitment from the LO, had a definite ideological goal, recruited individuals committed to the cause (rather than Weberian-style bureaucrats) and had enough power (in terms of regulation and resources) to achieve their objectives. The key was the Social Democratic Party's capacity to create a state agency that represented its values. The national labour-market board 'was a goal-oriented organization based on substantive rather than formal rationality', and the latter still prevailed within the National Education Board (Rothstein 1996: 171).

Even though no studies have been done treating the implementation of the ATP in the 1950s with similar theoretical objectives, it would be difficult to argue that the Social Democrats and the LO were not committed to this venture, considering the time and energy they devoted to the issue. Like the Rehn–Meidner reform programme, the ATP programme was designed by the LO, promoted actively by its leaders and is 'everyone's favorite story of a successful labor-initiatied reform' (Pontusson 1993: 556). It is, therefore, not surprising that it was difficult for the labour movement and the SAP to accept that the ATP needed to be reformed. As Anna Hedborg, a former Social Democrat minister and a central player during the pension reform of 1998, stated, 'it was hard and difficult for the Social Democratic Party to accept the reform of the ATP system, which is sort of a gold treasure for the party'.[14]

Indicative of a possible 'social-democratization' of the bureaucracy, Pierre presents few of the many accounts provided by non-Socialist ministers about the 'significant obstacle to policy reassessment and change' (Pierre 1995: 150) they faced once they took office. The problem was substantial because many of the individuals causing obstacles were not political appointees, but rather tenured senior officials. As is demonstrated further on in this chapter (see p. 117), the Ministry of Social Affairs was slow to propose solutions to resolve the difficulties faced by the ATP system. According to data gathered during interviews with the policy-makers involved in the pension reform process, many stated that civil servants from the ministry were very attached to the ATP, and it took them a while to accept that changes were necessary. The authority responsible for implementing pension policies, the RFV, was also very committed to maintaining the ATP system as it was. Its objectives were more transparent, and it advocated only those reforms that would not challenge the core of the system (i.e. parametric reforms).

Theoretical expectations

The Swedish case includes a non-potent, first ordering principle where labour-market partners do not exercise a collective veto point (as opposed to social partners in Belgium and France), resulting in a Parliamentary Integration relationship. However, a substantial number of veto players exist within the legislature (second ordering principle) consistent with a proportional influence vision. This is the foremost case illustrating why the nature of the veto matters more than its numbers, since a paradigmatic reform was introduced despite the large number of veto players.

The determination that Swedish labour-market partners do not have an effective veto point is explained by two complementary events. First, the implementation of the SAP–LO pension plan of the late 1950s led to the creation of a state agency responsible for the management and administration of the earnings-related pension plan (ATP). Thus, the public pension system became strongly anchored within the state, where labour-market partners have a minority voice.[15] This is contrary to the way policy-making happens within the unemployment domain, where labour-market partners retained a substantial role in the management and administration of unemployment insurance (Ghent system) (Bendz 2004). The institutionalization of the ATP within the state implied that the strength of the labour movement became intertwined with the civil servants having internalized their preference. When it became obvious that a reform was necessary, the first reaction of civil servants within the social ministry was to save the ATP system; hence the proposals to extend the contribution periods and the number of the best years utilized to calculate one's pension (see on p. 119). However, the economic crisis of the early 1990s led to a sharp increase in the number of civil servants involved within the ministry. A few of them came from financial ministries, which accentuated the possibility of promoting more extensive reforms (Marier 2005). Second, the participation and integration of labour-market partners within the decision-making process has declined sharply over the past 20 years (Hermansson *et al.* 1997), thus reducing the overall legitimacy and importance of corporatist arrangements. As a result, labour-market partners, and more specifically unions, do not possess a veto point and are not expected to play an important role in the Swedish pension reform process. Therefore, the first ordering principle should not affect this case because Sweden represents a case of Parliamentary Integration as opposed to one of Social Partnership (see Chapter 1).

The second ordering principle, however, is very important in the Swedish instance because the fragmentation of the legislature makes it impossible for a single political party to adopt legislation. The Swedish constitutional reform of 1970 resulted in a more competitive electoral environment, thus eliminating the prospect of continued SAP dominance (Andersen and Immergut 2006: 595). This implies that multiple veto players depend on the political coalition created. According to Tsebelis (1999, 2002), a high number of veto players complemented by large ideological differences should result in policies aligned with the status quo. Therefore, just as in Belgium, coalitions requiring a high number of diverse political parties should generate parametric pension reforms. The case of Sweden, however, clearly illustrates the limitations of this argument (and the relative importance of veto points as opposed to veto players) with the adoption of pension reforms that are the most comprehensive of any implemented by industrialized countries by five parties representing a broad political spectrum (Conservative, Liberal, Christian Democrat, Centre and SAP).

In contrast to Belgium, the unions' ability to interfere with the reform process was diminished significantly because politicians were able to keep them on the margins. Throughout the two most important committees working on the pension reform (Working Group on Pensions and the Implementation Committee), unions and employers were not directly involved in the negotiations leading to the pension reform proposal. It was actually very difficult for unions to seek the addition or removal of specific elements because changes required consultation among no less than five political parties. Thus, the main structures and elements of the pension reform presented in a 1992 sketch (and solidified in the 1994 proposal) remained relatively unaltered by those who opposed it.

Pension reform in Sweden ... a long march to an innovative pension system

Those seeking to criticize the 'garbage can' view of public administration would be hard pressed to find a more linear process than the Swedish pension reform process that lead to the 1994/1998 legislation. A pension committee (*pensionsberedningen*) stressed the need for reform and played an important ontological role in convincing various actors that such an undertaking was necessary. Further, it provided an opportunity for all political actors to present their views and initiate debate about the issue (SOU 1990[76]). Following the electoral victory of the bourgeois coalition in 1991, a working group (*pensionsarbetsgruppen*) on pensions that included all the political parties was organized to seek a compromise on this issue. Five of the seven parties agreed to a proposal in late 1992, which led to the presentation of a final report in 1994 (SOU 1994[20]) and to the adoption by the Riksdag of a legislative framework. An implementation committee that included many members of the working group was instituted following the 1994 elections, and it worked on the new reform until the final legislation was adopted in 1998.

The Swedish pension reform is very substantive; it did not limit itself to parametric changes, but rather instituted a whole new system whose features have already been exported to other European countries such as Italy, Latvia, Norway and Poland.

Time to reform the ATP (1982–90)?

In Sweden, consensus on the need for pension reform was established during the 1980s. The publication of both an RFV report in 1987 and a parliamentary commission's conclusions presented in 1990 left no doubt that it was time for 'a new war on ATP' (*Veckans Affärer*, 10 October 1990).[16] As indicated by the title of this *Veckans Affärer* article ('A New War on ATP'), it was far from obvious that a compromise would be achieved a few years later, as the stance of each political party seemed relatively unchanged from their original 1950s positions. This section analyses this important ontological period.

As part of its mandate, the RFV was required by law to publish a report every five years outlining the ATP's financial future and advising whether adjustments to contribution levels should be considered. The 1982 report presented a bleak picture of its future, stating that if the current economic stagnation were to continue, more than one-third of an individual's wage would be required to finance the system by the year 2030.[17] The report's conclusions led to much debate in numerous circles in early 1983. A central feature of this debate was the indexation of pensions. Unlike France, the United Kingdom and Belgium, in Sweden the pension system was already indexed to prices rather than wages; thus, the government should not have had to deal with this issue unless it wanted to readjust the living standards of retirees *vis-à-vis* current wage earners. Ironically, though, the economic crises of the late 1970s and early 1980s resulted in consideration of the reverse action: the possibility of indexing pensions in accordance with the movement of the economy and wages.

The Swedish government attempted to avoid the economic crisis by devaluing the Swedish krona, which led to a reduction in real wages and to severe inflation. Thus, while workers were faced with lower real wages, pensioners continued to receive the indexed pension increases. To reduce this growing gap between pensioners and the working population, the bourgeois coalition 'tricked' pensioners by not fully indexing pensions to price increases, hence leaving them vulnerable to harsh criticism from pensioners' organizations and from opposition parties like the Social Democratic Party and the Left Party. The former used this 'under-indexation' as an electoral issue and promised to properly re-index the value of pensions.

Another pension adjustment made by the Centre Party (the minority government) was the introduction of payment for contributions above the ceiling in 1982.[18] This affected mostly high-income earners and resulted in a hidden tax, as these payments did not result in increased benefits. The process came under intense scrutiny following a report published by the RFV in 1987 (see p. 118), as it helped to forge a consensus that pension reform was necessary. Due to its redistributive nature, the Social Democrats were quite fond of this progressive tax and had pledged to maintain it. This stance would turn out to be one of the adversarial points between the SAP and the bourgeois parties, who sought to revoke the tax during the negotiations of the Working Group on Pensions (*pensionsarbetsgruppen*) in 1991–4.

A few days following the election of the Social Democrats in 1982, the Minister of Social Affairs, Sten Andersson, announced the creation of a pension committee to review the pension system.[19] It would take more than two years for the SAP to establish the committee, as internal conflicts regarding the lack of substantial pension indexation paralysed the group (Lundberg 2001: 14–15). The committee began its work in November 1984 and included the labour-market partners (LO, TCO, SACO and SAF), other interest groups (associations for the disabled and pensioner organizations), representatives from various ministries (Labour, Finance and Social Affairs), the RFV and other experts. It was chaired by the State Secretary of Social Affairs Minister Sture Korpi, someone known to have a strong interest in pension issues. The mandate of the pension committee (*pension-beredningen*) was to evaluate and review the rules and past experiences of the current pension system. It also stated that the main elements of the basic and earned pension scheme (ATP) should be retained, and that the basic pension level should remain independent of previous employment and continue to complement the ATP pension. Methods of financing were also not to be altered (SOU 1990[76]). The committee's work went on for six years.

Many important developments related to the reform of the pension system occurred during that time frame. First, the LO began to promote the extension and deregulation of the AP-funds to save the ATP. This measure allowed the funds originating from the system's surpluses (prior to 1983, contributions outweighed the benefits paid out) to be invested in the stock market in order to increase their rate of return. The original purpose of the AP-funds was three-fold. The first was to compensate for a potential lack of savings that could result from the ATP system. Private savings actually decreased substantially, from 19.28 per cent of GDP in 1963–6 to 7.54 per cent of GDP in 1987–90 (Ds 1992[89]). Right-wing politicians were quick to blame the ATP system for this state of affairs, which was among the lowest in OECD (Organisation for Economic Co-operation and Development) countries. A second function was to smooth over any sudden change in the ratio between contributors and pensioners. Not surprisingly, the importance of each function was fiercely debated between the left- and right-wing parties. The Left emphasized the latter function and the importance of collective savings, while the Right continued to focus on the savings rate while reiterating that the best solution to increase savings was to encourage private, individual savings. Third, a portion of the AP-funds was employed to finance early retirement (Palme 2005: 47).

Many political actors, especially those on the Right, opposed the LO's proposal. More than any others, the SAF and the Conservative Party expressed strong opposition to investing the AP-funds in the stock market, fearing more control over the private economy by the state (*Affärsvärlden*, 18 May 1989). The Finance Ministry, even under an SAP government, favoured the extension of private rather than collective savings. The major criticism of the LO's plan, however, was that the value of the AP-funds would not increase enough to maintain the ATP system. Analysts claimed the AP-funds could disappear quickly if nothing else in the system changed. A government report published in 1987 stated that the first AP-funds would begin to lose money starting in 1995, as the sum of contributions and interest would not cover the costs of benefits. Thus, relaxing the rules of investment could lengthen the process, but not stop it, and a large increase in contribution rates would still be necessary.

The second wave of discussions surrounding the pension reform debate occurred as a result of the publication of the 1987 actuarial report by the RFV, which presented a rather grim picture of the ATP's future. For the first time, it demonstrated that even economic growth could not save the system, as it would lead to a high number of individuals being above the ceiling of 7.5 basic amounts. With 2 per cent economic growth, it was projected that 80 per cent of men and 66 per cent of women would be above the ATP ceiling.[20] In the long run, this would have made the ATP system a semi-basic pension, since most workers would surpass the contribution ceiling because the indexation was based on prices rather than on economic growth. Many projections accounting for a possible increase in the ceiling based on economic growth were presented to highlight the change in dynamics once that ceiling was adjusted. These findings made several of the proposals designed to save the ATP system, such as that presented by the LO, obsolete. Again, the RFV noted that slow economic growth combined with an ageing population would require a significant increase in contribution rates to maintain the system. This report was very important ontologically because it marked the beginning of a strong consensus that the ATP system had to be revamped.

The publication of *Allmän Pension* (SOU 1990[76]), the report from the Pension Committee, brought new proposals to the table and increased the frequency of discussions on reforming the pension system. Six members of that committee were interviewed and concurred that this commission was more a fact-finding seminar than a political commission seeking to alter the pension system, and it was clear from the very beginning that no political compromise would be found. It was even stated in the report's introduction that the commission's intention was not to reach a political compromise, but, rather, the report was to be the first step in the process of moving the discussion forward in another setting. Despite its limited role, this commission generated a consensus that pension reform was necessary, even though stark disagreements existed regarding the nature of the reform and the extent to which it should be undertaken.

Responses provided by the committee members highlighted some of the many differences between the political parties. All right-wing parties stated that people should not have to contribute above the ceiling since benefits ceased at that level (SOU 1990[76]: 577–8). Representatives from the Conservative and Liberal parties (Troedsson and Könberg, respectively) proposed increasing the pensionable age, possibly seeking private alternatives and putting forward plans to encourage investment in home ownership in order to reduce reliance on housing subsidies. They also advocated a stronger link between contributions and benefits (SOU 1990[76]: 577–80). Most of their positions were shared by the employers' organization (SAF) (SOU 1990[76]: 591–3). The Centre Party advocated a generous flat, basic pension. Representatives from the Left noted that removing housing subsidies would negatively affect many poor elderly people (SOU 1990[76]: 583–4).

The Social Democratic Party chaired the committee and therefore did not present a response to the report. However, the way the objectives and aims of the committee were framed made it obvious that it was not yet ready to abandon the ATP system. The leadership of the Social Affairs Ministry embraced a reform extending the 15/30 rule to a 20/40 rule. It became clear that Korpi had envisioned such an option with the publication of *ATP i takt med framtiden* in 1991 (Lundberg 2001: 17). Support for Korpi's solution was also firmly anchored within the Ministry of Social Affairs (Marier 2001: 106).

Adding support to the (perceived) strength and popularity of this solution within social democratic circles, the RFV actually proposed a solution to the pension dilemma with the political context in mind, as the director-general[21] and his deputy (Gustav Jönsson) found themselves at opposite ends of the political spectrum. Key elements of the RFV's proposal included incorporating a longer timeframe for the AP-funds to finance future pensioners, increasing the 15/30 rule to a 20/40 model, creating a new index level for both benefits and the ceiling based on economic growth, instituting a minimum basic pension requirement of 40 years residency in Sweden, reducing part-time pensions and increasing the legal pensionable age (*Riksförsäkringsverket* 1991: 15). Many elements of this proposal were quite similar to those Korpi advocated. The RFV's solution would resurface in later pension debates within social democratic circles.

All labour-market partners acknowledged the need to reform the ATP system. However, there was no consensus regarding the extent to which it had to be reformed and how that reform should occur, even among unions. This represented quite a shift from the late 1980s era, when many union members did not even acknowledge that there was a problem with the ATP and were actually still seeking better benefits from the system. The TCO, for example, hosted a conference during this period seeking ways to reduce the pensionable age. Prior to 1987, the LO still firmly believed that economic growth alone would save the ATP system.

Labour-market partners had divergent positions on how to reform the ATP. First, SACO and SAF stated that a new pension scheme should be based on a stronger link between contributions and benefits (SOU 1990[76]: 575). SACO's chief economist and member of the pension committee Jan Bröms discussed this concern in depth in his highly influential *Ur Askan av ATP*.[22] His book presented a new pension system proposal that reinforced the link between contributions and benefits by introducing the life-income principle (all earnings are included when determining benefit levels). In order to encourage personal savings, he also wanted to eliminate contributions above the ceiling that were not counted for pension benefits, a suggestion the SAF also made. Finally, Bröms also supported continuing a payg system and indexation based on the state of the national economy (the latter was also stressed by the LO and the TCO). The TCO's representatives to the pension committee, Ljung and Olsson, claimed that as more and more individuals contributed above the ceiling that basic amount risked operating like a tax. They also maintained that a pension system must include some form of redistribution between income groups in addition to distributing risk among the population (SOU 1990[76]: 589–3).

The publication of the final report (SOU 1990[76]) generated further discussions in the public sphere but also, importantly, within the government. The ministries of social affairs and finance were both seeking to initiate one more step towards reform. Anna Hedborg joined the Ministry of Social Affairs as State Secretary (replacing Sture Korpi), and led discussions among cabinet members from the Ministry of Finance and the Office of the Prime Minister. The LO also took part in many of these discussions.[23] With her nomination, the 20/40 option began to lose momentum despite her previous affiliation with the LO. The Ministry of Finance also began planning a possible reform, and was quite eager to do something immediately. Reform of the pension system would end up in the 1991 budget proposal written by the Ministry of Finance. Surprisingly, it would state that 'to stimulate a higher savings rate we ought to study the possibility of more funded options in more private and insurance ways than what we currently have with the AP-funds' (Proposition 1990/1: 34), which clearly went against the party line of sticking by the AP-funds. Although it is thought that the cabinet approved this proposition, people within the Ministry of Social Affairs were shocked by this statement as they felt it required more preparation. They also believed the issue should not be raised during an election year.

Politicians take control of the reform agenda (1991–4)[24]

The outcome of the 1991 election resulted in a return to power for the bourgeois parties after almost 10 years as the opposition. The victory was not complete, however, as they had to rely on the support of the (far-right) Ny Demokrati party, which entered Parliament for the first time. There was a strong conviction within and among the four coalition parties (Conservative, Liberal, Centre and Christian Democrats) that the turbulent coalition period of 1976–82 should be avoided. This goal was met, for the most part, but significant economic difficulties persisted, resulting in a sharp decline in output unseen since the 1930s, forcing the government to negotiate 'crisis packages' with the Social Democrats. This type of co-operation between the two sides of the political spectrum had not been seen since the World War II era.

There is no doubt that this context favoured the introduction of new ideas. A civil servant summarized the situation best by stating that, all of a sudden, 'anything was possible, you could notice this, feel it'.[25] It is worth stating that the Working Group on Pensions, created immediately after the election, began its work before the crisis and reached a compromise in its aftermath. Considering the adversarial atmosphere surrounding pensions in Sweden, the crisis surely made it easier to compromise and make important decisions. Nonetheless, it is worth emphasizing that the crisis may have facilitated the process, but it was not the reason for the pension reform. With the crisis over, each party involved had numerous occasions to withdraw from the agreement and none did, even though the Social Democrats came close in 1996–7. In the end, all parties were quick to affirm that the pension reform was not a crisis decision, but rather the continuation of a long process that began in the mid-1980s.

Working Group on Pensions

One week after the formation of the government in 1991, a Working Group on Pensions (WGOP – *pensionsarbetsgruppen*) was created by Bo Könberg, the new Minister of Health and Social Security. The aim of the working group was to present a proposal to Parliament on pension reform, which would make pensions 'more responsive to the general state of the economy, strengthen the link between contributions and benefits, and encourage an increase in long-term saving' (Ministry of Health and Social Affairs 1994: 5). In order to increase the likelihood of a compromise with the Social Democrat Party, Könberg based the guidelines on the budget proposition for 1991 (see p. 120).[26]

Drawing on his experience on the pension committee as the Liberal Party representative, Könberg sought to create another kind of committee to reach a pension compromise. He opted for a mixture of parliamentary commission and negotiation platform by setting up a working group. That way, he was able to create the smallest committee possible by inviting only political parties. Following the first meeting in December, it was decided that he would chair the group, something highly unusual by Swedish standards.

The labour-market partners were excluded, which drew some criticism but no strong protest on their part. This was in direct contrast with the instauration of the ATP system, where they were first asked to resolve the issue among themselves. Könberg was able to push them aside by claiming they were consulted during the previous pension commission and that it was now time for politicians to shoulder their responsibilities and enact those suggestions. A reference group including other social actors was created and consulted on a few occasions, but this group operated more as an information channel than as a forum for substantive participation in the WGOP's proceedings. Their exclusion from the WGOP was part of a growing trend that they should be involved in matters dealing strictly with the labour market. Since this reform did not involve the negotiated supplementary pensions from collective agreements, they were unable to muster a strong political claim for inclusion. Demonstrating the validity of this reasoning, Könberg attempted a similar approach with sickness insurance but was forced to change course and allow representation on the committee because they were involved in its management.

The individual parties chose their representatives for the WGOP. It is indicative of the importance of this new committee that most had previous experience with pension issues, and the parties chose people they knew to be amenable to compromise.[27] Whether the latter was achieved strategically or not is debatable, but it is clear the Conservative Party could have sent a more neo-liberal parliamentarian than Margit Gennser (Lars Tobisson, perhaps), while the Social Democratic Party could have sent individuals like Doris Håvik who were strongly opposed to the ATP system reform, but instead they sent Anna Hedborg and Ingela Thalén. Such personnel choices would have made it even more difficult to reach a consensus, and such a strategy could well have been employed by any of the main parties to ensure the failure of the committee. Thus, it appears that all parties acted in good faith with their nominations. Also important is the fact that both the Minister of Health and Social Affairs and the Minister of Finance came from the Liberal Party. Even though it remained a right-leaning party, it was much closer to the Social Democratic Party than the Conservatives, and it had a history of co-operation with the SAP.

The creation of the WGOP rejuvenated the pension debate. Clearly present in a much more direct manner was the link between reforming the pension system and increasing savings. This connection led directly to debates about the AP-funds, including the wage-earner funds within it and the role it could play regarding the future of the pension system. More interestingly, individuals who had served on the working group were again involved.

In a debate article, Hedborg and Thalén proposed to maintain the AP-funds and increase their assets by raising contribution rates by one extra point to build up a buffer for the upcoming demographic change. They agreed on the importance of savings but rejected the claim that it had to be in private hands. They stressed that dismantling the AP-funds would only make matters worse since it would reduce savings and lower pensions for women. Nonetheless, they allowed for the possibility of later breaking up the AP-funds into multiple funds to enable people to make their own choice of fund (*Dagens Nyheter*, 7 December 1991). While they expressed no doubt that the wage-earner funds belong to the pension system, they rejected the 20/40 option in a subsequent article by stating that it amounted to a simple reduction in benefits, one that would hurt women most without tackling the basic problems inherent in the system. They also issued a warning that funded options result in a pension level dictated by the market and emphasized the double-payment problem (*Svenska Dagbladet*, 8 May 1992).

Margit Gennser actively promoted her solution to the pension and savings problem. She stated on numerous occasions that more than 50 per cent of the Swedish population did not support the current ATP system upon its creation and that individual, rather than collective, savings were necessary to promote growth. It is indicative of the nature of the ideological divide that separated her from the social democratic position that she wrote a few articles in magazines and newspapers using the Thatcher reform of 1986 in Britain as her exemplar. People could choose whether or not to remain within the ATP system, newcomers to the labour market would have to select private options and the ATP system would be abolished in 20 years.[28] Acknowledging the double-payment issue, she advocated a solution that maximized personal savings even as it maintained previous commitments.

Despite these distinct ideological differences, a compromise seemed within reach a few months after the creation of the WGOP. The members felt that they had made such remarkable progress that they published the outline of a potential reform in a document in early September 1992 (Ds 1992[89]). Following many seminar-like meetings where various experts presented their views and proposals, the committee opted to publish some of the elements that were amenable to a consensus position.[29] The 89-page document provided a broad outline of the current and future state of the pension system, while highlighting the difficulties associated with the ATP system. It reiterated some of the earlier conclusions drawn by the previous committee, including the economic instability of the system, the weak link between contributions and benefits and the small savings incentive it provided. The fifth chapter presented the proposal for possible reforms. Many aspects of this section did actually form part of the new legislation on pensions that was introduced two years later. It maintained an income-related, mandatory pension system that had a guaranteed basic amount financed by contributions.

Two principal elements emerged from the proposal. First, there was the adoption of the life-income principle, where every krona contributed counted towards the calculation of an individual's pension. This implied a switch from a benefit-defined to a contribution-defined system. As a result of switching to life earnings instead of using the best 15 out of 30 years of employment, the working group introduced ways to grant pension points while individuals were unemployed, sick, on military service and caring for children. Second, it proposed the creation of a funded component on top of the payg system. No specific details were provided because no broad political compromise had yet been achieved. However, during the public conference presenting the outline, the bourgeois parties made it known that the group was studying the option of placing 10 to 15 per cent of future contributions in individual funded schemes (*Dagens Nyheter*, 1 September 1992). In addition to these two central elements, the working group raised the question of sharing pension points between married couples and proposed changing the indexation mechanism for pensions from prices to wages, or something else that was more in line with the economy's evolution.

The tentative proposal did not generate significant public debate for several reasons. First, Sweden suffered a difficult currency and economic crisis shortly thereafter, and the population was much more worried about that than they were about a possible reform that would not affect them for many years. Second, many individuals involved in the process claimed that the absence of political conflict diminished the story's appeal; it was boring and uneventful, thus there was less coverage. A quick look at the pension articles written during this period partly supports this hypothesis. The release of the outline was part of a day-long seminar on the subject; it got extensive television and press coverage, but there was little continuing interest. The number of articles on the WGOP was far greater at the end of 1993 when political conflicts arose and the TCO came out strongly against the reform.

The progress made in 1992 was not replicated in 1993. Stories began to emerge in autumn 1993 that the reform process was in trouble. Five important issues were proving quite difficult to resolve, resulting in a lengthy stalemate among the representatives of the five political parties. The first and most troublesome issue was the taxation of contributions above the ceiling. As stated earlier, contributions over a certain amount began to be taxed in 1982 by the Centre government[30] but did not offer any pension points. On one hand, the Liberals, the Conservatives and SACO consistently denounced this measure because it was not in line with the life-income principle, where every krona counts and every year worked earns pension points.[31] Könberg had the backing of the government to negotiate to have it removed. However, the Social Democrats were opposed because it represented a good progressive tax. All individuals above the ceiling are, by default, high-income earners, and their excess contributions cover pensions solely financed by the state (the new guaranteed pension, which replaced the basic pension). Wiklund, the committee representative for the Christian Democrats, crafted the compromise that both parties meet halfway with the support of the Centre Party (Lindbom 2001: 73). Thus, contributions remained, but at a discounted rate of 9.25 per cent.

The second issue was closely related to the first element mentioned above since it concerned the indexation of the ceiling. Originally, the bourgeois parties wanted to index it with prices, as was the case with the ATP system. As demonstrated by the RFV and economists, using that form of indexation meant that eventually virtually all income earners would earn an amount above the ceiling. The bourgeois parties' strategy was thus to keep a price index but remove the tax on earnings above the ceiling and replace it with funded options. This option was unacceptable to the Social Democrats, however, as it would result in the eventual transformation of the system into a large basic pension. It was thus important to create a ceiling that would be indexed to real wage growth. The social democratic option prevailed, and this outcome paved the way for the creation of a funded portion in addition to an earnings-related payg system.

The third contentious matter pitted the bourgeois parties against the SAP on the creation/extension of a funded component in the system. The Social Democrats defended the AP-funds on the basis that they were an important financial tool for the state as well as a collective saving instrument. It was clear from the bourgeois parties' perspective that no deal could be reached without granting a place for an individualized funded component (see Lindbom 2001). Even though the Social Democrats accepted this demand in late December 1993, it was a long process to maintain a high component of payg since the Finance Ministry also opposed a large public component. The Social Democrats were willing to accept a funded component, as long as it remained within a generous public system, and the Conservatives were willing to make this compromise, as 'it was very good for Sweden to have 5 million new capitalists who are saving in accounts'.[32] Initially, both parties settled for 2 per cent of the 18.5 per cent in contributions being funded and being part of the state pension system.

The fourth major issue was the amount of the guaranteed pension. Historically, the Centre Party promoted a high basic pension that could be complemented by private options (this was line 2 in the old ATP referendum). This policy preference had not really changed by the 1990s. Centre Party representative Åke Pettersson sought to increase it significantly from 51,000 Swedish krona (SEK) to SEK 80,000 (roughly $5,100 to $8,000) (*Dagens Nyheter*, 4 November 1993). Pettersson was unable to generate support from any party but the Christian Democrats. Frustrated, he came out publicly against the Conservatives, the Liberals and the Social Democrats for their lack of consideration for his position (*Dagens Nyheter*, 24 November 1993). The Christian Democrats withdrew their support for a high guaranteed pension in mid-December 1993 (*Dagens Nyheter*, 18 December 1993), marginalizing the Centre Party representative even further.[33]

Nonetheless, he obtained a small increase in the guaranteed pension of SEK 4,000 ($400).[34]

The final stumbling block concerned compensation for early childcare. In the previous system, such a measure was deemed unnecessary because the 15/30 rule would allow women simply not to include the years when they cared for children. However, in a system where life income is considered, compensation had to be offered for the interruption of a career due to unemployment, sickness, military service and childbirth. In this case, the influence of the Christian Democrats was most obvious. Key for them was to find a way to offer women the opportunity to stay at home and raise their children without being penalized for it by the pension system. This ran against the gender equality views of the Social Democrats and even the Liberals (Marier 2007). The SAP representatives felt it was important to maintain the individuality of the system and ensure that dependence on a husband was not more beneficial than a career in the labour market. Civil servants working closely with the WGOP produced more than 70 models for three options to resolve differences within the group. The final solution included a national income to be added during the child-raising years on top of any income earned during that year. Three options were made available to women (and men), and they had the option of choosing the one most favourable to them: (1) a supplement that raised pensionable income to 75 per cent of the average income for all insured; (2) a supplement that raised pensionable income to the income the insured person had the year before the child was born; or (3) a fixed supplement that reflected the earned income of one wage base amount. These rights were granted to the parent deciding to receive the child credit for up to four years after the birth.

In mid-January 1994, it was announced that an agreement had been reached (see Table 4.2). The WGOP presented three volumes summarizing their decisions and explaining their reasoning. They also presented impact studies of the new system (SOU 1994[20], 1994[21], 1994[22]). A few elements came as a surprise, such as the granting of pension points for education and the sharing of contributions by both employers and employees. The latter measure meant that employers would contribute less, with employees making up the difference. Employers would then be pressured to increase wages in order to compensate employees for that increased contribution.

In order to rush this agreement through Parliament before the end of the summer session (the last one before the elections), only six weeks was available for criticism and review of the documents. The members of the WGOP delineated eight minor changes to that proposal. One important point was that the group opted to discuss indexation later, stating that it would include price, wages or both. As was outlined in previous chapters, this is an important element over the long term that significantly impacts both benefits and costs. To resolve these issues, the WGOP announced the creation of an Implementation Group (IG – *Genomförandegruppen*) that

Table 4.2 Main features of the 1994 pension agreement between the Swedish government and the Social Democratic Party

- The new system is mandatory and covers the entire population.
- The new pensions are to be based on lifetime earnings on the basis of previous contributions (the so-called 'life-income' principle). This includes other social security benefits such as sickness and unemployment insurance.
- Military service and years devoted to raising children up to the age of four result in pension points.
- A flexible retirement age is instituted on an actuarial basis, meaning one can retire prior to age 65 but receive a lower pension. One could eventually retire later than 65 years of age and draw a larger pension.
- A guaranteed pension covers those who have made limited contributions and those with no contributions at all. Forty years of residency in Sweden is required.
- Contributions will eventually be shared equally between employees and employers. The ATP contributions came exclusively from employers.
- A contribution rate of 18.5% is instituted, of which 2% goes temporarily into a private savings account earning interest (National Debt Office).
- Pensions will be indexed according to both inflation and the evolution of real wages.
- Contributions are to be indexed according to many factors: life expectancy, mortality rate before retirement, income differences between men and women and future growth in real wages. Thus, the first pension is calculated according to the divisor.
- Contributions will be taken up to 7.5 basic amounts. This ceiling is indexed on the basis of real wages.
- Married couples can share their pension benefits on an actuarial basis; this means that men's points are worth less than women's points, since men have shorter lives, on average.
- The transition period will last 20 years. Individuals born between 1935 and 1953 will have their pensions based on both systems. For example, those born in 1935 will have 1/20 of their pension based on the new system, while those born in 1953 will have 19/20 of their pension based on the new system.
- The AP-funds will be used as a buffer fund.

Source: Reformerat Pensionssytem (SOU 1994 [20]).

would operate much as the working group had. In the end, the bill presented to Parliament was largely a matter of principle, as the technical details were left to be worked out later. Nonetheless, two principal changes were slated to come into effect on 1 January 1995. First, all individuals would have an individual contribution of 1 per cent of their gross wage. Second, the new calculation rules would begin to take effect (i.e. the life-income principle and points for studies, military service and childcare). The bill was adopted with an overwhelming majority (279 to 19) in early June 1994, and all parties agreed not to make pensions an electoral issue.

Implementing the 1994 Framework Legislation (1994–2001)

Contrary to expectations, it took four years to complete and implement the remainder of the agreement reached in 1994, rather than the single year that was expected. These four years were quite turbulent, and on a few occasions it appeared that the coalition behind the agreement was going to break up. The electoral victory of the Social Democratic Party in 1994 did not change the dynamic of the newly formed Implementation Group (IG), since it consisted of almost the same individuals as the Working Group on Pensions. Every member interviewed stressed that the election did not have any real impact on the continuation of the reform.

Several elements of the 1994 agreement were implemented in 1995. For example, pension points were first granted for education, military service and childcare. Out of the 18.5 per cent contributions, 2 per cent was confined to an independent agency (*Riksgälskontoret* – National Debt Office) that was investing for all Swedes while the decision on the structure of the funded part was put on hold. In the summer, the IG announced an agreement concerning the calculation of pension rights and the kinds of income that offered pension rights. Nonetheless, many decisions remained extremely problematic. The first decision of 1995 was to announce that the reform would come into effect only on 1 January 1997 rather than 1996. Other delays eventually pushed the starting date to 1999.

With opposition rising within her own party, Anna Hedborg asked for a break from the work of the IG in early 1996 in the hope of convincing the sceptics. The upcoming SAP congress in March was filling with motions quite critical of the 1994 agreement. Many of them, submitted mostly by the labour movement, actually advocated scrapping the whole agreement. The congress turned into a major challenge for the political coalition behind the pension reform. First, there was the cabinet reshuffle following the selection of Göran Persson to replace Ingvar Carlsson as prime minister. Persson was not very enthusiastic about the pension agreement of 1994, and his first action as prime minister did nothing to alleviate the critics' concerns (both Hedborg and Thalén were asked to leave the cabinet!). Thalén became party secretary, while Hedborg moved on to replace K.G. Scherman and became director-general of RFV. Thalén's replacement, Maj-Inger Klingvall, was not at all familiar with pensions. She would rely strongly on her secretary of state Hans Svensson. Thus, the whole group dynamic was altered significantly at a time where difficult issues still had to be resolved, which caused additional delays.

Second, in light of the strong opposition, the SAP leadership convened to gather opinions for an internal review on three central elements of the new pension reform: the creation of individual contributions, the funded system and the financing of the new system (*Svenska Dagbladet*, 22 March 1996). These were very sensitive issues for Social Democrats. The labour movement was opposed in principal to individual contributions. Funded options were supported as long as they remained public, and many uncertainties surrounding the financing of the new system and pre-pensions needed to be clarified (*Svenska Dagbladet*, 31 August 1996). The party waited until August to start the process and received more than 508 opinions on the matter by late December. The fact that the results were never published suggests that many of the opinions were quite negative.

The pressure to alter the pension reform increased within the SAP at the 1997 congress. Many motions sought to strike down the five-party agreement, while many others asked for a reform following the guidelines proposed by the RFV in 1991 (*RFV Anser* 1991[7] – see pp. 119–20). Fearing an embarrassing defeat on this issue, the party executive made a deal with some of the chief opponents of the agreement as the critics began to be heard on the congress floor. The compromise stated that: (1) the new system would guarantee a replacement level similar to the old ATP system, with 2 per cent growth; (2) low-income earners would be compensated if contributions were raised; and (3) people could choose to invest their 2 per cent in a public fund. If they wanted to change to a private fund, they would have to request it (*Dagens Nyheter*, 13 September 1997).

The other members of the IG condemned the SAP's actions throughout this period, and few meetings with the SAP representatives and the prime minister were held to ease tensions. The bourgeois representatives stressed on numerous occasions that the pension agreement could not be reformed without them. Additionally, they emphasized that the funded component was not negotiable and that there were other elements that they did not like, as the reform was based on a compromise. The five parties met two days after the conclusion of the 1997 SAP Congress to discuss the future of the group. The IG released a statement maintaining that they would continue to work within the framework of the five-party agreement to resolve the remaining questions. The four bourgeois parties noted that everyone had a veto in the negotiations (*Göteborgs Posten*, 16 September 1997).

The delays resulting from internal struggle within the SAP and the cabinet reshuffle led to another race against the clock, this time to salvage the 1994 deal. Members of the IG met on several occasions in autumn 1997 to resolve their differences. Following an in-depth analysis conducted by experts within the civil service (Ds 1997[66]), their first decision was to further increase the guaranteed pension by SEK 1,067 ($1,000) and to abstain from including private and occupational sources of retirement revenue in the means test associated with it. The WGOP opted to transform the universal basic pension into a means-tested pension. Thus, in the new Swedish pension system high-income earners would not receive a guaranteed pension. The logic behind this was that as income grows, the guaranteed pension diminishes. A line in the 1994 agreement stated that voluntary occupational pensions negotiated by unions and employers could be used towards calculating the guaranteed pension. This element attracted strong negative reactions from labour-market partners who considered collective pensions to be part of wages and believed it was not logical to include this collective pension but not private pension plans.

The IG experienced significant difficulty reaching a compromise to introduce individual contributions in the new system so that employees and employers would contribute the same percentage (9.25 per cent). To increase the chances of resolving this problem, the group narrowed the range of possibilities to three. The first option was to compensate for the imposition of individual contributions by granting a wage increase. This was the original agreement, and it was supported by the Conservatives, the Liberals and the Christian Democrats, but it had been rejected by the Social Democratic Party leadership at its last congress. Margit Gennser had intimated that she was willing to review this aspect, but Bo Könberg continued to be very attached to the split. This had previously been rejected by all labour-market partners, but was now accepted by the employers (SAF). The second option was presented by the social democratic government and was supported by the Centre Party. A sickness insurance contribution of 5.95 per cent paid by wage earners would be given to employers in return for a similar contribution to pensions. The remaining 2.3 per cent would be obtained via a wage increase and the use of the tax system. The last option was to shelve the whole proposition and leave all contributions with employers.

In order to clarify each position and provide the group with criticism and comments on all three options, the proposals were sent out for opinions (*remiss*). The SAP government, fearing another deadlock, decided to move ahead by sending their proposal for parliamentary review, a move contested by the Conservatives, Liberals and Christian Democrats (*Dagens Nyheter*, 14 November 1997). In early December, the responses further clouded the picture. Not only were political parties divided on the issues, but so were public authorities. The IG had made no progress at all.

At the end of December, all five parties held a press conference promising not to make pensions an electoral issue (*Svenska Dagbladet*, 29 December 1997). Intense negotiations followed New Year in 1998, and an agreement was reached on 9 January 1998 (see Table 4.3), just three days after it was announced that the negotiations could end up as nothing more than a huge political fiasco because of deep differences (*Expressen*, 6 January 1998). The social democratic option was selected to resolve the issue related to individual contributions. In exchange, the bourgeois parties gained another 0.5 per cent in the funded system. This action was condemned almost immediately by the Finance Ministry since it accentuated and accelerated the depletion of AP-funds to finance the transition to the new system. Once again, this pension bill gathered strong support in Parliament: 257 MPs voted in favour, 17 voted against and 16 abstained.

Resolving the question of the funded portion turned out to be easier than originally anticipated, despite much divergence in the two main political blocks. The Social Democrats sought to transfer responsibility for managing the funded component to the AP-funds, while all four bourgeois parties reiterated their preference of keeping the management of the various funds as far away as possible from the state. The European Union was indirectly involved in resolving parts of this conflict via its convergence criteria for EMU, which Sweden was attempting to follow to ensure its

Table 4.3 Main features of the 1998 pension agreement in Sweden[1]

- The new system is mandatory and covers the entire population.
- The new pensions are to be based on lifetime earnings on the basis of previous contributions (the so-called 'life-income' principle). This includes other social security benefits such as sickness and unemployment insurance.
- Military service and years devoted to raising children up to the age of four result in pension points.
- A flexible retirement age is instituted on an actuarial basis, meaning one can retire prior to age 65, but receive a lower pension. One could eventually retire later than 65 years of age and draw a larger pension.
- A guaranteed pension covers those who have made limited contributions and those with no contributions at all. Forty years of residency in Sweden is required. *Occupational and private pensions do not count towards the means test.*
- A contribution rate of 18.5% is instituted, *of which 2.5% goes into interest-earning private pension fund(s) chosen by the insured. The supervision of the funded part is granted to the Premium Pensions Administration (PPM). Those who do not select a fund will have their money managed by the seventh AP-fund by default.*
- *The question of how much of this contribution will be paid by employers and how much by employees will be decided later. By the year 2000,* the total contributions will be divided equally between employees and employers (9.25% each).
- *Contributions are to be indexed according to the general earnings trend. If real earnings rise, the value of pensions will also rise. If they fall, the pension's value will be lower in terms of purchasing power than when the contribution was paid. Once a person retires, the value of their pension is calculated according to the aggregate pension assets collected. For the payg component, assets will be divided by a coefficient based on life expectancy and a notional future growth factor of 1.6%.*
- *Pensions will be indexed at a rate corresponding to the general earnings trend minus 1.6%. If growth equals 2% in a given year, the pension will rise in real terms by 0.4%. If, on the other hand, growth is equal to 1.2%, pensions will not be fully compensated for inflation (or reduced in real terms).*
- Married couples can share their pension benefits on an actuarial basis. This means that men's points are worth less than women's points since men have shorter lives, on average. *This can only be done with the money contributed to a privately funded account.*
- The transition period will last 20 years. Individuals born between *1938* and 1953 will have their pensions based on both systems. For example, those born in *1938* will have 1/20 of their pension based on the new system, while those born in 1953 will have 19/20 of their pension based on the new system.
- The AP-funds will be used as a buffer fund.

Source: The Pension Reform. Final Report, June 1998.

Note:
[1] Words in *italic* indicate changes that were made to the 1994 agreement.

admission into the Euro-zone remained a political rather than an economic decision. The option favoured by the bourgeois parties would have resulted in the AP-funds (included in the state's finance) being drained over time if there was no substitution included in the state budget. This meant a sharp decrease in public resources, making it much more difficult for the state to meet the EMU criteria. This forced the bourgeois parties to accept the creation of an independent agency within the state, instead of leaving the funded part entirely to the private sector, a solution much more in keeping with the Social Democrats' preference.

Thus, the compromise led to the creation of the Premium Pension Authority (*Premiepensionsmyndigheten* – PPM) that would be responsible for ensuring that the money was transferred to the selected fund or funds. Another point of the agreement was the creation of a seventh AP-fund that enabled funds to be used to purchase stock-market investments by individuals who did not select a private fund. However, a restriction was included: once an individual selected a private fund, he/she could no longer revert to the public fund (seventh AP-fund). Therefore, not selecting a fund was equivalent to choosing the public fund. Despite an aggressive campaign to encourage citizens' active participation, 33 per cent followed their lead in 2000 (Weaver 2004: 42). In 2003, only 9 per cent of new entrants made an active choice (Palme 2005: 47).

As a result of the sprint marathon to maintain the five-party consensus, some technical issues were not fully resolved when the 1998 legislation was introduced. Following the election, the IG continued working to implement the automatic balancing mechanism, to plan the use of AP-funds to finance the transition to the new system and to find a solution to raise individual contributions to 9.25 per cent. With respect to the last item, no solution has been found, and individual contribution rates remain at 6.95 per cent for employees, leaving employers to contribute the remaining 11.55 per cent.

The automatic balancing mechanism required substantial work from experts within the Ministry of Social Affairs, the result of this work being two reports (Ds 1997[66], 1999[43]). There was a genuine commitment from the members of the committee to create an indexation mechanism that guaranteed the financial future of the system while considering social elements, such as intergenerational fairness for the individual, notionally defined contribution accounts created on the basis of the life-income principle (i.e. the earnings-related component of the new pension system). The automatic balancing mechanism relies on the size of the buffer (AP) funds remaining to finance pension liabilities considering changes in various elements such as employment, earnings and fertility. Thus, pensions may be reduced in the event of poor economic performance. Following the adoption of the ensuing legislation in 2001, a commission was set up to study what to do with surpluses. In 2004, that commission published a report suggesting the surplus should be redistributed in the form of both increased pension benefits and pension credits for those currently contributing (SOU 2004[105]). However, the balance ratios of the AP-funds have since diminished substantially, thus reducing the likelihood of a surplus (Anderson and Immergut 2006: 651).

The other principal issue involved the use of AP-funds to finance the transition period and compensate the government for taking on the responsibility for risks such as early retirement/invalidity no longer covered by the new pension system. This element was very controversial, with early estimates suggesting a transfer of SEK 300–350 billion to the state (Ds 1998[7]). By January 2001, SEK 258 billion had been transferred, resulting in a sudden reduction of its debt by 23 per cent of GDP. Despite the IG's commitment to pursue the transfer, no other sums have been transferred following numerous criticisms of the amount being transferred and the increased likelihood that the depletion of the buffer fund might trigger the automatic balance mechanism (Anderson and Immergut 2006: 649).

Opposing the Working Group on Pensions and the Implementation Group

The lack of traditional political conflicts and the economic crisis meant that the Working Group on Pensions was not a high-profile organization, despite the political tensions historically associated with pensions in Sweden (the 1958 pension reform required two elections and a referendum to settle it). Nonetheless, the group's work did not go unchallenged, despite the fact that five of the major parties supported it. The main criticisms concerned gender issues, education, the life-income principle, the costs of the new system, the difficulties of challenging members of the group, the introduction of individual contributions and the creation of a new indexation system. In line with the theoretical framework developed in Chapter 1, this section focuses on the opposition generated by the labour-market partners (first ordering principle) and the political parties (second ordering principle). They were not the only actors who attempted to alter the pension system, but they were, by far, the most influential. Elderly organizations, for example, played a marginal role despite their representation on the IG in 1996, because current retirees would not be directly affected by the new system. Within the state apparatus, the Ministry of Finance also played a role by ensuring that the costs of the new pension system would not worsen public finances in the long run (see Marier 2005).

Könberg's successful creation of a WGOP and IG that excluded the labour-market partners confirms the efficacy of the theoretical framework's contention that the latter, owing to their outsider status, did not effectively influence pension reform. Labour-market partners were only able to stop proposals directly involving private pensions obtained via collective agreements because they could genuinely claim that they are not part of the public domain. For example, when Anna Hedborg acknowledged that voluntary occupational pensions would be integrated into the system to calculate the size of the guaranteed pension on national television in 1995, the public's reaction was harsh and forced politicians to change course.

The main difficulty thus involved the political parties. Representatives had the support of their leaders, but other Members of Parliament and party members sometimes intervened to oppose the compromises being forged. Opposition was most pronounced within the SAP and the Conservatives. The Green Party and the Left Party both opposed the reform proposal and were thus not involved in the WGOP. Their criticism focused on the negative impact of the reform on women and the lack of solidarity measures ensuing from the construction of personal pension accounts. However, they could not alter the process since they accounted for less than 20 per cent of all seats in the Riksdag.

Position of labour-market partners

The foremost decision concerning the participation of labour-market partners was their exclusion from the WGOP and the IG. The advantages of being included in the group go beyond having an influential role during the negotiations, as such a role also provides members with access to all documents and analyses performed by the civil servants attached to the group. In many cases, these documents offer the best source to critique a proposal. The exclusion of the labour-market partners from the working group must be considered an important part of this process, as it had the effect of substantially limiting their influence. Frustrations built up rapidly, and the TCO's president would be the first to complain about his access to members of the WGOP in September 1993:

> The doors of the Working Group on Pensions are almost always closed to the labour-market partners. Therefore, we do not know exactly what is going to be proposed.
> (*Dagens Nyheter*, 12 September 1993, Debatt; my translation)

Not surprisingly, labour-market partners were able to successfully oppose measures that directly affected the wage bargaining elements negotiating exclusively between unions and employers (see Table 4.4). Besides obtaining the guarantee that private occupational pensions would not count towards the means test for the guaranteed pension, labour-market partners were able to derail the recalibration of contributions. Following the surprise announcement in 1994 that contributions were going to be split evenly between employers and employees (as opposed to the ATP, where employers paid all contributions), the SAF responded by stating that it was not at all obvious that wages would rise if contributions were reduced. A few weeks later, its confrontational tone had decreased, but the SAF still claimed that a one-for-one krona exchange might not be possible, since other social contributions were higher due to the wage increase (*Dagens Nyheter*, 19 February 1994). This element of the reform was seriously jeopardized when the LO expressed its opposition to employee contributions in principle. It also questioned how this would work in practice (*Göteborgs Posten*, 15 February 1994). The TCO criticized the proposal on the basis of its marginal effects. Further wage increases would be required to maintain the same net wage. A principal reason mentioned was that an increase in income incurred higher taxes (*Dagens Nyheter*, 20 June 1994).

Labour-market partners changed their tone once it became clear that the government would bear the costs of any adjustment necessary to implement this change.

The most interesting aspect of the pension reform remains its disproportionate impact on labour-market partners. Despite all the articles discussing the main advantages of Sweden as a universal welfare state where occupational divisions are minimized, opposition was in fact structured along occupational lines (see Table 4.4). The LO was the only organization to give its full support to the new pension proposal. Interestingly, it was also the most subdued during this whole period. According to Lundberg, there was a pre-negotiation between the leadership of the SAP and the LO to support each other throughout the process to avoid internal conflict between those supporting the reform and those seeking to maintain the ATP system (Lundberg 2001: 27). Despite frequent contact between the central office and the two SAP representatives, it is difficult to conclude that the LO was actively involved in the proceedings for many reasons. First, being outside the committee implied that the LO had to rely on the Social Democrats and the so-called reference group to obtain documentation and other information regarding the committee's progress. However, many documents were not made available, making it difficult for critics to argue against the pension groups. Regardless of the ties between the LO and the SAP, such contacts cannot replace full participation on a committee. The LO's surprised reaction to the introduction of employee contributions suggests that it was not fully aware of all the decisions being made. Second, the foundation of the new system was negotiated in December 1993 and early January 1994. These negotiations were fairly quick and intense, diminishing the input of any external players. In addition to this obstacle, the LO had another major preoccupation during this period: the resignation of its president, Stig Malm. As a result, this was a turbulent period within the LO executive, and pension reform was not the main priority at that time.

Despite the support granted by the LO's central office, the LO members were very critical of the pension proposal. This became obvious during the internal review of the SAP in 1996 and during both congresses in 1996–7. The LO federations were also divided, thus further marginalizing its position. It had the support of its largest federation, Kommunal Förbundet (which was also the foremost women's federation), but not of Metall's, the second largest union within the confederation.

The consequences of switching to the life-income principle within the new pension system were a chief contributor to the divisions within the LO. Interestingly, comparisons to the old ATP system made it easier for members of the WGOP to demonstrate that typical LO jobs, where individuals start working at a young age without sharp increases in their wages, would receive an equal exchange for their contributions. The old ATP system favouring brief careers with fast-rising wages contributed to the accentuation of inequalities among occupational groups, with professional women

Table 4.4 Positions of labour-market partners on specific issues proposed by Swedish *Pensionsarbetsgruppen* as outlined in *Sammanställning av Remissyttranden över Pensionsarbetsgruppens Betänkande Reformerat Pensionssytem*

	Life-income principle	Pension rights for children	Pension rights for studies	Pension rights for insured	Indexation based on state of economy	Basic pension	Transition rules	Splitting contributions 50% each	PPM
LO	Support – if considers redistribution based on sickness, unemployment …	Support	Support	Support	Support	Support	Support	Opposed	Support – still prefer use of AP-funds
TCO	Opposed – based on labour market of yesterday, short work life heavily penalized		Support – should be increased and granted for part-time studies	Support – should be based on insured income	Support	Support	Opposed – need review	Opposed	Leads to a decentralization of savings
SACO	Support – even though it hurts academics (low early wages)	Opposed – wants change (not equitable for men and women)	Support – should be increased and granted for part-time studies		Support		Mild support – period should be prolonged by five years	Mild support – many complications for this transition	Support
SAF	Support	Opposed – benefits without contributions	Opposed – benefits without contributions	Opposed – did propose an alternative solution	Support	Opposed – too high		Support	Support

Source: (SOU 1994 [20])
Note: * People on unemployment or sickness insurance.

benefiting the most. Women with precarious jobs had in fact benefited the least from the previous system, as they obtained only 0.64 krona for every krona paid into the system (SOU 1994[22]). The WGOP, and more particularly Hedborg, argued convincingly that the new system was better than the previous one in terms of gender equality. Three female-dominated unions within LO added credibility and support to the WGOP's point of view by endorsing the proposal on the grounds that their members typically have long careers and low wages (*Dagens Nyheter*, 11 April 1994).[35] The WGOP acknowledged that women earn less than men, resulting in different future pension treatment, but stressed that this was a labour-market issue and not a pension one.

In another instance, typical Metall workers operating in manufacturing and heavy industry tend to retire early, which penalizes them further. They pronounced themselves against the reform, even though their leaders at first supported the proposal. Metall claimed that many workers – close to 50 per cent – are forced to retire at 60 owing to the physical toll their work entails and would thus be heavily penalized by the new system. Metall proposed to lengthen the rules of the old system to 20/40 instead of adopting the life-income principle. It was also very critical of the introduction of employee contributions (*Göteborgs Posten*, 19 January 1997).

The TCO had been opposed to the reform from 1992 on. Broadly speaking, the TCO lost what it gained in the 1950s when its support was needed to create the ATP system. It was no secret, even then, that the 15/30 rule was created to secure the vote of a large portion of its members. The social democratic representatives were able to secure the LO's support in part by demonstrating that TCO-type jobs had been advantaged under the ATP. This is extremely important since the new system, in fact, results in an increase in the length of contributions. By demonstrating that the LO's members would be relatively better off, the Social Democrat representatives were able to secure their support.

With the support of SACO, the TCO also focused on the lack of compensation for periods spent in education and training. The WGOP originally refused to give compensation for education because it results in higher income, generating a higher pension in a system based on contributions. But the TCO stressed that the relationship between higher education and higher income is not automatic. It strongly criticized the fact that those who start working directly after high school might get a higher pension than those who opt to study longer (*Dagens Nyheter*, 29 November 1992). The WGOP eventually added pension points for education. However, this was highly symbolic since the pension points given are based on a low fictitious income of SEK 20,000 ($2,000) annually.

Though SACO remained positive with respect to the foundation of the system, it also came out against the pension proposal. Its negative input was based on the fact that many questions needed to be clarified, such as the financial consequences the system would have for the state's budget.

SACO claimed that this could result in higher taxes (*Dagens Nyheter*, 7 April 1994). Despite certain aspects, such as the non-contributory elements that it deemed expensive, the SAF ended up supporting the splitting of contributions between employers and employees and was relatively supportive of the reform. It would not be active in the process beyond ensuring that wage bargaining agreements remained outside the scope of the new reform and that changes to the contributory structure would not negatively affect its members.

Internal critics: the Social Democratic and Conservative parties

These two parties were really the only ones among the five political parties backing the agreement to question the pension proposal presented by the WGOP and the IG. Despite continuous support from the party leadership and executive, the work of Anna Hedborg and Ingela Thalén was increasingly criticized within the SAP. Its women's association was strongly opposed to the life-income principle. Many MPs under Karin Wegestål's leadership began to question the actions of their representatives and criticize the reform. Nonetheless, the party leaders elected to go ahead with the pension proposal.

As noted earlier, the SAP congress of 1996 and 1997 almost forced the government to break the agreement with the four bourgeois parties. Much criticism emerged during the congress of March 1996, including several motions to scrap the agreement. Anna Hedborg presented the reform to the congress and spent a lot of time defending the position taken by the party. In the hope of appeasing opposition within the party, the leaders agreed to conduct broad-scale consultations with its members, even though the framework of the agreement had been approved two years earlier. This strategy backfired, however, as most comments were quite negative. Adding fuel to the fire, Klingvall refused to publicize the results of the inquiry.[36] More than 15,000 members participated in various forums, producing more than 500 official submissions of opinions. According to Lundberg, around 80 per cent of the opinions regarding the new system were negative and advocated changing the parameters of the ATP system instead (Lundberg 2001: 43). The reform proposal sketched by the RFV in 1991 became the alternative model for the opposition.

The result was a stormy congress in 1997 – 28 motions were very critical of the new pension system, while 17 asked that the pension agreement be dismantled and replaced with a reform based on the ATP system (Lundberg 2001: 42). An influential member of the government, Thage G. Petersson, and Metall's representative Göran Borg, who had been advocating the dismissal of the proposal, saved the agreement thanks to a compromise struck during the early stages of the debate on pensions.

Margit Gennser also faced opposition within her party. The critics were mainly from a group led by Lars Tobisson and individuals within the government's office (Rosenblad) who had been advocating either a fully funded system or a larger funded component. Lars Söderstrom, who had been advocating a fully funded system himself, eventually supported Gennser and convinced the others to do the same by emphasizing the tax reduction (the 50 per cent reduction in contributions collected above the ceiling) and the closer link between contributions and benefits.[37] Tobisson also ultimately supported Gennser, and his support was essential, as other influential party members, such as Bo Lundgren and the then prime minister Carl Bildt, were more critical of the pension proposal.

Swedish reform: a system shift?

When all was said and done, Sweden ended up creating a whole new pension system rather than simply fixing some parameters, as France and Belgium had. The issues raised by such an undertaking are far greater relative to the aforementioned countries. The implementation of the Swedish reform was very complex and difficult. Numerous reports outlining technical details were published, and the final legislation comprised 1,091 pages, excluding the annexes. This is in direct contrast to France's experience when it introduced pension reforms in 1993. When asked about implementation and legislation, a member of the Balladur cabinet replied that 'it was easy, I wrote three lines!' Given this state of affairs, it is difficult to support Pierson's interpretation that the Swedish case was stable, not to mention his conclusions, where he states that 'the pension reform introduced in June 1994, based on extensive consultations among the major parties and the representatives of labour and capital, seeks to get Sweden's public pension system on a stable, long-term footing without challenging its basic principles' (Pierson 1996: 172–3).

The consequences of the new system are multiple and complex (for a detailed overview, see Palmer 2000 and Palme 2005). The automatic balancing mechanism of the pension system ensures the financial sustainability of the system by avoiding potential increases in contribution rates. Further, a pension-debt adjustment mechanism was created for those whose retirement income relied, solely or in part, on the ATP (individuals born before 1953). Both measures attempted to ensure a stable contribution rate of 18.5 per cent. With 1 per cent growth, contribution rates would have had to rise to 24–29 per cent by 2030 in the old ATP system, while they would have required a level of 18.5–22 per cent with 2 per cent growth (Palmer 2000: 22). It should be noted that the financial sustainability of the old ATP system improves rapidly with growth rates above 2 per cent. However, the generosity of benefits also declines rapidly owing to its indexation to prices.

Individual benefits in the new system are also extremely difficult to predict since they will include a portion based on notionally defined contributions and another based on the performance of privately managed financial investments. The first component is very sensitive to the indexation mechanism, which includes growth and fertility rates along with labour-market performance (including compensated leave for childcare and disability). The second element depends on the success of the stock market and the selections made by each individual. As a result, individuals contributing the same amount in the new Swedish pension system may collect different retirement incomes, based on how they managed the second component. If we compare the new system with the ATP, individuals with a long career with a stable wage will now do better than those with short careers and fast-rising wages, due to the replacement of the 15/30 rule with the life-income principle.

The introduction of means-tested benefits has drawn a lot of criticism because it attacks the universality principle previously associated with the basic pension in the ATP system (Lindbom 2001). This measure was established despite the fact that the literature on the subject emphasizes the relationship between means-tested benefits and poverty among the elderly (Korpi and Palme 1998). However, as was accurately noted by Palme (2005), the design of the guaranteed pension excludes occupational and private pensions, thus erasing the disincentives to save that are usually associated with means-tested benefits.

The Swedish pension reform represents a blending of the three positions that were debated during the ATP conflict of the 1950s. It includes a large payg component guaranteed by the state, a relatively high guaranteed pension (albeit means tested within the public system) and a funded component. By default, such a metaphor implies the acknowledgement of a system shift towards the right, since right-leaning parties were not able to integrate any of their preferences in the 1950s. The introduction of a funded component into the state system was the principal item that had to be accepted by the Social Democrats to achieve this agreement. It is worth noting, however, that the life-income principle does not necessarily represent an anti-social democratic element. Contrary to the misleading picture of Sweden and its generous welfare state, the system encourages and pushes people into employment, not into accepting passive handouts. When replying to the gender critiques, for example, Hedborg was quick to point out that employment, and not the state or a rich husband, was the most effective way for women to acquire independence.

Why did the Social Democrats agree to such a change?

By agreeing to the reform of the entire pension system, the SAP opened the door to the demands of the four bourgeois parties. We must then ask why they did so? First, Sweden has had a tradition of solving crises by consensus that was severely tested in the early 1990s when it entered a dreadful recession. The government adopted a major crisis package and it was supported by the Social Democrats. Thus, contact between the opposition and the government was quite frequent and hence conducive to continued compromise. Even though the work of the committee began prior to that economic crisis, it reinforced the necessity to do something about pensions. The long-term vision required to introduce a new pension system also increased the need for co-operation.

Second, one can question why the Social Democrats would agree to change the system. It is often mentioned that the Social Democrats have been in office for all but a few years since World War II, but a closer look at the chronology presents another perspective. For the period 1976–94, the bourgeois parties held office for a total of nine years (1976–82 and 1991–4), the same length of time as the Social Democrats had (1982–91)! At the beginning of the negotiations, the Social Democrats' popularity was extremely low and the chances of gaining office seemed weak. Despite the SAP's desire to reform the pension system according to its preferences, it had to acknowledge the possibility that a future bourgeois government could do the same and that this likelihood was currently much stronger than it would be in the future. Thus, the maintenance of a strong payg component required broad political support to ensure its long-term viability. The politics of pensions in the United Kingdom (see Chapter 5) supports this hypothesis. This is one of the foremost reasons why the Social Democrats accepted the proposal, even though all the polls in 1994 switched in their favour.[38] Even though the then party leader Carlsson was sceptical that an agreement could be reached among the largest parties, he was still extremely careful in selecting the SAP representatives. Hedborg and Thalén were chosen for upcoming difficult negotiations within the working group and the party (Lundberg 2001: 25). This selection demonstrates that the SAP was serious about reaching a compromise. It could just as easily have selected members critical of the need to reform the pension system, such as Doris Håvik, who had been the vice-president of the Social Security Committee in Parliament. The negotiations would have gone nowhere, and the SAP could have campaigned on a platform of saving pensions. From this perspective, one has to wonder what Persson's actual motivation was when he appointed Klingvall as Social Affairs Minister in 1996 and a pensioners' representative to the Implementation Group during the same year.

Third, why did the Social Democrats stand by the agreement in 1996 and 1997 when it became evident that grassroots support was, at best, questionable? The costs of renouncing the pension agreement increased as time went on. Had the Social Democrats opted to renounce the five-party agreement, they could have faced stark public criticism for leaving the pension agreement as it was when a pension reform was widely understood to be necessary. These costs were considered quite substantial and might have been overestimated, but no party wanted to be blamed for the failure to reach an agreement. This runs contrary to Pierson's (1996) argument, since in this instance avoiding a painful reform was deemed more harmful than enacting one.

Fourth, the SAP would have faced many difficulties in pushing through its own preferences. Even the internal opposition admitted as much by pointing towards possible coalitions the party could make to avoid dealing with the Conservatives. For example, the president of Metall, Göran Jonnsson, was highly critical of both the Centre and Conservative parties because both favoured only a basic system of social protection. Thus, he advocated a new deal with only the Liberals and the Left Party (*Svenska Dagbladet*, 14 January 1997). Even if we accept the unlikely possibility of co-operation among a tripartite agreement that would include the Left and a bourgeois party, reopening negotiations with a new party while seeking the co-operation of a bourgeois party would have resulted in further delays. Moreover, it did not provide any guarantee that a new coalition would be able to generate a system shift soon afterwards. The bourgeois parties would most likely have sought to reform any system adopted unilaterally by the SAP.

Finally, the alternative to the pension proposal was built on shaky ground. Social democratic representatives had stated on numerous previous occasions that the old ATP system would crumble in the near future and that it was unfair to the LO workers. Turning back the clock to defend it would have resulted in a serious credibility dilemma and even more internal conflicts. The mass media would have had a field day bringing back old comments made by the SAP representatives from various pension commissions.

Conclusion: a surprising lack of union influence

A Parliamentary Integration relationship facilitated the enactment of major pension reform without much input from the labour movement. This concluding section first discusses the impact and the reasons for this surprising lack of influence and then concentrates on the elements explaining how the large number of veto players was overcome, thus justifying the Committee label attributed to Sweden in Chapter 1.

This chapter (and to some extent the entire book) challenges previous studies that highlight the participation and importance of the LO in the Swedish pension reform process (see, for example, Anderson 2001). The standard reply to any denial that the LO was actively involved is to answer with a typical M. Olson (1965) argument: the concentration of interest results in a stronger political position where conflicts can be internalized because of the notably hierarchical structure of unions. Thus, a compromise can easily be reached where losses are spread out in a corporatist way.

As mentioned prior to the discussion of the pension reform process, this position is becoming increasingly difficult to support. First, the role of labour-market partners within both the decision-making process and the state apparatus has declined significantly. Analysing a wide range of indicators and factors related to Swedish corporatism, Hermansson *et al.* conclude that the participation and involvement of labour-market partners within the decision-making process has decreased significantly in the past 20 years (Hermansson *et al.* 1997: 378). On this subject, Jan Bröms, chief economist with SACO, mentioned that, in the past, unions had experts like him actively participating in various commissions and inquiries. It was not unusual for an expert to be involved in several inquiries at the same time. It is indicative of the changing involvement of labour-market partners with the state that Bröms was only involved in one committee when he was interviewed for this book, and he sat in because of his expertise with the subject matter rather than his union affiliation.[39] Labour-market partners now tend to confine themselves somewhat more strictly to more narrowly defined labour-market issues.

As a result of the ATP, a universal pension scheme was created and confined to the state. The LO trusted the state and it sought to (and did) 'capture' the state (see Rothstein 1996). Thus, its proposal was to build such a scheme within the state rather than apart from it. This is in stark contrast to France, where unions were highly critical of the state and its overwhelming presence. Thus, they constantly sought to obtain control of occupational pensions and keep the state away from them.

These two factors can explain why the labour movement's protest was very mild when Könberg announced the creation of the WGOP. Only when it became clear that the new system meant a reduction in pensions for its members did the TCO criticize its exclusion in 1993. During an interview, a member of the WGOP neatly illustrated the reasoning behind the exclusion of labour-market partners by stating that it would have been impossible to exclude them if Sweden had Finland's system, because theirs is administered by the labour-market partners.[40]

Thus, throughout the later part of the pension reform process, the LO's influence would be generated via its links with the Social Democratic Party rather than the state. This is why protests from LO members were directed towards the SAP congresses rather than the pension group directly, as would have been the case in France. Historically, this is nothing new. Korpi (1983) and Esping-Andersen (1985) claim that the rise of the Swedish welfare state was dependent on this collaboration. However, for this equation to work, the SAP had to be able to sustain a lengthy political dominance. The constitutional reform of 1974 created a far more competitive environment where such hegemony could not be replicated (Anderson and Immergut 2006). By the early 1990s, it was not clear that they would govern for two consecutives terms, let alone a third, after the bourgeois coalition of 1991–4. As was underlined by Rothstein (1996) and Lindqvist (1990), control of the state bureaucracy combined with significant participation in its workings is also an essential element and could have presented another line of resistance. As mentioned earlier, the Ministry of Social Affairs experienced a stark increase in the numbers of staff, including a few from the Ministry of Finance. These shifts helped decrease the attachment to the ATP system within the department (Marier 2005).

As a result, the LO's influence in the deal cannot have been very strong, especially if we compare it to the critical role it played in the creation of the ATP system in the late 1950s. Of course, it had close contacts with the

Social Democrats, who were aware of the LO's preferences. For example, they had plenty of time to discuss the outline published in 1992. However, these discussions and contacts could not disguise the fact that it was not participating directly in the negotiations. The two most serious rounds of negotiations (December 1993/January 1994 and January 1998) occurred in a very short period of time, decreasing the likelihood of external consultations. In addition, the LO was experiencing a leadership change in December 1993. Once the agreement was concluded, the LO, like other parties outside the five main parties in the WGOP, were faced with a *fait accompli*. It could comment negatively on specific aspects or ask the SAP to seek certain modifications pending approval of the other parties within the WGOP, but it was forced either to accept the package or to reject it.

The second major element, often stated as a major difference between Sweden and other countries, is the universal nature of the welfare state, partly the product of a highly centralized labour movement. This results in a welfare state supported by all citizens, as they all receive benefits from it (Rothstein 1998). This chapter raises doubts about the validity of the universal argument in times of retrenchment. The creation of a universal income-related pension programme was the result of an occupational coalition of blue- and white-collar employees. The Social Democrats and the LO needed the support of the TCO members, many of whom already had occupational pensions, to ensure that it could emerge with a sufficient majority to beat the opposition. The Social Democrats agreed to the 15/30 rule in order to gather the TCO's support for the supplementary pension and expand the size of its electorate (Svensson 1994). The fact that TCO-type jobs benefited most from the previous system is no surprise; the ATP system was designed to solicit their support, not to improve the situations of women or of those facing long periods of unemployment, and so on. Of course, they also benefited from the system, though not as much in relative terms.

The new pension system came into effect because of the opposite action, and an occupational logic led the LO to support the system. As is the case in France, blue-collar unions (FO and CGT) were strongly opposed to any increase in the length of contribution period because many of their workers already had difficulties reaching the 37.5 contribution years required, and many were counting on early retirement. Despite having a better situation than their French colleagues, the average retirement age of LO members was still below 60, and many workers were drawing pre-pensions. The new pension system, with its life-income principle, has the same effect as an increase in the required number of years to obtain a full pension, but it was not criticized as heavily as it was in France. Why? At the expense of TCO members, the LO was the relative winner in the new system. The five-party agreement meant that the support of the TCO was not as crucial as it had been when the ATP system was created. It could no longer play the role of being the centre element sought by two blocks opposing each other.

However, the LO's support was more important because of its connection to the SAP. The five-party coalition was, moreover, able to sell an extension in the length of the contribution period by stressing that the previous system disadvantaged them. Statistics demonstrated that they were financing the pensions of the TCO's members, who were eligible for a higher pension even though they might have contributed a similar amount. This was a powerful argument to justify counting all contributions made to the system. It was also enough to silence those who criticized the fact that many LO members could end up with small pensions because they tended to retire sooner. The latter argument struck a chord among industrial workers, but could not outweigh the relative gain accruing to other professions within the union (regional government employees and retail and service-sector employees).

How could so many veto players generate such a substantial reform?

A central aspect behind Sweden's reform was the cohesiveness and chemistry of the pension groups. Helping to develop this chemistry were the institutional manoeuvrings of Bo Könberg, who created an unusual working group rather than an official inquiry. The small group was comprised exclusively of politicians and experts, which was conducive to a seminar-like atmosphere, generating an abundance of open discussion among the members. As Gennser noted, 'it was really like we were sitting at a seminar at a university and we were discussing how to find a solution. Of course, I had to look at my customers and they had to look at their customers. But, I mean, we had to find a solution'.[41] The group approached the reform as an intellectual problem, with issues to be resolved one by one. The fact that Könberg was a liberal minister also helped to bridge the differences between the Social Democrats and the Conservatives. Both Hedborg and Gennser gained a reputation for being social engineers, and members learned to trust one another (*Dagens Nyheter*, 12 April 1994; *Affärsvärlden*, 15 November 2000).

This cohesiveness was very evident to those outside the group, such as labour-market partners, the Ministry of Finance and those politicians who were opposed to the deal. They demonstrated great resolve to stick together, often speaking with a single voice. Complaints highlighted that speaking to different members of the group did not really change their response. Some comments from opponents almost gave the impression that they were part of the same political party. It would be difficult to envision such a coalition in a Social Partnership structure.

5   United Kingdom
A marriage with the private sector?

Introduction

Public pension policy in the United Kingdom is distinctly different from the previous three cases because it has never had the chance to mature. Its most consistent feature is its strong reliance on the private sector, with the state seeking to minimize its responsibilities (Nesbitt 1995: 141). This could be partly explained by the combination of a parliamentary system and a first-past-the-post electoral formula that favours a bipartite system and a single-party majority government with a strong executive. Policies seem to be more easily changed due to the competitive and confrontational aspects of British politics. With more than 100 parameters involved in the calculation of one's state pensions (Pensions Policy Institute 2006: 1), this policy type has generated 'the most complex pension system in the world' (Pensions Commission 2004: 210). The United Kingdom example defies popular arguments in the retrenchment literature, which stresses that the high accountability and visibility of the executive constrain the government's actions because it cannot easily avoid blame (Pierson 1994, 1996; Vail 1999). This chapter challenges these assertions by highlighting successful retrenchment efforts that have left Britain fighting to save the elderly from poverty rather than seeking to reduce the cost of pensions. Numerous reforms were undertaken by successive Conservative and Labour governments that resulted in severe distrust of the state for not providing dependable information to guide citizens regarding how they should plan their retirement.

Theorizing pension reform within the British context

The British state: an elusive player

Unlike discussions of French politics which almost always begin with the state, it is extremely difficult to find similar input regarding British politics. Using Krasner's (1976) typology, the United Kingdom is clearly a weak state, and the extent to which it has sought to change the behaviour of private actors has actually been quite limited by international standards. There was no strong, dominant state to challenge organized interests as was the case in France, Spain or Italy (Birnbaum 1988: 75). Since private actors tend to play a much larger role in the United Kingdom than in other European states, it is no accident that the burgeoning literature on policy networks took root in the United Kingdom.

The United Kingdom did not need to use welfare as a tool to support the creation of the state the way Bismarck did in Germany. This might be explained by the fact that state formation was accomplished relatively easily in Britain compared with the continental countries. A strong state was not necessary to create unity, as was the case for states seeking to incorporate territories from the city belt (Rokkan 1999). Thus, while everyone acknowledged it had a role to play, social policy was never firmly linked to the state (Ashford 1986: 76).

The United Kingdom is the country where Friedrich List's ideas never stood a chance in the face of a deeply embedded *laissez-faire* philosophy. The combination of the elitist nature of policy-making and the solid entrenchment of individualistic assumptions within the society resulted in a lack of drastic government welfare action even during periods of persistent social need such as the mid-19th century (Ashford 1986; Polanyi 1944). As King noted, the strength of liberal ideas had an impact similar to that of institutional arrangements in shaping debates and policy options. Labour has not been strong enough politically to alter this liberal legacy (King 1995: 203) and would have needed a long period of political hegemony to reverse the Conservative's head start. This contrasts sharply with the Swedish case, where the Social Democrats were able to secure successive electoral victories and extend their political base successfully by promoting encompassing programmes (Svensson 1994).

Moreover, despite being an international political and economic hegemon (Gilpin 1987), the benefits of this power were not translated into better social policies. The United Kingdom's vast international expansion implied a policy of open trade that benefited London's financial district, the City, and those with strong interests abroad – a policy that was not reversed even though it resulted in a long period of decline. It also resulted in a very powerful Treasury that was fearful of budget deficits and of public finances that could impede its international interests (Gamble 1994).

The political system also prevented the establishment of a universal and generous public pension system. In fact, a coherent public pension system never took form due to ever-changing relevant legislation. As discussed in Chapter 1, a first-past-the-post electoral system encourages the formation of single-party governments where negotiations with other parties are extremely rare. Further, the British executive possesses significant power and faces limited checks and balances compared to other democracies (Heffernan 2005: 67). In constrast to the United States, where the president must deal with Congress and an activist Supreme Court, the British executive must ensure the support of Parliament, which is usually controlled by its own party. Recent research points towards even more centralization of power in the hands of the prime minister at the expense (mostly) of the cabinet through governing practices introduced by Thatcher and Blair (Foley 2000; Hennessy 2005). These include the involvement of non-state actors, the creation of non-traditional commissions and the inclusion of non-experts within consultative processes and the formulation of public policies.

As Steinmo convincingly demonstrated in 1993 with respect to tax policies, the establishment of long-term policies is extremely difficult within this political context, since new governments can effectively alter pre-established legislation, and often do. The development of public pensions is an illustrative case in point. A pension truce has never been achieved and the British pension system is utterly complex as a result. On one hand, the Labour Party actively tried to expand the public pension system by encouraging the creation and expansion of a public occupational plan, while the Conservatives, on the other, fought to ensure a significant private component within the pension system and sought to limit the scope of public benefits.

The Conservatives' lengthy tenure proved fatal to Labour Party projects owing to the strength and growth of private occupational and individual pensions. The state remains quite active in promoting private solutions, since one-third of pension contributions to private plans come from con-tracted-out rebates given to individuals and enterprises as an incentive to invest in a particular pension system (Pensions Commission 2005: 73). Nonetheless, Labour actively ensured that a stronger public component, including occupational pensions (such as SERPS – State Earnings-Related Pension Scheme; and S2P – State Second Pension), was developed. Further, the Labour Party tried to introduce stricter rules governing private pensions. Not surprisingly, due to the numerous reforms of the past decades British citizens are very confused when it comes to retirement questions and trust in private pensions is higher than for public pensions (Taylor-Gooby 2005: 221).

The relationship between the social partners, and their relationship to the state

Consistent with a Parliamentary Integration type, the United Kingdom lacks the involvement of unions and employers within the policy process compared with the other three cases examined. Unions and employers never became social – or labour-market – partners, as they did in continental Europe and Scandinavia. Thus, even when co-operation reached its peak in the British political system during the 1960s and 1970s, these interactions were never fully institutionalized. They were considered legitimate and institutionalized by British standards, but their role never really went beyond the exchange of information and inquiries, and rarely featured active participation in policy-making and implementation (Olsen 1983: 167). It is far easier to exclude actors involved in this type of relationship than those who have had longstanding participation in committees and agency boards. The Conservatives under Thatcher and subsequent Conservative and Labour governments have, in fact, been able to do this very effectively by creating pension committees and commissions that do not include both employers and employees, such as the Inquiry into Provision for Retirement in 1983 and the recent Pensions Commission, which submitted its first report in 2004. The latter included former representatives of both employers and employees, but they acted independently.

The influence and political strength of the main union, the TUC, traditionally came from its relationship with the Labour Party. However, unions actually tried to divorce labour problems from social issues (Ashford 1986: 315), and the Labour Party also sought to distance itself from the TUC by appealing to broader audiences (Ashford 1986: 210). Nonetheless, when members became disenchanted with employers and with the levels of workers' pensions, the TUC turned to Labour and obtained some results. First, in the aftermath of World War II it pressured the Labour Party to reduce the length of the transition period to allow pensioners to receive a contributory flat-rate pension after 10, rather than 20, contribution years (Heclo 1974: 256–7; Baldwin 1990: 117–26). Second, it advocated the creation of a public, earnings-related pension scheme that included an opt-out clause for workers already covered by private schemes. Despite these developments, it must be emphasized that, relative to the other cases studied in this book, the TUC cannot be considered a major player in expanding public pensions, owing to a lack of will and of political power. For example, there was a lack of interest on the TUC's part when the idea of a mandatory public occupational scheme was first proposed in the late 1950s, while its Swedish counterparts were actively pushing the Social Democrats to introduce just such a scheme. With regards to political power, the TUC has also not been formally involved in pension commissions; nor has it been closely consulted in the past 25 years. Ironically, despite the presence of successive Conservative governments from 1979 to 1997, the Confederation of British Industry (CBI) suffered a similar fate.

Bureaucracy

Social policy departments in the United Kingdom have been inherently weak, both historically and by international standards. As Heclo stressed, they were ill equipped to deal with emergent social problems such as pensions; the insufficient resources allocated to social policy were the prime reason for the lack of consideration of a contributory pension scheme in the early 1900s (Heclo 1974: 302). The first pension expert group (Pension Provision Group, PPG), established soon after the Labour Party's victory in

1997, initially faced the challenge of acquiring missing and disparate data. This was mentioned as a principal reason few recommendations were made. Frustrated with this state of affairs, the PPG eventually created an independent Pensions Policy Institute (PPI) to partly alleviate these difficulties. The creation of the more ambitious Pensions Commission in 2002 specifically addressed the general lack of knowledge about the British pension system.

Currently, the two main bureaucratic actors are the Department for Work and Pensions (DWP)[1] and the Treasury. The role of the DWP (then the Department of Health and Social Security, DHSS) was severely marginalized by the Thatcher government and only recently regained some of its influence. As is demonstrated in the following pages, the Conservatives successfully kept them away from the elaboration of pension policy. Following a reorganization of the department in 2002, the 'newly' created DWP was quite active in the policy-making process for matters related to occupational pensions. It has, however, left the Treasury in charge of state pension initiatives even though this leadership has been contested, as evidenced by numerous accounts stressing conflicts between the two public organizations (see, for example, *Financial Times*, 3 November 1998; *Financial Times*, 18 December 2002). The DWP's influence has recently been heightened by hosting the secretariat of the Pensions Commission, which served as the basis for its elaboration of the White Paper entitled *Security in Retirement: Towards a New Pensions System* (Department for Work and Pensions 2006b[0]). In the latter case, the Treasury was consulted and kept informed of the progress made, but the initiatives clearly came from the DWP.

The influence of the Treasury is such that it would not be an overstatement to suggest that nothing gets done without its approval. The Treasury's strength has seriously constrained the expansion of social budgets and programmes (Heclo 1974; Ashford 1986: 236). Bonoli goes so far as to claim that it represents a veto point in British social policy-making (Bonoli 2000: 84). The Treasury is considered the main actor in the development and reform of social policies, including pensions. This arrangement has been reinforced by successive Labour governments. Prior to a serious prioritization of pensions by Prime Minister Tony Blair, the prerogative to alter pensions within the British executive rested largely with the Chancellor of the Exchequer, rather than with the prime minister (Hennessy 2005: 10). As with other domestic issues (Heffernan 2005: 65), the Prime Minister's Office could not ignore the Treasury when dealing with pensions. In contrast to the Swedish Working Group on Pensions (see Chapter 4), the Treasury was an important actor in the main inquiry into pensions and often brought discussions to a halt when they were linked to tax issues. It was also able to impose a zero-cost constraint on pension discussions and intervened successfully when proposals accompanied by an increase in public expenditure were presented.

Theoretical expectations: does a cabinet type result in unlimited powers?

The United Kingdom is the example where the most policy change is expected because the government does not have to deal with vetoes. The term social partners (see Chapters 2 and 3) is simply not employed in the United Kingdom, reinforcing the notion that both unions and employers' associations are interest groups seeking to influence the state, rather than partners co-operating with it in the elaboration of policies. Recent Labour Party governments have been more prone to discussing policy issues with both unions and employers than the Conservatives, but this is a far cry from their institutionalization within the policy-making process. The structure of the British pension system grants a significant role to employers and employees when it comes to private occupational pensions (and these are quite substantial in the United Kingdom), but their role is extremely limited (though not non-existent) when it comes to public pensions, given that the state is the primary contributor. Thus, the UK represents a clear case of Parliamentary Integration, since unions and employers do not represent a veto point (Immergut 1992).

Reinforcing the powers of the government in making policy, a majoritarian vision strongly entrenched within British politics generated single-party executives with no veto players (Tsebelis 1999, 2002). Negotiations with other parties only occur when majorities are exceptionally slim or when they dissipate, such as during the later months of John Major's period in office, in which case an additional party might be considered a veto player. However, this is a very rare event in British politics. In all instances highlighted in this chapter, the opposition was unable to influence the policy choices of the government and had to wait for an electoral victory to do so. Thus, the long-term implementation of a pension policy is linked closely to the electoral fortunes of the party in power.

Given this extreme centralization of power, the most potent political conflicts are internalized within the cabinet. When it comes to pensions, these have usually involved the prime minister and the chancellor to the exchequer, while the Secretary of State for Work and Pensions is allied with one or the other of these.

Reforming pensions in the United Kingdom ... too much policy change?

This section discusses the various pension reforms introduced by Conservative governments from 1979 to 1997 and concludes with a brief analysis of the Labour period (1997–). In light of the history of pensions in the United Kingdom, analysing the actions of the Labour government is useful, since both parties have traditionally overturned whatever changes the previous government made to pension plans. However, the changes made by Conservative governments, when combined with the length of their stay in office, means any policy reversal will be extremely expensive. Thus, the policy options available to the Labour government were seriously constrained, and the core of the important changes made during the 1980s remains untouched.

Even though this book has not tackled the second pillar of pension systems, i.e. the occupational pension schemes available within the private sectors, it must be included in the discussion of this example, given that SERPS allowed occupational schemes to operate alongside the state scheme. Consequently, the private sector is a key political player in the United Kingdom because it has a vested interest in the current system.

The new Right wave hits pensions subtly … but efficiently (1979–83)

The adoption of the SERPS in 1975 marked the end of a long political battle between the Labour Party and the Conservatives. Despite minor objections, the Conservatives at the time supported this legislation in order to break the period of uncertainty faced by the insurance industry (Nesbitt 1995: 14; Pierson 1994: 58). Pensioners participating in the plan would have received benefits equal to 25 per cent of their 20 best years of coverage, adjusted to reflect increases in the cost of living. This reform also encouraged employers to 'contract out' of the public scheme by creating their own pension plan as long as they could guarantee a minimum pension equivalent to the one offered by SERPS. If the opt-out clause was used, contribution rates were reduced by 2.5 per cent for the employee and 4.5 per cent for the employer (Bonoli 2000: 60). This clause was introduced because of the high number of individuals already contributing to private pension schemes and because trade unions, especially those in the public sector, already had a strong vested interest in them and they wanted opt-out options (Fawcett 1995: 160). This incentive led to an increase in the number of workers relying on private schemes from 50 per cent to 67 per cent (Williamson and Pampel 1993: 54–5).

When Margaret Thatcher took office, she brought in a government strongly committed to reducing the size of the public sector and granting as much control as possible to the private sector. As Pierson stressed, pensions seemed 'a dubious target for reform' (Pierson 1994: 58). Benefits were quite low by international standards; the replacement rate of 25 per cent is by far the lowest amount in comparison to what is offered by the other three countries analysed here. The replacement rate for a single person was considered to be 33 per cent in 1980, compared to 66 per cent in France. Being married did not significantly improve one's position, generating only 47 per cent, compared to 75 per cent in France (Walker 1991: 20). Further, the heavy reliance on the private sector with respect to occupational pensions implied that the state's future payments would not be as extensive as was the case in continental countries. The Thatcher government's first budget in 1979 suggested that pensions would escape the reformist wind engendered by the Conservatives' victory. Aside from unemployment insurance, social security was left relatively untouched (Nesbitt 1995: 34–5).

The pension truce would be short-lived, however. The 1980 budget introduced a change in the indexation modality for both the basic and the SERPS pensions. Chancellor of the Exchequer Howe suspended the higher-price or wage-inflation indexation introduced by Labour in 1978 and replaced it solely with price indexation. In order to minimize opposition, the government sold this as a temporary measure, claiming that wage indexation would be reintroduced once the economy improved (Nesbitt 1995: 35–6). But the government never followed through, and Labour promised to re-establish that link once back in power.

As is demonstrated by the French example, switching to price indexation has significant financial consequences.[2] Already by 1989, a married couple received 25 per cent less than what they would have obtained under the previous indexing mechanism (Walker 1991: 26). Assuming an annual growth rate of 2 per cent, the replacement rate of the basic pension would decline by 50 per cent by the year 2020 (Pierson 1994: 59). Pierson refers to this measure as an 'implicit privatization', as it further encouraged the citizenry's reliance on the private sector to compensate for the loss of these benefits (Pierson 1994: 59). Fawcett (1995) goes further by arguing that this reform was the most drastic of all pension reforms undertaken by the government. With a price tag of £4–5 billion per annum, it is unlikely that any future government will seek to alter it (Fawcett 1995: 165–6). Accordingly, the Labour Party removed the restoration of the more advantageous indexation in its 1996 programme, and subsequent Labour governments have not altered Howe's measure.

More discussion of pensions took place during the remaining years of the first Thatcher government. One of the first things Thatcher did was to commission a study of the difference between public- and private-sector occupational pensions. She expressed her concerns regarding the generous pension schemes enjoyed by civil servants on numerous occasions. Their occupational pensions provided strong guarantees that no private occupational pension scheme was able to match in the subsequent decade due to rising inflation. Contrary to Thatcher's expectation, the Scott Report produced by this inquiry did not condemn the public-sector pension treatment, but rather argued that private-sector employees should be treated better (Nesbitt 1995: 36–7). A government that was aggressively seeking ways to reduce public expenditure and public intervention was unlikely to want to increase its role in occupational pensions, and the Scott Report was deposited at the very bottom of the government's drawer.

The key pension issue dominating the political agenda was the problem of 'early leavers'. As a consequence of their dependence on occupational pensions rather than the state pension, employees' pensions became tied in with their employers. Thus, unemployment or going to work for a different company often resulted in the loss of significant pension benefits from one's previous employers. Employers embraced occupational pensions as an effective way to maintain loyalty among their members and were reluctant to alter them significantly (Bonoli 2000: 73). It was clear early on that the government and Secretary of State Norman Fowler gave the private market every opportunity to find a solution to this problem. However, with the continuous silence of the market, the pressure to take action began to mount on the government. The early leavers were indirectly subsidizing other pensioners, and addressing their concerns implied either a rise in contributions or a decline in the benefits to employees with long and stable careers – both of which were unpopular concepts.

The 'early-leavers' problem slowly became associated with another potential issue, the maturation of SERPS. Thatcher's Conservative government was anxious to increase individual responsibilities and reduce dependence on the state, and the White Paper *Growing Older*, released in 1981, was extremely clear on these objectives. It emphasized that pensions needed to be reformed for the following reasons: (1) individuals should obtain more rights and responsibilities over their pension; (2) SERPS was likely to become very costly in the future; and (3) early leavers were a problem. According to Nesbitt, the paper was 'high on ideology and low on substance', and it 'indicated quite clearly that economic considerations must take precedence and that social needs would be met as a consequence of lower inflation and increased growth' (Nesbitt 1995: 37). Perhaps as a result, the government remained silent on its pension ambitions prior to the 1983 elections, which produced a majority of 188 seats for the Conservatives.

Seeking permanent change (1983–97)

The re-election of the Conservative Party allowed it to focus on longer-term policies and eased the fear that the following government could alter changes it might introduce. Further, due to the size of its majority, the tone and attitude of the government – as well as its policy orientation – became increasingly uncompromising and more ideologically driven (Nesbitt 1995: 57–8). As is demonstrated in the following pages, pension policy did not escape this new reality.

Following a failed, last-ditch effort to resolve the issue of early leavers through a meeting at the DHSS in September 1983 and pressure from the prime minister and the Chancellor of the Exchequer to reduce the long-term costs of SERPS, Fowler decided to create a special inquiry to deal with pensions. On 22 November 1983, the Inquiry into Provision for Retirement was formally launched; its composition was announced at the same press conference (Nesbitt 1995: 60–5).

As Fowler delineated in an interview, a principal motive behind the inquiry was to reach a favourable political decision: 'I had to make proposals – not only proposals I believed in and supported but proposals which I could get past my colleagues' (cf. Nesbitt 1995: 68–9). To achieve this goal, he set up the inquiry in an unorthodox manner. First, Fowler shied away from creating a royal commission or an internal committee, since they would have been comprised of civil servants. Despite claiming that he did so because pensions were not a high priority for the DHSS, his motives clearly seemed intended to push them aside. As his assistant secretary, he appointed Nick Montagu, a new member of the department. As highlighted by Nesbitt, 'he had only recently joined the DHSS and therefore had not had time to be socialized into their particular culture. Nor had he had time to establish formal or informal relationships with interested parties' (Nesbitt 1995: 68). The expertise and analysis of the DHSS was simply ignored during this period, at least with respect to pensions.[3]

Second, Fowler appointed important members of the pension industry to work with Conservative MPs. However, core social security actors, such as the Social Security Advisory Committee (SSAC), the CBI (the main employers' association) and the TUC were left out, although they were consulted (Nesbitt 1995: 71). Their influence would have been negligible in this process, at any rate, considering the positions of both the SSAC and the TUC to maintain SERPS and not introduce personal pensions. The TUC simply refused to discuss the introduction of personal pensions at all (Bonoli 2000: 77–8). Third, to raise the profile of the inquiry and marginalize the groups that were not invited to participate, Fowler organized three public sessions. Finally, he created a sub-group comprised predominately of economists to discuss the possible implementation of personal pensions. The sub-group's purpose was mainly to provide Fowler with the evidence he needed to proceed with this policy – and SERPS was not on the group's agenda (Nesbitt 1995: 74). He granted a very short timeframe during which interest groups could present evidence on this subject prior to the beginning of deliberations. Given that the budgetary impact of proposals considered by the inquiry was not published until two years after the fact (Nesbitt 1995: 73), one would be hard pressed to argue that they influenced the committee's work.

While influenced by different institutional constraints, Fowler's actions bear a strong resemblance to those of Könberg in Sweden during the early 1990s, when the latter instituted the Working Group on Pensions (see Chapter 4). Both actors sought to maximize the likelihood of reaching a politically acceptable proposal. They did not employ the usual commission channels, making it easier to pursue their policy objectives. They were also able to exclude specific actors, especially employers and trade unions. Obviously, Fowler found it easier to find a political solution because he had only his own government to please, though he was required to acknowledge the pension industry, which had supported the Conservatives. Thus, he did not really have to come up with a specific document or report, but, rather, a proposal to be negotiated within the cabinet. Könberg, on the other hand, had to generate political consensus among five parties, a much more difficult task considering that the proposal had to be a great deal more definitive. Nonetheless, both commissions were extremely important as they set the political agenda for pension reform and their proposals became the basis of future legislation.

Most of the discussions in the Inquiry into Provision for Retirement centred on: (1) the impact of population ageing on the future costs of SERPS; (2) the introduction of personal pensions; (3) the early-leavers problem; and (4) the age of retirement (Nesbitt 1995: 76–7). Upon the release of figures estimating the future costs of SERPS in 1984, the government was quick to interpret them as an intolerable financial burden requiring immediate attention. Broad objections by political opponents, independent commentators and academics alike would do little to stop the government's campaign against their future expense (Bonoli 2000: 63). The Treasury added support to the achievement of these goals with the publication of the Green Paper *The Next Ten Years* in the same year, wherein it advocated significant public spending reductions. Thus it, too, was keen to reduce the costs of SERPS (Nesbitt 1995: 82–3) and pressured Fowler to generate savings from social security in the order of 5 to 10 per cent (Pierson 1994: 60). It is worthwhile stating that, in contrast to Sweden's pensions committees, the Treasury was a present and effective actor at a very early stage. It firmly objected to any propositions resulting in more public expenditures and blocked any discussion of taxation, claiming that subject was reserved for the Treasury only (Pierson 1994: 70).

On 3 June 1985, Fowler released the long awaited Green Paper on pensions, which was supposed to be the outcome of the discussions held by the Inquiry into Provision for Retirement. In a nutshell, the Green Paper advocated eliminating SERPS and replacing it with personal pensions, an idea that had been proposed earlier by the Conservatives' own think-tank, the Centre for Policy Studies (CPS), and the Institute of Directors (IoD). Fowler's propositions soon faced a mountain of criticism from both traditional opponents of the government (trade unions and the Labour Party) and supporters of the party (the pension and insurance industries and the CBI). Even more unexpected is that the fiercest opposition actually came from within the government: the Chancellor of the Exchequer, Nigel Lawson.

It comes as no surprise that the Labour Party, the TUC and the anti-poverty lobby were quick to express their disapproval of Fowler's plans. The Labour Party, with the support of the TUC, had just recently launched SERPS as part of the pension consensus and was inclined to try to keep it alive. The Shadow Secretary of State for Social Services Michael Meacher publicly criticized the proposal as being 'the re-introduction ... of Victorian values in an invidious distinction between deserving and undeserving poor' (cf. Bonoli 2000: 75). Labour promised during their annual congress soon afterwards to reintroduce SERPS if they won the next election. The TUC was also strongly opposed to Fowler's intentions. In the early 1980s, it actually tried to raise SERPS' replacement rates to 33 per cent (Bonoli 2000: 77). Implicitly relating the Green Paper to the 'pension consensus' of 1978, the TUC claimed that the proposals represented a 'colossal breach of faith on the Government's part' (cf. Pierson 1994: 61). The anti-poverty lobby criticized the government's plans on the basis that they were detrimental to those with precarious employment (an argument supported by the Conservative Institute for Fiscal Studies [Pierson 1994]), and maintained that they would end up with lower benefits than with SERPS (Bonoli 2000: 78).

What was more surprising, however, was the amount of opposition the Green Paper attracted from traditional Conservative supporters, including core members of the inquiry. First, insurance companies and the private pension industry were not very pleased at the prospect of incorporating poor risks into their plans. Many individuals contributing to SERPS have erratic careers and are likely to be expensive clients with almost unattainable expectations. The National Association of Pension Funds (NAPF) expressed concerns about the wisdom of such a plan if the Labour Party was just going to repeal it once in office, and asked for a longer period of study (Bonoli 2000: 75). More importantly, Stewart Lyon, a member of the inquiry and a representative of the largest pension fund in the country, also expressed disapproval, further claiming that such proposals were never analysed by the inquiry body (Pierson 1994: 62).

Second, the CBI opposed the proposals because they challenged the current order of occupational pension schemes and left them with the double-payment problem, wherein they would have to pay for current employees and those already retired. According to the *Financial Times*, the estimated costs to employers of scrapping SERPS would be £1.5–2 billion (cf. Pierson 1994: 61). Both employers and insurance companies expressed their concerns regarding the administrative difficulties they would experience during that transition period (ibid.).

In the face of the Treasury's strong opposition, the death of Fowler's proposal became a certainty. According to both Nesbitt (1995) and Bonoli (2000), the Treasury expressed its opposition to the Green Paper prior to its publication. Thatcher chaired a meeting on this matter in early 1995, where the Treasury is said to have initially endorsed the move. However, it soon realized that scrapping SERPS implied an immediate increase in expenditure, a fact acknowledged even within its report. This is the direct consequence of abandoning a payg system. The government would have had to continue paying retirees who had contributed earlier to SERPS without receiving any off-setting contributions from current workers. The Chancellor of the Exchequer therefore opposed it. Highly indicative of the extent to which Fowler's proposal was contested, the Conservatives' own social security officials opposed the Green Paper (Walker 1991: 27). Interestingly, Thatcher continued to support the elimination of SERPS (Nesbitt 1995: 87).

Following the uproar caused by the Green Paper, the government withdrew its plans to eliminate SERPS. Nonetheless, this did not stop its effort to significantly alter pension policies. The White Paper *Programme for Action*, released in 1985, included new proposals designed to make SERPS unattractive to future contributors while encouraging a further expansion of the private sector with the introduction of personal pensions. These had the advantage of being portable, thus facilitating movement within the labour market, but more importantly they offered a solution to the early-leavers problem. The elements included in the White Paper were eventually adopted by Parliament in 1986 within the Social Security Act and were implemented in April 1988 (Nesbitt 1995: 89–90).

The measures related to SERPS included decreasing the value of the replacement rate from 25 to 20 per cent and extending the period upon which benefits were based from the best 20 years to lifetime earnings. Those who retired prior to the year 2000 were exempted from these measures, as the transition phase was set to occur between 2000 and 2010. Equally important, these new SERPS measures resulted in a reduction in the guaranteed minimum pension (GMP) that occupational pensions had to guarantee when contracting out employees, as long as they continued to guarantee the post-retirement value indexed to prices, up to a maximum of 3 per cent (Nesbitt 1995). This new threshold made it more likely that small employers could establish new occupational plans and avoid SERPS. The White Paper also introduced personal pensions with a special incentive for individuals to contract out of SERPS. The rebate discussed was in the range of 2–3 per cent for a period up to 1992–3. Finally, survivors' benefits were cut by half (Nesbitt 1995).

The Social Security Act of 1986 put a serious dent in the state's role in the provision of pensions. All SERPS and survivors' pension proposals from the White Paper were included in the new legislation, and the conditions affecting personal pensions were more precisely defined. Individuals were granted the option to opt out of either SERPS or occupational schemes (depending on their current affiliation) with an advantageous rebate of 2 per cent. Employers were also given an incentive – a 3.8 per cent rebate on their contributions. This combined contribution rebate for the state came to a total of 5.8 per cent,[4] and the option was offered only for a limited time (April 1988 to April 1993). Such generous (and expensive) conditions designed to reduce the appeal of SERPS indicate the government's commitment to expanding personal pensions.

A direct consequence of the new legislation was a 33 per cent loss of contributors to SERPS (Bonoli 2000: 80), but it is important to note that the new legislation challenged both SERPS and occupational pensions. Employers could no longer force employees into their occupational schemes, and they could not stop an employee from switching to personal pensions. Thus, the new legislation also had the effect of stopping the growth of occupational pensions, a measure that corresponded with the Conservatives' views on promoting individual ownership.

The new legislation was better received than the Green Paper, yet it did not lack critics. First, the CBI and the NAPF criticized the new bill because it extended the 2 per cent rebate into occupational pensions and challenged the pension order. Many occupational schemes were benefit-defined and thus enjoyed an internal solidarity that was threatened by exit options. Both organizations preferred an initiative limiting personal pensions as a third pillar rather than instituting them as a competitor to occupational pensions (Bonoli 2000: 75), but they nonetheless supported the changes made to SERPS. In response to the Green Paper, the CBI actually suggested that the timeframe over which benefits were calculated should be increased from 20 years to the entire career, and that there should be a 50 per cent cut to survivors' benefits (Nesbitt 1995: 89). Second, both the Labour Party and the TUC continued to criticize the government. Labour promised to stop the implementation of the new legislation if it was elected prior to 1988 (Bonoli 2000: 76). After failing to capture office, Labour was forced to accept the new pension landscape without being able to alter it significantly when it returned to power in 1997 because of the large costs and administrative difficulties that would have resulted from a policy reversal at that time.

Consequences of the 1986 legislation

This section assesses the impact of the Social Security Act of 1986 on individuals, groups of individuals and the state. Its calculation extended beyond a simple cost/benefit analysis. It reinforced the importance of the private sector in the provision of pensions by making SERPS less attractive while simultaneously promoting personal pensions. As Nesbitt noted, SERPS became the 'scheme of default' for those who were unable to join an occupational scheme or find an appropriate personal pension plan (Nesbitt 1995: 95). The introduction of personal pensions had important implications for those who adopted this method of securing their pensions. In contrast to many occupational pensions and SERPS, personal pensions are based fully on contributions and carry no guarantee of a minimum level of benefits. The flip side of obtaining greater personal choice is that all the risks associated with the investments are borne by the individual without any guarantee from the state.

The first element worth mentioning is that, surprisingly, the state ended up spending more rather than less money with the introduction of the new scheme. Personnel at the DHSS did not foresee that personal pensions would be so popular. The department estimated that roughly 500,000 individuals would opt out of SERPS during the period 1988–93. However, more than 4 million individuals chose that option, and most replaced them with personal pensions (Nesbitt 1995: 98), owing to an aggressive campaign by private pension providers combined with the government's generous incentives (Bonoli 2000: 80).

As a result of that misjudgement, the total cost of the rebate amounted to £9.3 billion, while the savings from SERPS amounted to only £4.3 billion. Thus, the government was left with a deficit of £5.9 billion (National Audit Office, cf. Ward 2000: 140). Nonetheless, the government is expected to obtain more savings since expenditure is expected to plummet to £7.1 billion by the year 2021, down from a pre-reform estimate of £16.4 billion (Pierson 1994: 63–4). Ironically, the total expected savings over a period of 35 years (£9.3 billion) barely cover the incentives provided by the government during the period 1988–93 (£9.3 billion). Therefore, the 'astronomical cost' of SERPS was never eliminated, but rather displaced into the hands of individuals who opted to change and support personal pensions, resulting in a regressive transfer. The money saved was taken away from those remaining in SERPS to subsidize those who elected to have personal pensions.

Second, as highlighted by the Maxwell affair, the private sector's irresponsible behaviour in many cases resulted in heavy losses for many individuals. Financial service companies sold personal pensions very aggressively and, according to a study undertaken by the Security and Investment Board, 91 per cent of personal pension sales were made without adhering to standard business rules (cf. Ward 2000: 141). Nurses and steelworkers were convinced to leave generous occupational schemes in favour of less profitable personal pensions. Many individuals with precarious positions and low wages left SERPS for personal pensions despite the negative repercussions of that choice.[5]

Finally, the overall effect was relief from the difficulties in meeting the financial challenge created by the ageing population, as many estimates suggested a reduction in costs (OECD 2005). However, the meagre benefits offered by SERPS and the limited protection available to those with precarious career patterns imply that funding will most likely be required to alleviate the poverty of many elderly people (Pensions Commission 2005).

Explaining the passage of the reform

In terms of retrenchment, the effects both of the Social Security Act of 1986 and of basing the indexation of pensions on prices in 1980 represent the most drastic reductions in benefits implemented in the four countries compared in this book. The prudent and careful approach adopted in the other three countries is in direct contrast to the uncompromising method the Conservatives used to push the 1986 legislation through. Interestingly, pension reforms in the United Kingdom represent the only policy area where even Pierson acknowledges that far-reaching cuts were made (Pierson 1994: 53). This section explains how such reforms were possible.

Nesbitt argues that a policy community that strongly supported the individualization of benefits was formed in the early 1980s. Fowler sought to integrate them to shape his own policy agenda. The nature of these contacts was considered quite informal; individuals were considered more important than the organization they represented. His conclusion stresses that the policy community of the 1980s was very different from that of the 1970s, which relied more on the DHSS and on institutionalized support from the TUC (Nesbitt 1995: 142–5). Nesbitt's explanation centres on their participation within a policy community, but it lacks a complete understanding of the political process. The individuals whose roles were upgraded during the process all had one thing in common: they supported Fowler's views. Because it refused to co-operate with the government and its views were directly opposed to those of the Conservatives, the TUC never took part in this policy community. Fowler kept the DHSS at bay, probably because its views were closer to the maintenance of the 'pension consensus' than his were. Nesbitt's detailed analysis suggests that it was Fowler and his government who controlled the policy agenda.

Pierson argues that 'Thatcher did not always get her way, but she controlled the political agenda and ultimately engineered a major transfer of responsibility for retirement provision to the private sector' (Pierson 1994: 53). Contrary to his expectations, Thatcher engineered a very visible and unpopular policy, yet she was not punished for it in the following election. Pierson and Smith claim that Thatcher's limited progress was the result of an unpopular welfare state in the United Kingdom (Pierson and Smith 1993: 513). However, it is difficult to support this thesis given that more than five million people opted for personal pensions (Bonoli 2000).

Pierson (1994) emphasizes five reasons why British pensions deviate from his general theoretical framework as it is summarized in his first chapter. First, the system was quite fragmented between the private and public occupational schemes. Walker, who criticizes functionalist theories that consider the elderly as a single unified group,[6] had already made that argument; prior to Thatcher's reform, there was a pre-existing social division with white-collar employees benefiting from occupational and private pensions while others – blue-collars, unemployed and those with precarious employment – had to rely on the state (Walker 1991: 23).

Second, Pierson pointed to the pre-existing, extensive private market that made expansion easier. It would have been much more difficult for the government to introduce market solutions had the pension system been solely within the public realm. Third, it was easier to index the basic pension alongside prices because it was not earnings-related. Fourth, in contrast to other occupational schemes in Europe, SERPS' financing structure remained part of the state's financial structure (including other pension programmes), making it difficult to present an accurate portrayal of its financial state. Finally, SERPS had not had the chance to mature, thus somewhat reducing the cost of the double-payment problem (Pierson 1994:

71). These difficulties were stressed in a subsequent paper with Myles (Myles and Pierson 2001). Thus, compared with Sweden, there was no talk of the limit under which contributions could be made to the private sector.

Fawcett (1995) claims that Thatcher's pension policies did not mark a radical break with previous Conservative governments, thus challenging the distinction made by Pierson (1994) between the politics of expansion versus the politics of retrenchment of the welfare state. For example, Fawcett indicates that privatization was at such a high level that Thatcher's expansion of it was not truly a radical move, but instead was simply the continuation of a trend (Fawcett 1995: 153). Araki follows similar logic when he concludes that the Conservatives persisted in strengthening the private sector's role in the pension field (Araki 2000: 617). Thus, the attitude of the Conservatives was not that different from that of their predecessors. What distinguished this period, however, was their 18 years of uninterrupted political power which effectively protected their reforms from Labour Party alterations.

Adjusting the pension reform of 1986: can the private market be controlled?

Fowler's 1986 changes became more likely to last with the re-election of the Conservatives in both 1988 and 1992. Following a wave of scandals related to both private occupational and personal pensions, the government weathered the storm by strengthening the rules in the Pension Act of 1995, but the Conservatives' commitment to the market remained undaunted. During the 1997 election, they proposed to suppress both SERPS and the basic pension (Reynaud 1997: 43). Once in office in 1997, the Labour Party had little choice but to accept the Conservatives' policy legacy.

The first of many subsequent pension scandals coincided with the death of newspaper tycoon Robert Maxwell on 5 November 1991. Maxwell had removed close to £1 billion from the pension funds of his employees in order to keep his businesses afloat (Bonoli 2000: 81), even though this transaction went against what is considered appropriate practice. His companies were later dissolved, resulting in a huge loss to current and future pensioners. The estate originally claimed that only £8.75 million could be recovered. Eventually that amount increased to close to £100 million, but accounting fees of more than £300,000 per working day in the year following Maxwell's death were taken directly from the pension funds recovered, reducing the hopes of proper compensation. Fearing liability, the government refrained from intervening decisively by creating a trust fund (Nesbitt 1995: 136–8).

More worrisome was the fact that the legislation in place could not have prevented such a scandal even if actions had been taken by the appropriate regulatory agencies (Nesbitt 1995: 136–7; Bonoli 2000: 81). Thus, most of that decade was devoted to establishing stricter rules to avoid the abusive behaviour of private companies for both occupational and personal pensions.

Few commissions were established to analyse both the Maxwell affairs and the irresponsible selling of personal pensions, which the government dealt with in very different ways. First, for private occupational pensions it introduced a Pensions Act in 1995. The act constrained self-investment of pension funds on the part of employers by introducing a 5 per cent limit. The limit was enforced by trustees, one-third of whom had to be elected. A new regulatory board was also instituted alongside an emergency fund to be used when schemes become insolvent (Bonoli 2000: 82). Far from simply restricting employers' practices, the 1995 Pensions Act further promoted the private sector by eliminating the GMP requirement, thus totally severing the link with SERPS. Starting in 1997, private occupational schemes had to demonstrate that they offered benefits similar to SERPS, but pensions had to be protected against inflation up to a limit of 5 per cent instead of 3 per cent (Fawcett 2002: 15; Araki 2000). Further, the incentive rebate was changed to make it age-sensitive, with the end result being that those aged 47 and above could get 9 per cent out of the 10 per cent paid out to a private insurance company if they decided to opt out of SERPS (Ward 2000: 142). Finally, to conform to the European Union's directive regarding the equal treatment of men and women, women's retirement age was to be increased gradually until it equalled men's. In direct contrast to Belgium, this measure generated almost no debate.

Second, the government opted to ensure that private companies find their own solutions to the irresponsible marketing of pensions without intervening legislatively on the issue. The government continued to avoid imposing new restrictions on insurance companies, pressuring the guilty into correcting their mistakes instead, even though mounting evidence stressing dubious sales practices by insurance companies surged (Ward 2000: 142). As in the case of the 'early-leavers' problem, this approach was deemed highly unsuccessful, with only 2 per cent of the 1.5 to 2.5 million Britons waiting for compensation being satisfied prior to the election of 1997 (*Le Monde*, 24 November 1997).

New Labour, new era?

Even prior to its election in 1997, it was obvious that the Labour Party was not going to repeal most changes made by the Conservatives and reintroduce prior preferences, as doing so would have been extremely expensive. Reintroducing a strong public occupational scheme also did not appeal to a party eager to demonstrate that it could be 'financially responsible' (see Ross 2000a). Nonetheless, this did not imply that the 'new' Labour would stand idly by; the objective of ensuring that 60 per cent of income originated from private savings, as opposed to the then figure of 40 per cent, signalled that reforms were forthcoming. First, immediately after their election victory, the government actively pursued the companies that were failing to compensate the victims of the personal pension scandal. It fined companies and published the list of late compensators every month (*Le Monde*, 24 November 1997).

Second, Secretary of State for Work and Pensions Alistair Darling asked seven industry leaders to form a Pension Provision Group (PPG) and take a leadership role in analysing various options and proposing solutions to the pension problem. Following its resistance to the introduction of the pension credit (see on pp. 164–5), the Labour Party disbanded the PPG in 2000. The creation of the PPG was not in vain, however, as it led to the formation of the Pension Policy Institute (PPI) in 2002 to strengthen non-partisan expertise and facts about pensions. It received financial support from diverse sources such as the TUC, CBI, Association of British Insurers, insurance and consulting companies, NAPF and Age Concern (a leading charity for pensioners); it even wrote commissioned reports for the DWP. This broad support made the PPI a key player in the debate. Despite being a private actor, it established a reliable and accepted expertise, somewhat similar to the Swedish *Riksförsäkringsverket* (its National Insurance Board – see Chapter 4), a public organization responsible for the management of public pensions. Like RFV, its recommendations were openly challenged by various political actors, but its analyses were utilized and considered seriously by various public offices and by the Pensions Commission.[7]

Third, and more importantly, Labour presented a Green Paper entitled *A New Contract for Welfare: Partnership in Pensions* in 1998, wherein it announced a major reshaping of pension policies. Pension reform was presented as being necessary to restore faith in the system, and many elements contained in the Green Paper were legislated in 1999 in the Welfare Reform and Pensions Act. Blair clearly restated that the Labour Party saw the private sector as the primary source of pension provision, and that the state would intervene only when the market failed:

> We are building a new contract for pensions between the State, the private sector, and the individual. We believe that those who can save for their retirement have the responsibility to do so, and that the State must provide effective security for those who cannot.
>
> (Department of Social Security 1998: iii)

The new legislation altered the means-tested assistance programme and introduced a more generous state pension scheme called the State Second Pension that would eventually replace SERPS for low-wage earners and provide flat-rate benefits. Further, the 1999 legislation implemented a new form of private pension – stakeholder pensions – designed for those without the opportunity to join an occupational scheme but who could not afford a personal pension.

The minimum income guarantee (MIG) introduced means-tested benefits that were more generous than the previous income support, which were expected to be indexed to average earnings in the future. The MIG was replaced by the pension credit in October 2003 to ensure that retirees with low savings received some help as well. In contrast to the MIG, the pensions credit used only 40 per cent of private savings instead of its full value to calculate whether or not someone qualified for this means-tested benefit.

The S2P targeted those earning less than £9,000 per annum, a situation experienced by roughly 9 per cent of men and 17 per cent of women working full time (Rake *et al.* 2000: 303), and improved benefits substantially. For example, someone earning £9,000 could receive a pension worth double the pension amount SERPS offered. Further, non-contributory benefits were granted for those experiencing periods of sickness, childcare and invalidity, as if they had earned £9,000 (Department of Social Security 1998). The government's optimism was not shared by everyone, however. Because S2P is price indexed, its value relative to wage earners slowly declines. In a study analysing the effect of the Green Paper on low-wage earners, Rake *et al.* argue that the combined benefits of both the basic pension and S2P will be slightly higher than what would be offered by the MIG, and the latter would be necessary to avoid a relative drop in benefits. Thus, it is expected that many will not benefit from their investment in S2P, resulting in a *de facto* new flat-rate pension for the poorest (Rake *et al.* 2000: 299–300, 313). This is a long way from the aims of SERPS when it was introduced in the late 1970s.

The Labour Party's response to personal pensions was a stakeholder pension that targeted those earning between £9,000 and £18,500 per year. This group of wage earners rarely has access to occupational pensions, and personal pensions are considered ill-equipped to tackle their needs since it yields high administrative costs for low-income earners, and because career interruptions engender penalties (Department of Social Security 1998: 5). Stakeholder pensions still rely on the private sector, but the government played a more active role in advertising the schemes that meet its standards. Thus, the principal behind it is similar to the one the International Organization for Standardization (ISO) established for private companies, except that the government, rather than an international agency, sets the standards. The requirements are that the pension schemes offered carry a yearly administrative cost of less than 1 per cent of the value of the fund, charge no fee when the pension is transferred elsewhere (most likely the case when one changes jobs) or when payments are not made, and the schemes must be willing to accept contributions of £20 or more, though some may accept less. As part of the strategy to ensure lower administrative costs, employers that do not offer occupational schemes to their employees will have to provide a stakeholder pension and collect the contributions for it. The trustees must also be independent and have no relationship to the employer. Finally, new incentives were introduced to encourage savings in these schemes (Department of Social Security 1998).

The government closely examined the issue of compulsion for the poorest workers with respect to both occupational schemes and stakeholder pensions.

This was a position endorsed by the NAPF that would have required a reversal of the 1986 legislation introducing personal pensions. The inability to agree on this point led to the resignation of the Minister for Welfare Reform Frank Field (*Financial Times*, 20 November 1998). With the Conservatives very clearly stating that making them compulsory would effectively amount to a new tax, Labour has shied away from this policy option.

The government's plan met with opposition from the NAPF and numerous occupational (and personal) pension providers, who complained that the stakeholder pension initiative could threaten existing schemes since it encouraged workers to leave their plans. This position was shared by the PPG even as it stressed that the new legislation was a step in the right direction. The group also stressed the proliferation of tax regimes for pensions, which could lead some employers to restrict or abolish their pension schemes (*Financial Times*, 5 March 1999). Further, Rake *et al.* argue that in order for the stakeholder pension to render low-wage earners ineligible for means-tested benefits, they would have to earn a lifetime wage approaching that of the average male (Rake *et al.* 2000: 315)! A similar critique was raised by the Liberal Democrats, who noted that the stakeholder pensions, the State Second pensions and other provisions are price indexed, while the pensioner poverty line rises with earnings. This has the potential to extend reliance on means-tested benefits (*Financial Times*, 3 March 1999).

Consequences of the 1999 reform

Even though the reform is fairly recent, emerging trends led to criticism concerning the need to more forcefully address the fragile state of public pensions, prompting a broad consensus that more substantial reforms were required. Three specific points are worth stressing. First, the adoption and utilization of the pension credit has earned Gordon Brown high praise for efficiently assisting current poor retirees, especially women. However, it has also been vigorously criticized by a wide range of policy actors who focused on its cost over the long term, its impact on savings for low- to middle-wage earners and the low take-up of this benefit. Due to a lack of private savings and the price indexation of public pension programmes, an increasing number of individuals are expected to rely on means-tested benefits. Already 31 per cent of pensioners are relying on one (or a combination) of the three means-tested benefits offered to them (pension credit, housing benefit and the council tax benefit) (Department for Work and Pensions 2005). This does not include the fact that numerous individuals do not apply for these benefits even though they might be entitled to them (for various reasons ranging from ignorance to stigma), an omission that leaves them living in poverty. For example, the take-up rate for the pension credit oscillates between 58 per cent and 66 per cent of those eligible for it (Department for Work and Pensions 2006b), and the government forecasts a 75 per cent take-up in its budget. Thus, a reversal of this situation combined with a future cohort of pensioners with fewer private resources and a basic state pension indexed to prices rather than earnings could significantly increase the reliance on means-tested benefits in the future. The *Financial Times* claimed that Blair had been advised that close to 82 per cent of pensioners could be relying on such benefits by 2050 if current policies are maintained (*Financial Times*, 13 March 2002).[8] It is difficult to calculate the budgetary impact of the pension credit since it does not factor in future projections, and the Treasury has indicated that it might be indexed to prices rather than earnings starting as early as 2008.

More worrisome is the negative impact the pension credit has on savings. According to pension industry leaders, the increasing use of means-tested benefits provides disincentives to saving, particularly for low- to middle-wage earners. The pension credit results in an effective loss of about 40 pence of every £1 saved. Thus, the incentive to save is very limited, especially since older workers already know that means-tested benefits will most likely be necessary. According to a survey conducted by the ABI, 58 per cent of individuals stated that the pension credit would put them off saving (*Financial Times*, 25 October 2003). A report commissioned by the DWP demonstrates that the impact of the pension credit on savings is somewhat exaggerated, but this is likely to change in the future with the prospect a drastic increase in the number of pensioners living on means-tested pensions (Sefton *et al.* 2005). As a result, the Treasury is now one of the only policy actors defending the pension credit.

Second, the stakeholder pension has not generated the result envisioned by the government. Instead of becoming the private pension tool of the future for low- to middle-wage earners, it has added an additional element of confusion for employers, and contributions have been scarce, especially among small companies. Most schemes are 'empty shells with no contributing members' (Pensions Commission 2004: 92); only 4 per cent of small companies contribute. Further, there has not been any noticeable increase in pension savings as a result of the stakeholder pension (Pensions Commission 2004).

Third, contrary to the objectives of the government to ensure that 60 per cent of retirement income originates from private sources, many have returned to the public contributory scheme, the S2P (formally SERPS). This is largely because the number of employers who provide generous occupational schemes and lower rebates for those opting out in favour of occupational and/or private pensions has decreased significantly. As of the mid-1990s, close to 30 per cent of the population contributed to S2P, as opposed to 20 per cent contributing to SERPS (Pensions Commission 2004: 70–1). In early 2002, many insurance companies began to advocate switching to the public scheme for men aged 54 and over and women aged 49 and over (*Financial Times*, 13 March 2002).

Finally, the presence of the state has been considered more important given the numerous difficulties experienced by occupational schemes, even though the state is now among the least trusted to deliver on pension promises.[9] A change in actuarial rules in 2001 alerted companies and authorities to the fact that many occupational schemes faced a severe crisis. A survey of the 100 largest British companies revealed that only two were not experiencing a pension deficit (*Financial Times*, 8 September 2004)! As a result, final salary schemes (i.e. defined benefits) have been closed to most new members, while existing members in numerous companies have been forced to accept a reduction in benefits. Active membership in defined-benefit schemes has decreased 60 per cent since 1995; only 14 per cent of new employees have been allowed to join, and these were almost exclusively from within the public sector (Pensions Commission 2004: 84). This information corresponds to the results of a survey of 300 companies conducted by the Association of Consulting Actuaries. That survey noted that 42 per cent of employers sought to reduce pension spending, while 51 per cent wanted to reduce pension liabilities (*Financial Times*, 24 March 2002). This trend is worrisome in the long run because final salary schemes were the most generous of the lot, and most were replaced by significantly scaled-down, defined-contribution schemes (Pensions Commission 2004: 85). It is worth noting that the voluntary approach already results in 33 per cent of workers not making any contribution at all to a private pension scheme (Pensions Commission 2004: 63). Thus, the state is likely to play a more forceful role in the near future to compensate for the looming shortage of retirement income.

Company closures have already prompted government action to ensure that future and current pensioners with company schemes will not be left penniless. The Pension Protection Fund was created as part of the Pensions Act of 2004, providing assistance of up to £25,000 to employees whose employer went bankrupt and left an under-funded pension fund.

The Pensions Commission

While it had set an objective of seeing 60 per cent of retirement income coming from the private sector, the Blair government realized that its efforts were falling short and opted to create the much publicized Pensions Commission in 2002. The creation of the commission came at a time where disagreements between Blair and Brown, as well as within the Treasury, regarding how to increase private savings – especially among the low- to middle-wage earners – became public (see *Financial Times*, 18 December 2002).[10] Headed by Adair Turner (former DG of the CBI) and assisted by Jeannie Drake (a former president of the TUC) and John Hills (a professor at the London School of Economics), the aim of this commission was to analyse 'the adequacy of private pension savings in the United Kingdom and to advise on appropriate policy changes, including whether there is a need to move beyond the voluntary approach' (Pensions Commission 2004: v). From the commission's inception, it became obvious that the entire pension system was going to be scrutinized, given the interdependency of public and private schemes.

The commission presented two reports, as well as a brief response to the critics. The first report, published in 2004, provided the most detailed assessment of the British pension system. It stressed that to deal with population ageing issues, adjustments should have been made 20 years ago. It noted that the government now faced a significant dilemma and would have to do one of three things: accept that there would be poorer pensioners in the future, raise public and/or private assets for pension and/or increase the retirement age. It also emphasized that the number of employers providing generous pensions was declining, as was the number of generous state schemes. As a result of changes to the structure of employer-provided pensions, defined-benefit schemes were replaced by defined contributions, and 75 per cent of these provided inadequate coverage, meaning close to 9 million workers were not saving enough (Pensions Commission 2004). Government officials, employers, trade unions and pension industry leaders conducted broad consultations in the aftermath of this preliminary report; this led to the more politically potent second report – filled with precise recommendations – that Labour presented after the elections of 2005.

Three elements of the second report stand out. First, probably inspired by the Swedish experience of creating individual accounts administered indirectly by a state agency (PPM – see Chapter 4), the Pensions Commission proposed the creation of a National Pension Savings Scheme with a minimum contribution of 8 per cent of a worker's wage to be financed by the employee (4 per cent), the state (via a 1 per cent tax rebate) and employers (3 per cent). This method would ensure easy access to private savings while minimizing administrative costs. Workers would automatically be enrolled into this system or into a high-quality, employer pension scheme, yet they retained the right to opt out.

Second, the Pensions Commission recommended building on the actual public schemes to create a generous, non-means-tested, flat-rate pension plan. In order to achieve this objective, the commission proposed that the basic state pension be indexed according to earnings, rather than price; this measure already had the explicit support of numerous policy actors such as the CBI, TUC, PPI, NAPF and ABI. The commission also advocated an increase in the rights available to individuals under this pension provision by introducing compensation for career interruptions such as unemployment and care-giving responsibilities in an attempt to reduce indirect entitlements (e.g. spousal benefits). Rather than scrapping the S2P, the commission sought to accelerate its transformation into a flat-rate system by freezing the upper earnings limit for S2P accruals in nominal cash terms. Whatever the means used, the commission deemed it imperative to provide a generous flat-rate system and improve the treatment of workers facing career interruptions. Finally, it stressed that a combination of additional public resources alongside an increase in the state pension age was required –

directly challenging the notion that state spending on pensions was likely to rise minimally within the next 50 years.

Following intense discussions between Tony Blair and Gordon Brown, the government presented the much anticipated White Paper, *Security in Retirement: Towards a New Pensions System,* in May 2006. Inspired by the Pensions Commission, the government proposed the implementation of a new pension system in 2012 (the long delay being largely the result of negotiations between the Treasury and the Prime Minister's Office). The new system is expected to include a new scheme of personal accounts with automatic enrolments for those earning between £5,000 and £33,000 per annum, with an 8 per cent contribution rate (4 per cent from individuals, 3 per cent from employers and 1 per cent as a tax rebate). The structure of the agency responsible for managing the accounts is yet to be decided. The White Paper also proposed the alteration of S2P, transforming it into a flat pension to top up an accrued basic state pension. Finally, the government proposes to increase the retirement age to 66 from 2024 and up to 68 in the year 2044 (Department for Work and Pensions 2006a).

The lengthy delay in implementing the core elements of the pension plan, especially the improvements to the basic state pension, has been criticized by the opposition as unacceptable. The reliance on means-tested benefits is expected to rise significantly until 2012, reducing savings incentives further for upcoming retirees (*Financial Times,* 16 November 2006). Moreover, the final structure is expected to be adopted in the next session of Parliament, thus raising doubts about its implementation by either the Conservatives or Labour. In the latter case, Gordon Brown, the new prime minister, was a strong critic of the Pensions Commission, and he will no longer have an incentive to adhere to old compromises negotiated with Tony Blair.

Conclusion: the politics of Wimbledon?

The past 10 years resulted in controversy over the game of tennis, particularly at the 'fast grass' court of Wimbledon. New technology transformed the game of tennis into a game of serves which are now so powerful that exchanges are a rare event. Thus, recent Wimbledon champions have all been great servers. Pension politics in the United Kingdom shares many of the problems facing the game of tennis. The party holding the reins of power can send powerful serves that are difficult to return. However, once a serve is lost, the other player gets the opportunity to serve and has an excellent chance to succeed. The key is to hold on to the serve as long as possible in order to control the match.

The only pension truce in British politics lasted from 1975 to 1979! Both Labour and Conservatives have been serving new pension reforms on an ongoing basis for most of the post-World War II period. The Conservatives provided the private sector with an important share of responsibility with respect to ensuring provision for retirement, but this was not because their plan was better. They were simply able to generate a tie-breaker by holding on to their serve for 11 years after the introduction of the Social Security Act of 1986 (17, actually, if one considers indexing the basic pension to prices). In order to get back into the game, the Labour Party had to agree to play according to the rules established by the Conservatives. Once in the game, Labour added three new types of pension schemes, complicating the pension field even more. Not surprisingly, this issue must still be resolved, and the adoption of the proposals presented by the Pensions Commission represents a step in the right direction. Nonetheless, as it pushes the implementation date well past the next election (2012), the new Pensions Bill may be shelved in favour of another plan if the Conservatives return to power.

This assessment is the continuation of a long historical tradition where social polices have been confrontational, yet confined to Parliament. This is clearly explained in Ashford's analysis of the development of social policies between the years 1890 and 1950:

> British social politics never lost its adversarial character and social policies continue to be treated as a reserve for political and parliamentary bargaining. British institutions seemed condemned to marginal and partisan attacks on basic social and economic questions so that even some of the most notable success, such as the NHS, [National Health Service] have been constantly disrupted by political attacks from both left and right. ... In a sense, the complexities of French politics were reproduced within social policies while the British rather ingenuously set out to simplify social politics and policymaking.
>
> (Ashford 1986: 310–11)

In the United Kingdom, a political party faces relatively few constraints once it is in power and controls the political agenda. It does not have to negotiate with other political parties unless there is a coalition government, which rarely happens. The opposition can highlight the failures of a government, but it cannot really alter policy choices. Unlike in Belgium and Sweden, legislative power is centralized within a single party and the support of other parties is not required. Also, the state's administrative capacities are such that pension expertise has historically come from the outside (Heclo 1974). This allows the government greater flexibility, since it can choose to rely on experts who already agree with its principal policy positions. The individuals who ended up being actively involved in the formal policy process when Fowler was secretary of state were highly supportive of the extension of private provisions, the reduction in the size of SERPS and personal pensions. The implementation of the Inquiry into Provision for Retirement also demonstrates the extent to which the bureaucracy can be disregarded. Fowler appointed an individual who had just arrived at the DHSS as assistant secretary with little difficulty. Moreover, the DHSS Research Unit was not even consulted when Fowler elaborated his Green Paper (Nesbitt 1995: 68). The creation of the Pensions Commission did, however, somewhat alter this trend by creating a strong pension expertise within the DWP, rather than outside the government; a public expertise later employed by government officials to draft the 2006 White Paper.

As a result of the Parliamentary Integration relationship, social actors can be more readily avoided than their French or Belgian counterparts. It must be noted that both the CBI and the TUC were not granted a seat at the Inquiry into Provision for Retirement. Nesbitt emphasized that contacts between these two groups and the government became more informal in the 1980s, again indicating their weak degree of institutionalization. These two groups were never formally involved in the creation of policy. Their participation tended to concentrate 'upon information exchanges and inquiries, and that kind of participation less often includes policy formation and implementation' (Nesbitt 1995: 167). This type of institutionalization makes it easier for politicians to discard them than the French or Belgian forms of institutionalization. The recent Pensions Commission included prominent figures from among both employers and employees, but their report is not binding. Neither is it a commitment for future consultation. In fact, both representatives acted independently, and they did not represent their former associations' views and positions.

Owing to the lack of veto points (Immergut 1992) and to the executive's centralized power, who forms the government significantly impacts the extent and the degree of influence unions and employers have. In the elaboration of SERPS (Walker 1991: 21) the TUC was an important actor, and its leader traditionally met the prime minister at Downing Street for beer and sandwiches in the 1960s and 1970s (Nesbitt 1995: 142–3), but he was completely ignored as soon as the Conservatives were elected. Thatcher's hostile attitude towards the unions added more impetus to keep the TUC out of the policy process. Interestingly, the CBI was not particularly influential in the process, either. It favoured maintaining strong occupational pensions and retaining personal pensions as a third pillar, but not as a competitor of its schemes. Neither the TUC nor the CBI had this sort of influence with New Labour.

Finally, as in the case in the reintroduction of workfare, institutional legacy can play a role in assisting those working towards retrenchment (King 1995). The importance of the private sector within the pension system really helped the Conservatives pursue their agenda. As is underlined by Fawcett:

> the legacy of past policy meant that there was an absence of well-established and powerful interests in defence of the state sector. The strength of the private sector and the corresponding weakness of the state sector meant that the Conservatives did not face 'veto points' or interest groups which would obstruct their agenda. Ironically, the major

interest group that blocked certain policy proposals was the insurance industry itself.

(Fawcett 2002: 11–12)

Few policy constraints are notable and apply to both parties. First, the Treasury continues to play a dominant role regarding social policy by ensuring that public finance will not be committed to large new expenditures. The resistance of the Treasury is far from being a new phenomenon and is one of the main reasons the British state never accepted a large expansion of the public pension system (Heclo 1974). Second, as stated by Fawcett in the quotation above, private companies are now so involved in pension provision that they cannot be ignored; they represent a powerful source of opposition. If the implementation of the 2006 reform grants a managerial role to the pension industry and the state continues to provide minimal public benefits, it may soon have a veto point.

6 Conclusion

Comparative tests of the hypotheses and their application to other industrialized countries

Introduction

The aim of this chapter is two-fold. First, it seeks to compare and analyse the hypotheses presented in Chapter 1. Despite the difficulties inherent in comparing pension policies, the theoretical framework used in this research shows much potential. The process by which pensions are being reformed tells us a great deal about the breadth of the reforms, with the institutionalization of political actors being the key independent variable. Null hypotheses are also studied and dismissed. Second, a brief exploration of how the theoretical framework might be applied to other countries is presented, along with avenues for future research.

Review of the hypotheses

This section analyses the hypotheses presented in Chapter 1. Each individual hypothesis is stated and then discussed according to what was learned from the four cases studied.

> Hypothesis 1: Parliamentary Integration structures are more conducive to programmatic pension reforms than are Social Partnership structures, given that the latter have more inherent veto points.

This is the main hypothesis of this book (also referred to as the first ordering principle). Based on the four cases reviewed here, we can affirm the hypothesis associated with a Parliamentary Integration structure. Both the United Kingdom and Sweden, two cases having that structure, did successfully introduce programmatic reforms (see Table 6.1). The Thatcher governments in the United Kingdom actively promoted the private sector by making the public scheme unattractive while simultaneously offering generous tax benefits as an incentive to join private schemes. The TUC and the CBI, to a lesser extent, were pushed aside during the discussion and elaboration of these pension reforms. Even though the TUC was not in principle opposed to the idea of privatization, because many of its white-collar workers were benefiting from generous occupational pensions it really had no say in the matter, as the Conservatives were committed to reducing the unions' political influence. More radical reforms were blocked by the Treasury, which feared an escalation of the public deficit in order to finance the transition costs incurred by the elimination of SERPS. Its elimination was also opposed by the pension industry, which feared having to integrate 'bad' risks into its pension schemes.

Successive Labour governments promulgated their own versions of pension schemes by first seeking to reinforce public schemes via the introduction of the S2P (a modified version of SERPS), the pensions credit and the stakeholder pension in 1999. These policies did not eliminate the prospects of increased reliance on means-tested benefits in the upcoming years, and so the government established an ambitious Pensions Commission. Most of the elements the commission proposed were adopted in 2007, including the introduction of a more generous basic pension, an incremental increase in the pensionable age and automatic enrolment (with an opt-out clause) into contributory pension funds co-financed by individuals (4 per cent), employers (3 per cent) and the state (1 per cent). Given the current design of the pension savings scheme and its relatively late implementation date (2012), its introduction may hinge on the electoral prospects of the Labour Party, as predicted by the hypothesis regarding a Parliamentary Integration type of relationship in a two-party system.

In the Swedish case, the Minister of Health and Social Insurance was able to keep both unions and employers in a marginal position during the negotiations surrounding the reform of the entire pension system. By creating a Working Group on Pensions rather than a commission, the minister successfully reduced the number of individuals serving on the committee, thus enhancing the likelihood of arriving at a consensus. Among those excluded were unions and employers. Despite their mild protests, it was understood that it was the state's responsibility to change the system. It was argued earlier in this book (pp. 112–4) that this was a consequence of the late 1950s pension reform, which granted extensive responsibility to the state in the administration and financing of pensions. Unions and employers were not granted administrative responsibilities.[1] Once a compromise was reached among the politicians working on the committee, it was extremely difficult to change specific elements, since it implied a reopening of the negotiations among the five political parties. Swedish Members of Parliament were able to defend their proposals owing in part to the expertise they gained via the workings of pension committees.

Not surprisingly, discussions of the pension systems in the United Kingdom and Sweden have moved from the need to reform to the efficiency of previous reforms. The reforms introduced in these two pension systems offer a high degree of uncertainty to individuals regarding what they can expect in the way of retirement benefits. Both systems emphasize tightening the link between contributions and benefits, resulting in an individualization

Table 6.1 Comparative analysis of the successful pension reforms introduced in Sweden and the United Kingdom (Parliamentary Integration)[1]

| | Parliamentary Integration | |
	Sweden	United Kingdom
Pension reform name	• 1994/1998 – New Pension System	• 1980 – Budget • 1986 – Social Security Act • 1995 – Pensions Act • 1999 – Welfare Reform and Pensions Act • 2006 – Pensions Bill
Pension reform content – main elements	• 1994/1998 – Entirely new system. Increase in the length of contribution (from 30 years using the best 15 to the life-income principle); compensatory measures introduced for childcare, studies and military service; new indexation mechanism based on economic growth, prices and population ageing; 2.5% to be invested in the private sector; instauration of a means-test for the guaranteed pension; flexible retirement age.	• 1980 – Pensions are indexed solely on prices. • 1986 – Decrease in the value of the replacement rate for SERPS (from 25% to 20%); reduction in the minimum pension that needs to be guaranteed by private occupational pensions; introduction of personal pensions with fiscal incentives reaching 2–3% alongside rebates reaching 3.8% for the employers. • 1995 – Constraints on self-investment for occupational pensions and creation of a regulatory board. • 1999 – Introduction of the stakeholder pension and of the second state pension. • 2007 – Introduction of a new system of personal accounts, rise in the basic state pension, reform of the second state pension, increase in the retirement age.

Consequences	• 1994/1998 – Due to the extent of the changes, its strong connection to the state of the economy and its reliance on the stock market, the outcome of the reform is difficult to assess and/or predict.	• 1986 – Dependence on the private sector for the bulk of pension provisions. Public policy shift from providing pensions to regulating the private sector in these functions.

Consequences

• 1994/1998 – Due to the extent of the changes, its strong connection to the state of the economy and its reliance on the stock market, the outcome of the reform is difficult to assess and/or predict.

• Expected to lose: those with broken careers; blue-collar workers prone to early retirement; white-collar workers who were benefiting from the 15/30 rule of the ATP system (e.g. female university professors).

• Expected to benefit: those with steady careers and low wage progression.

• Buffer fund created by the old system is scheduled to disappear to finance the transition to a private component.

• 1986 – Dependence on the private sector for the bulk of pension provisions. Public policy shift from providing pensions to regulating the private sector in these functions.

• Expected to lose: those making poor occupational choices; those with broken careers (especially with long periods of unemployment); those who invested more in SERPS.

• Expected to benefit: those with good occupational plans; those who play the market successfully.

• 2007 – Those who had invested more in SERPS will see their benefits decrease; low-income earners will have better access to private pensions; those relying on the basic state pension will see their income rise.

Inclusion of employers and unions

• Exclusion/informal: A reference group was set aside – unions and employers did not participate in the negotiation of the new system; influence filtered by the political parties (e.g. LO via SAP). No veto points.

• Excluded: Neither unions nor employers were active players during the preparation of the legislation; nor were they very involved with the commissions studying reform proposals. No veto points.

Number of parties involved

• 1998 – 5 (SAP, FP, M, Kd, C)

• 1980 – 1 (C)
• 1986 – 1 (C)
• 1995 – 1 (L)
• 1999 – 1 (L)
• 2007 – 1 (L)

Notes:

L = Labour; C = Conservatives.

[1] This table is not exhaustive. For a more detailed analysis of the reforms, please consult the relevant chapters.

of risks even though the guarantor of pensions differs – state vs private market. The long-term generosity of pensions, however, depends on different sources. In the United Kingdom, it is the value of the investments that guarantees the level of benefits, while Swedish benefits are adjusted according to an index that emphasizes both the state of the economy and the ageing of the population, with private pensions playing only a minor role.

Social Partnership results in parametric reforms

France and Belgium were limited to parametric reforms (see Table 6.2). Governments have not been able to produce changes to the pension system as a whole, but, rather, were co-opted into adjusting existing parameters. The easiest way to explain this outcome is that there are simply too many different types of actors to consider implementing a new system. The formal inclusion of social partners in the reform equation plays a significant role, since unions and employers serve different interests than do political parties. For example, neither is preoccupied by re-election. Further, their ideas regarding the best way to reform pensions are distinctly different. On one hand, unions tend to emphasize past promises/commitments made by previous governments, and they act very defensively. Regardless of the country, all unions stressed the fact that growth could at least partially compensate for the ageing population, and that the forecasts presented tend to over-exaggerate the pension crisis. On the other hand, employers are using the pension crisis as a means to negotiate lower labour costs. They stress the importance of not increasing employers' contributions due to the detrimental effect such actions have on the economy.

It might seem that the importance of social partners has been misconstrued in the French case owing to the importance of the state and the lack of the social partners' genuine concerted efforts. However, social partners manage the programmes, even though they do not control the pension-related rules and regulations; they are thus very aware of the activities related to this field. Both employers and unions pay close attention to the government's actions and are actually hostile towards its involvement in this policy area. The reason the Balladur and Raffarin reforms survived while Juppé's did not is related to Matignon's consultations with the social partners prior to enacting the reforms. The Balladur and Raffarin cabinets knew that the measures introduced had the support of at least one of the three major unions (CFDT), while Juppé did not even bother to discuss reform with any of the social actors.

In Belgium, the situation is somewhat different because the state is less powerful. The channels of communication between social partners and the government are always open. As compared to the other three cases, much of the discussion and debate occurred behind closed doors. Interestingly, some of the media scoops or leaks related to ideas for reforms were strongly

Table 6.2 Comparative analysis of the successful pension reforms introduced in Belgium and France (Social Partnership)[1]

| | Social Partnership | |
	Belgium	France
Pension reform name	• 1996 – Colla Reform • 2001 – Silver Fund and second pillar	• 1993 – Balladur reform • 1995 – Juppé plan • 2003 – Public-sector scheme reform
Pension reform content – main elements	• 1996 – Alignment of the pensionable age for women to make it consistent with men; reduction in the indexation rate for contributions made between 1955 and 1974. • 2001 – Government money put aside to create a buffer fund; creation of a second pillar managed by social partners.	• 1993 – Increase in the length of contribution (37.5 to 40 years); benefits based on the best 25 years of contribution instead of 10; price indexation instead of wage indexation; creation of a retirement fund. • 1995 – Increased managerial powers granted to the Parliament. • 2003 – Increase in the length of contribution period for public-sector employees (both sectors from 2009 to reach 41 years in 2012). Public sector: decrease in the coefficient used to calculate pensions. Private sector: increase of 0.2% in the contribution rate starting in 2006. Increase in the level of minimum pension (with increase in the minimum contribution). Penalty for early retirement and bonus for years worked beyond usual retirement age.

(continued on next page)

	Social Partnership	
	Belgium	France
Consequences	• 1996 – Limited due to the long transition period and other social benefits that will compensate for the loss of pension for women – exceptions are women with long careers, who may lose up to 11% in pension benefits. • 2001 – Nil. The buffer fund consists of government bonds. Same effect as paying back the debt right away; second pillar does not resolve any difficulties associated with the first pillar but adds extra retirement income.	• 1993 – Biggest impact comes from the price indexation of pensions (close to twice the savings generated by the other two measures combined). Pensions may decline by an average of 26% *vis-à-vis* average wages over a period of 50 years depending on the duration of benefits. • 1995 – No financial impact, but the Parliament further constrains the managerial duties of the social partners. • 2003 – Decline in benefits for both private and public sector, especially for those without a lengthy and continuous career (affecting especially women and younger workers).
Inclusion of employers and unions	• Constant social dialogue between the government and the social partners, which act as veto points.	• Institutionalized dialogue between the social partners and the government. Government may act alone – the absence of consultation can be costly (e.g. events of December 1995). Veto points.
Number of parties involved	• 1996 – 4 (PS, SP, CVP, PSC) • 2001 – 6 (PS, SP, VLD, PRL, Agalev, Verts)	• 1993 – 1[a] (RPR–UDF) • 1995 – 1[a] (RPR–UDF) • 2003 – 1[a] (RPR–UDF)
Worth noting	• Public-sector schemes have not been reformed despite being more generous.	• Some public-sector schemes have not been reformed despite being more generous.

Notes:

[a] Due to the 'permanent' coalition between the RPR and UDF, they are considered to represent one party (see Chapter 2 for further explanation).

L = Labour; C = Conservatives. 1 This table is not exhaustive. For a more detailed analysis of the reforms, please consult the relevant chapters.

opposed by the unions, leaving little doubt regarding the leak's origin. Thus, once the government tables a bill, broad support is already guaranteed.

Obtaining widespread consensus on the coalition government's actions in Belgium is easier than those advocating the use of veto players would think. The *déclaration gouvernementale* provides the blueprint for the arrangements agreed to by the governing parties. A logrolling of policy choices then occurs as each side bargains and negotiates for what it most wants. This type of behaviour is problematic for issues that arise suddenly, but pension reform does not fall into that category. Nonetheless, pension reform remains difficult in this type of system because social partners have the opportunity to intervene and interfere with arrangements political parties have already agreed to. As they are involved in the process from beginning to end, radical proposals are not even considered. This explains why a programmatic reform like the kind implemented by the coalition of political parties in Sweden is not feasible in Belgium.

> Hypothesis 1a: Reforms are most likely to occur when unions have a co-operative relationship with the state (e.g. Belgium) compared to a confrontational one (e.g. France).

As implied in the above discussion, unions are insiders in the policy process in Belgium but they are outsiders in France, even though both have managerial responsibilities and can claim to be 'legitimately' involved. Including the unions in the development process helps to ensure 'smooth' implementation as the government secures their support ahead of time. In the French case, the government consults, but it is expected to make the final ruling. More uncertainty regarding the kind of response it will get is the usual result. Owing to the fact that unions have traditionally defended the pension system and opposed government actions in this respect (at least in principle), the Belgian government should have more success implementing pension reforms, but, contrary to expectations, France has been more successful than Belgium.

Both the Balladur and Raffarin reforms introduced much more substantive changes than the Belgian reform of 1996 since the long-term effects of the latter were off-set by other social measures, and they were smaller in scope and breadth to begin with. Nonetheless, it is worth noting that the Balladur reform was already *de facto* implemented in Belgium, since its pension system had fewer advantages to start with. It was already price indexed and it had a contribution period of 45 years (compared to 40 years in France with the Balladur reform). When it comes to the public sector, Juppé's 1995 reform attempt had the indirect consequence of muting the Belgian government's reform efforts with its public servants.

> Hypothesis 1b: Assuming that Rothstein (1996) is correct about the possibility for unions and social democratic interests in Sweden to

capture the state, then the state's expertise is more likely to be accepted and trusted by unions in Sweden than in France, where the French state has a confrontational relationship with unions.

Few economists (Tamburi 1999; Legros 2001) have examined the importance of institutional credibility when seeking to reform pensions. People are most likely to distrust politicians if there is a 'credibility gap', meaning that there is not a popular institution attached to a specific policy area. The evidence provided here supports this thesis. France and Sweden remain polar opposites. In the former, a vast amount of energy and a large part of the debate surrounding pensions is related to the government's expertise and the accuracy of its projections. It is not an accident that many French people are confused about the need to reform the system. It has been difficult for citizens to trust French politicians for two main reasons. First, the state does not manage the system and has a difficult time 'selling' the need for reform when the unions who co-manage the plan with the employers argue otherwise, especially when both draw their conclusions from the same pool of information. Muddying the waters even more is the fact that the French population is divided when it comes to assessing who should be responsible for pension policies; 35 per cent believe the state should manage the pension system, compared to 34 per cent who favour the social partners. Thus, the decision regarding who conducts, chairs and performs the statistical analysis is highly politicized and controversial. Second, the constant reliance on commissions, many of which are considered external to the workings of the state, clearly highlights the lack of institutional leadership. Over a 16-year span, 13 commissions have presented reports, and no consensus has yet been achieved. What is even more worrisome for the average citizen is the fact that many reports have reached distinctly opposite conclusions. For example, the 2000 Teulade Report, with its emphasis on the need to develop policies promoting economic growth rather than altering the pension system, negates virtually all of the conclusions presented in the 1999 Charpin Report, which prescribed specific reforms to the pension system (see Chapter 2).

Many of these political issues are absent in Sweden because of the high level of trust placed in the national insurance agency (*Riksförsakringsverket*, RFV) and in the various departments. None of the individuals interviewed contested any of the analyses presented by those offices. Many competing alternatives coming from various parties were actually analysed by the same people. Further, 'external' expertise has been incorporated within the committee and complemented rather than challenged. Critics focused instead on the consequences of the reform, using the numbers and analyses provided by the state agencies.[2] All of this has important consequences, especially when compared with France. First, the endorsement of the reform by all offices adds credibility to the actions of the committee members because citizens trust them; they are highly credible, and the RFV is not nearly as politicized as the Bureau du Plan in France. The fact that the RFV was the first to state that pension reform was necessary helped politicians a great deal, as they did not then have to pursue blame avoidance strategies. All agreed that a reform was necessary, and so it did not become a vote-losing proposition.[3] Second, more political energy was spent discussing substantive issues, such as what elements should be included in or excluded from a reform, because the playing field itself was not being challenged. Third, when the credibility of an 'analysing agency' is not questioned, a committee is taken far more seriously because there is less chance that an alternative group will challenge its findings later, which is precisely what occurred after Charpin published his report in France (Marier 2005).

> Null Hypothesis 1: The higher the number of political parties within a government, the less likely it is that a programmatic pension reform will occur.

This hypothesis is rooted in rational-choice literature, which emphasizes that the higher the number of veto players (Tsebelis 1995), the less likely it is that substantial policy reforms can be undertaken. For example, both Alesina and Perotti (1995) and Mattson (1996) argue that coalition governments have more difficulty maintaining fiscal discipline because negotiations among the political parties within the coalitions result in higher spending. This argument has been challenged by Hallerberg and von Hagen (1999), who emphasize the possibility of reaching a binding agreement within a coalition government, and by Peters (1997), who stresses the possibility of logrolling as a way to tackle difficult decisions (see Chapter 1).

The empirical evidence presented in this book supports the latter argument. A grand bargain among five key parties in the Swedish Parliament resulted in one of the most radical pension reforms in Europe, while consecutive single-party governments in France faced deep opposition even while trying to introduce less drastic parametric reforms. The new Swedish system is full of compromises, and many of the issues were resolved in a logrolling fashion. For example, a significant public component was retained in exchange for a private savings account within the pension system (see Chapter 4). Even in Belgium, the difficulties are attributed to the social partners rather than the governmental actors. The leadership of the Flemish Socialists has not been questioned by other political parties in the coalition, who are more concerned with their preferred issues (see Chapter 3). As indicated by the main theoretical framework of this book, the important issue is not the number of veto players, but rather the nature of the veto. The institutionalization of social partners within a pension system is more problematic than having many parties within a governmental coalition.

Null Hypothesis 2: Based on Tsebelis (1999), a broad political coalition that includes ideologically polarized political parties is unlikely to yield a (major) pension reform.

In light of the Swedish pension reform experience, this hypothesis cannot be supported. Even Belgium, with its current rainbow coalition composed of Socialists, Liberals and Greens, challenges this hypothesis, since a consistent reform effort is present within the government. It is the Social Partnership structure that mostly constrains Belgian governments and not the number of parties within them.

Hypothesis 2: The impact of pension reforms should be very limited in the consensual type of reform-making and most extensive in the cabinet style. The overall reform ranking should be as follows: cabinet > committee > social conflict > consensual.

Application: Belgium should be the case closest to the status quo, and the most extensive reform(s) should have occurred in the United Kingdom. Overall, the ranking of the four pension reforms should be as follows: United Kingdom > Sweden > France > Belgium.

This is the combination of both ordering principles: Parliamentary Integration vs Social Partnership and proportional vs majoritarian vision. It is argued that the number of veto players within a parliamentary assembly has an impact as soon as it is combined with the structural pattern of the relationship. Thus, a high number of veto players might not be overly cumbersome within a Parliamentary Integration structure, but a Social Partnership structure amplifies the difficulties associated with negotiations among the political parties. For example, in the latter case, unions might effectively pressure socialist parties to act in a 'socialist' manner, or they might simply veto reform projects (see Chapter 1).

As expected, the most radical reforms occurred in the United Kingdom. The Thatcher government actively promoted more reliance on the private market, making it nearly impossible for a successive government to re-establish a public system. The early years of the Labour Party entrenched the reforms enacted by the Conservative governments by not seeking to recreate another strong public system. Most of the debate currently addresses how private pensions should be regulated in order to ensure a financially secure retirement for citizens now investing heavily in the private sector. The 2007 reform, despite increasing the value of the basic state pension, confirms the private pension plans' predominant role by introducing a new pension scheme that automatically enrols individuals, whose contributions are then invested in private pension plans. The unions and employers were simply not involved in the main committees studying pension reform, and the participation of political parties in opposition was negligible (see Table 6.1 and Chapter 5).

The Swedes enacted the second largest number of changes to their pension system by creating a whole new pension system, which will be implemented over the next 20 years. Among the most important improvements to the new scheme is the introduction of a funded account representing 2.5 per cent of the 18 per cent of contributions levied. Nonetheless, it is important to emphasize that the new system creates notional accounts, where all contributions are counted towards one's pension; this is a substantial change from having benefits calculated on the basis of the 15 best years in a 30-year (or more) career. Furthermore, the basic pension is being replaced with a means-tested, guaranteed-income pension. The latter measure breaks the universal nature of the previous system, where every citizen received the same basic income. This shift could have negative consequences in the long run, since countries offering means-tested benefits such as the United States and the United Kingdom tend to have the lowest levels of support for their welfare state. It is the universalistic nature of the Swedish welfare state that led to its strong public support (Rothstein 2001). It should be pointed out, however, that the means test applies to pensions earned within the public system. This form of means testing is less intrusive and does not discourage private savings (Palme 2005). As stated earlier, the influence of unions and employers was limited, owing to their exclusion from the main negotiations among the political parties. They were faced with a final version that could not really be altered, since changes would have resulted in reopening a complex compromise.

It is more difficult to assess whether Belgium or France ranks third because the changes made in France already existed in the Belgian system. Nonetheless, the Balladur reform results in more important changes since, in contrast to Belgium, generous early-retirement options do not exist to cushion the alterations in the public scheme for private-sector employees. The three measures the Balladur government took (see Table 6.2) will result in lower pension benefits for a large segment of the population, especially if one considers the evolution of pensions versus that of the average wage. Further, the French government successfully reformed its civil servants' pension system with the Raffarin reform of 2003, while the status quo prevails in Belgium.

Pension discussions involve social partners who contest the legitimacy of the state in this respect, resulting in highly publicized conflicts between governmental actors and the social partners. From the public stance of social partners, it is difficult to assess what is truly acceptable as a reform and what is not. What is clear, however, as was demonstrated by the events of December 1995, is that the social partners cannot be ignored.

Social partners are actually more powerful in Belgium because they are very much a part of the policy process. As a result, conflicts are internalized, and the government's actions rarely occur without their prior consent (or mild opposition). Social partners can also influence the outcome of coalition negotiations by pressuring related political parties to address the concerns of their electoral interests. For example, the Socialist ministers have had to defend their negotiation stance within the government and with the unions.

Following the guidelines of the *déclaration gouvernementale*, the Minister of Social Affairs has had to present proposals to the other members of the coalition prior to seeking their approval with the social partners. This adds another element of complexity to the process, which can be partially negated by logrolling (see p. 181). The end result is a policy process which progresses '*à petits pas*' (in small steps). The 1996 reform was enacted after an extended period of negotiations even though it had to be brought in because of an earlier European Court of Justice ruling. The compensation package introduced (or maintained) with this reform resulted in a near status quo. Ironically, it is women with lengthy careers (and hence higher contributions) who have been most affected by it. The reforms that followed (the creation of the Silver Funds and occupational pensions) did not alter the current public system in any way.

> Hypothesis 2a: Unions will be better equipped to block drastic reforms when they are institutionalized within the Social Partnership model regardless of union density.

> *Application*: Unions are more likely to have a disruptive role in Belgium than in Sweden, despite a similar level of unionization.

Belgium and Sweden present a very fruitful comparative exercise to test this set of hypotheses. Both cases have very generous pension systems and high levels of unionization. Further, in both countries the state has historically sought to incorporate the unions within their policy process, and the unions consented because the state was not perceived as a threat as was the case in France. However, as evidenced by this research, Belgian unions had more input into the pension reform process than did their Swedish counterparts because they could interact with policy-makers while proposals were being considered. Swedish unions had to deal with a *fait accompli* where they could only accept or reject the agreement. The fall of corporatism and the resulting responsibilities given to the state when the pension system was extended in the late 1950s explain the relative lack of union input. The unions played a stronger role within the political parties, where they almost forced the SAP to backtrack on its earlier agreement with the four bourgeois parties.

> Hypothesis 2b: Regardless of the number of veto players (Tsebelis 1999), it is more difficult to generate a pension reform with the social conflict type than with the committee type.

Application: France is expected to have greater difficulties in generating a reform than Sweden even though it has fewer veto players.

This is another test of the concept of veto players. On one hand, even though Sweden is not a case where coalition governments have occurred on a regular basis, the occasions where a single party can push its own agenda through without the support of at least one other party are rare. In the early 1990s, when the Working Group on Pensions was initiated, the support of as many as five parties was necessary to obtain a majority. An extensive pension reform was successfully instituted despite the larger number of approvals needed in the Swedish example. On the other hand, unitary French governments have been unable to launch equivalent reforms. The argument presented in this book is that the institutionalization of social partners in the French case goes further towards explaining why it has been more difficult to alter the system than do the number and type of possible vetoes.

Hypothesis 2c: The cabinet type generates more extensive reforms than the social conflict style because the latter faces veto points.

Application: The United Kingdom should be able to generate more extensive reforms than France because it does not have a structured relationship based on Social Partnership.

This is also an interesting comparison since, according to the literature on the 'new' politics of welfare, both countries should have a lot of difficulty reforming their system because accountability can be readily traced back to a single party in power; the government cannot blame another actor or political party for a retrenchment measure (see Pierson 1994). Thus, any change to the pension system resulting in negative consequences can influence voters' choices in a subsequent election. However, the United Kingdom has introduced radical pension reforms and the Conservatives did not pay the price in the following elections. Even in France, the popularity of the Balladur government did not decline as a result of the 1993 pension reform. This explanation does not help us determine why the United Kingdom introduced such radical reforms, while the Balladur government, committed to introducing private options, could not do more than alter three parameters.

Both governments faced a divided opposition and used it to enact their reform policies. In the United Kingdom, the stark reduction in public benefits was made possible because a significant portion of the population already relied on private benefits. In France, wage earners and retirees are enrolled in different pension schemes based on their occupational status. The *régime général* represented the easiest target because of a lower unionization level and the presence of a co-operating union (CFDT) that was strongly established in the private sector. The main difference is that France still had to negotiate with its divided opposition because of Social Partnership. The United Kingdom could be more dismissive as it is the sole manager of public pensions, representing a Parliamentary Integration structure.

Hypothesis 2d: The consensual type leads to more reform difficulties than the social conflict type because it has more veto players in a similarly structured relationship (Social Partnership).

Application: Belgium is expected to experience more difficulty generating reforms than France.

This is a test of the second ordering principle. In this case, both countries have a social partnership structure, meaning that they must take the unions and employers into account throughout their decision-making process. The main difference between the two countries is that France can have a prime minister who decides to act '*à la* Bonaparte', as Juppé did in 1995 (Vail 1999), while such action could never have been taken in Belgium. There, any ministerial proposal must receive the approval of other coalition members. Further, pension reform has tended to be included in the *déclaration gouvernementale*, meaning it becomes a matter to be negotiated among the coalition members in the formation of a government. Thus, the government's position can be advanced more forcefully in France than in Belgium.

Hypothesis 2e: The committee style leads to more reform difficulties than the cabinet type because it has more veto players in a similarly structured relationship (Parliamentary Integration).

Application: Sweden is expected to experience more difficulty generating reforms than the United Kingdom.

This is clearly supported by the analysis presented in Chapters 4 and 5. Both countries introduced substantial changes to their pension systems, yet the way this was achieved varied a great deal because of the number of veto players in each setting. The Thatcher government was uncompromising and first sought to scrap the public system. It was the intervention of the Treasury, foreseeing a substantial rise in public expenditure, that stopped this proposal from going through. Plan B was still very beneficial to the private sector to the extent that it jeopardized the viability of the public system in the long run. The return of the Labour Party to power resulted in two more rounds of pension reform, culminating in the 2007 pension reform.

In the Swedish case, a single political party cannot have that kind of latitude. The key difference was that the SAP had to negotiate and compromise with the bourgeois parties to reform the whole pension system.

Thus, the final agreement does not represent a solution advocated by any single political party, but rather a collage of wishes from each of the five involved. This explains why it took longer for Swedes to enact a reform. This is also, however, the strength of the Swedish policy-making process. Policies tend to be more stable in the long run than in the United Kingdom, because an agreement like the pension reform of 1994/1998 is unlikely to be altered once a new government comes to power.

Extending the theory to other industrialized countries

In order to assess the potential of the theoretical framework, a brief survey of reforms in other industrialized countries supports the main arguments developed in this book, though a few cases raise interesting questions. To facilitate their analysis, these cases are analysed according to their cell (committee, consensual, cabinet and social conflict) and are presented in Table 6.3.

Committee

This cell includes other Scandinavian countries such as Norway, Denmark and the Netherlands. Moreover, owing to the powers attributed to the second chamber, the United States would be included in this group, since a single party is unlikely to have sufficient support in both houses to unilaterally introduce its own pension plan. The strange nature of the Dutch pension system results in its inclusion in this cell. A brief survey of recent pension reform initiatives in this country supports the theoretical framework introduced by this research.

Table 6.3 Types of pension reform in North America and Western Europe

Democratic visions	Institutionalized structure of relationship	
	Parliamentary Integration 'in the state'	Social Partnership 'out of the state'
Proportional influence visions	committee • Sweden • Norway • Denmark • Iceland • Netherlands • USA	consensual • Belgium • Italy • Germany • Spain • Portugal • Austria • Finland • Switzerland
Majoritarian visions	cabinet • United Kingdom • Canada/Québec	social conflict • France

In December 2004, Norway presented a White Paper addressing pension reform based on the recommendations of its Pension Committee, which was comprised of experts and politicians. The policy process and the reform itself closely resemble Sweden's. The main exception was the active participation, early on, of the Ministry of Finance in the process. Social partners were not included in the discussion groups and held few meetings with core members of the committee. Neither were they present during negotiations. Norway's proposal is extremely similar to the recent Swedish pension reform in the following ways: (1) it introduces the concept of the life-income principle; (2) it has a flexible retirement age and a means-tested pension for those with insufficient contributions; (3) it grants pension points for childcare; (4) its indexation is based on life expectancy and the current state of the economy; and (5) part of its contributions will be funded by the government (NOU 2004[1]).

Iceland, Denmark and the Netherlands actually have very similar pension structures. In all three, strong private occupational pensions were established alongside a universal basic pension providing a replacement income of more than 40 per cent of employment income (OECD 2005). Thus, occupational and private pensions play a more important role in these countries. In all three cases, labour unions pressed employers to create occupational pensions to assure a higher replacement wage. Similarly, in all three, occupational pensions are included within wage bargaining agreements. The existence of these fully funded occupational schemes (administered privately by social partners) allowed governments to reform their public system – managed by the state – by diverting adjustment costs to them (Herbertsson *et al.* 2000; Haverland 2001; Green-Pedersen and Lindbom 2006). This was an easy political solution that could be agreed upon by coalition governments. As stressed by Myles and Pierson (2001), the existence of these fully funded schemes reduced the financial liability of public pension schemes. However, a reduction in the level of protection offered by public schemes increases the pressure on the occupational schemes, since fund managers must either be better performers or seek additional contributions. The evidence supports the thesis that social partners do not have a veto point in these jurisdictions when it comes to the public system.

The United States represents a special case due to democratic institutions that, in effect, function like a bicameral parliamentary system. Thus, for example even when the Presidency and the House of Representatives are controlled by one party, another party may have the majority in the Senate. Complicating matters further, party discipline is not as rigid as in other industrialized countries. In essence, the United States cannot be considered to have a proportional vision. On the contrary, American politics is highly polarized with regard to pensions, echoing a majoritarian vision. The United States represents a clear case of Parliamentary Integration; the management and responsibilities of social security lie clearly with the state. As Béland stressed, social partners do not have a veto point when it comes to managing social security (Béland 2001). The Democrats' response to the upcoming difficulties of the social security system has been to adopt the 'Canadian' solution by investing excess contributions in funded schemes. Republicans have opposed this 'socialization' of investments, opting for private (and individual) options. Divided governments and the fear of negative electoral consequences have thus far contributed to legislative inaction (Pierson 1996; Béland 2005). The decreasing returns provided by social security since the 1980s will likely prompt further debates and proposals in the near future (Peters 2005).

Cabinet

As a result of federalism and the nature of the Canada Pension Plan (CPP), provinces can actually challenge plans brought forward by the federal government. However, in order to be efficient, they must represent a broad coalition, approaching unanimity; a rare feat in Canada. The electoral system usually produces single-party governments, even though the recent regionalization of Canadian politics is currently challenging the party system. The Liberal Party of Canada introduced a reform in 1998 resulting in a 76 per cent increase in the contribution rate and penalizing pre-retirement. Further, it instituted the Canadian Pension Plan Investment Board, an independent agency, to invest excess contributions in the stock market. Contrary to what has been happening in countries such as the United Kingdom and the United States, pension privatization never took a prominent place in the policy debate to reform the pension system. The policy crusade undertaken by the Alberta government and the Reform Party to establish private solutions fell on deaf ears within the federal government for two reasons. First, the federal government could not convincingly state that its financial situation was too critical to save the CPP, since it had been generating surpluses (Weaver 1999) and would finally give the provinces something concrete on which to base their claim that the federal government was cutting into social programmes. Second, Québec quickly and publicly announced that it would not support such a plan. It also rejected proposals made by federal bureaucrats to reduce the replacement rate and increase the retirement age. In the aftermath of the 1995 referendum, the federal Liberal Party did not want to provide any more ammunition to the Parti Québécois government that might justify a rupture with the rest of Canada (Béland 2006). Finally, further privatization was not supported on the grounds that transition costs, like those experienced by the United Kingdom in the mid-1980s, were excessive.

Consensual

Numerous analyses have discussed the difficulties of continental European countries to reform their welfare states (Esping-Andersen 1996; Pierson

1998; Ferrera and Rhodes 2000; Hinrichs 2000; Pierson 2001; Schludi 2002; Natali and Rhodes 2004). The role and importance of social partners has been noted as a strong obstacle to pension reform. Recent accounts of pension reforms in the *consensual* type indicate that negotiations with social partners occurred in Italy, Germany, Austria, Spain, Switzerland, Finland and Portugal (Bonoli 2000; Hinrichs 2000; Reynaud 2000; Scarborough 2000; Rhodes 2001; Schludi 2002; Swank 2002; Natali and Rhodes 2004). For example, typical of the consensual style, Austrian reforms (2000 and 2003) involved extensive negotiations among political parties and the social partners. The reforms are clearly parametric and include incentives to delay retirement, changes in the indexation formula and lengthy implementation periods. The federal nature of Germany and Switzerland made it more difficult to initiate reforms (see, for example, Bonoli 2000; Haverland 2001). Interestingly, despite not being recognized as corporatist and having weak institutional features (with the potential exception of Social Partnership in a few policy areas), Italy, Spain and Portugal have recently become very involved in reforming their welfare state (Rhodes 2001). Even though the consensual type of pension reform generally applies, Germany and Italy represent problematic cases.

First, Germany has traditionally followed a consensual style. A broad parliamentary coalition supported by social partners led to parametric reforms in both 1976 and 1989. The 1989 reform introduced an indexation based on net (instead of gross) wages, a reduced replacement rate, an increase in taxes and social contributions, and an increase in the reference age for retirement to 65. This reform was expected to ensure the financial viability of the system for at least a decade, but the reunification of Germany rapidly altered this outcome (Haverland 2001). The *consensual* type was abandoned in the late 1990s. Social Democrats and Christian Democrats entered into a heated competition to reform the welfare state, and public pensions did not escape the trend. The Christian Democrats first sped up the implementation of the 1989 reform and introduced a new indexation method that included a demographic factor. This new indexation was removed by Social Democrats following their election in 1998, but they opted to replace net wage indexation with an inflation index and devised a new pension formula providing a replacement rate of 64 per cent rather than the traditional 70 per cent (Haverland 2001; Hinrichs and Kangas 2003). Despite much criticism from social partners and the opposition on another reform package in 2001, the Social Democrats and the Greens altered their stance but were still able to introduce three major changes: the introduction of a minimum pension, a (voluntary) funded component with tax benefits and an indexation change (Hinrichs and Kangas 2003).

Italy represents a case where the consensual type of pension reform actually led to extensive programmatic changes rather than parametric alterations. All successful reforms involved the active participation of labour union experts. The most notable intervention remains the Dini reform of

1995, which transformed the pension system into a defined-contribution system (similar to the Swedish life-income principle), and implemented a reduction in seniority pensions and a clearer differentiation between soli-daristic and non-solidaristic features. Berlusconi attempted to secure another reform in 1994, but opted to confront unions in the process, leading to a response similar to the one Juppé faced in 1995 (Natali and Rhodes 2004). It should also be noted that the Italian reform efforts were rooted in the public finance marathon to meet EMU criteria (Pitruzzello 1997). This incentive was much more influential in Italy than in France, since few believed Italy would be able to meet the criteria and join the Euro-zone, and so the threat of being left out was genuine. On the other hand, the creation of a European currency without France's involvement was never a viable alternative.

Despite the challenge these two cases pose to the theoretical framework developed in this study, it is only fair to note that two distinct political crises affected them: German reunification and Italy's march into EMU. These are both exceptional events that would be difficult to account for with any theoretical model aspiring to create generalizable theories.

Key policy implications

Owing to the difficulties associated with institutional structures, the options available to policy-makers remain varied. Few conclusions can be drawn on the basis of pension reforms implemented in industrialized countries. First, in order to reform public pensions, one has to recognize the limitations of one's structure. A state that has delegated substantial authority to social partners in the past must continue to include them in the decision-making process. This implies that a coherent strategy is more likely to be successful if it entails a series of small steps and/or other policy issues where there is more negotiating room. In the long run, states can try to minimize the impact of the social partners by taking more responsibility within the overall system. The revision of the social budget by Parliament, as illu-strated by the Juppé plan, represents this type of strategy. Albeit less likely in this day and age, a possible alternative would be to grant more respon-sibility to social partners so that they are responsible for a larger share of the work of reforming the system. This action was proposed by the then French prime minister Bérégovoy in the early 1990s in a desperate attempt to salvage the fortunes of the Socialist government. The social partners' reaction was quite negative, however, as they understood clearly that responsibility for future unpopular decisions would lie with them. The Dutch and Danish reforms, where reforms to the public pension systems forced changes to funded occupational pensions that were administered and controlled by social partners, illustrate this dilemma.

The fact that it is easier to reform pensions within a Parliamentary Inte-gration structure can also be a disadvantage. The United Kingdom's pension system is excessively complex because no previous pension policies had the opportunity to mature, owing to the constant changes that accompanied each new government. Given the long-term vision necessary to deal with the field of pension policy, this outcome is quite undesirable. The potential costs of this type of uncertainty were actually a key factor behind the resolve of the five Swedish political parties to reach a compromise. Both socialist and bourgeois parties feared that a future government would undo a unilateral decision, thus resulting in an unstable policy regarding a hotly disputed political issue.

Second, and building on the latter point, policy changes can be made regardless of the structure. Reformers are more likely to succeed within a Parliamentary Integration structure if they opt to overhaul the system or make explicit reforms. It is worth noting that both Swedish and British reforms tackled some of the previous systems' financial shortcomings even as they introduced new difficulties. For example, despite all the efforts of the pension committee in Sweden, there is no guarantee the new system will prove itself sustainable in the long run. It remains to be seen whether or not politicians will have the courage to let that automatic indexation of pensions occur when the country falls into a recession.

Ingenious ways to reform the pension system within the Social Partnership structure can be devised, even though one cannot be as explicit as in the previous cases. For example, the Belgian reforms have put the burden elsewhere (pre-retirement), which may be easier to reform in the future, and have introduced new programmes (occupational pensions) to compensate for a future lack of adequate replacement wages. Simply privatizing a component of the public scheme would not have generated support, but the creation of a new pillar earned widespread approval. In the end, both policies achieve a similar aim: increasing the percentage of private savings in the system.

Notes

Introduction: policy change in difficult times

1 Even though the UK and Sweden are not part of the Euro-zone, both countries have sought to keep the Economic and Monetary Union question a political one through attempts to adhere to the convergence criteria.

1 The origins of diversity in pension reform processes: a theoretical approach

1 Less than 5 per cent of all policy-makers interviewed in Belgium, France, Sweden and the UK dispute the necessity of reforming pensions. These individuals were usually politicians positioned to the left of Social Democrats and trade unionists.

2 Pierson alludes to this in *Dismantling the Welfare State*, wherein he states that one of the principal reasons for Thatcher's successful reformation of the public pension scheme in Britain was that it had not yet reached the same level of maturity as social security had in the US (Pierson 1994: 71–2).

3 A parametric reform implies an alteration of existing parameters within a pension programme, such as a rise in the contribution rate or a lengthening of the contribution period. A programmatic change introduces a new programme that replaces an existing one.

4 Ross argues that the long transformation of Labour into 'New Labour' is a case in point.

5 Even though this is less applicable than in the US, parties may adopt specific policies in order to raise financial support for their re-election (Mayhew 1974).

6 He restricts himself to a discussion of five reform options: shifting financing from payg to funding, increasing the age of retirement, targeting benefits, changing the benefit formula and changing the indexation mechanism (Bonoli 2000: 23–7).

7 A reform does not have to cut expenditures. However, since most difficulties are related to expected increases in the cost of pensions during the period studied, reforms are often associated with retrenchment measures.

8 These are graduates of the *École Nationale d'Administration*, the highly selective public administration school that most senior civil servants and numerous politicians attend.

9 Benefits have been granted on the basis of employment, not citizenship. The coverage is based on the occupations of the employees and varies from one profession to another. The financial and administrative roles of the social partners in these countries tend to be relatively high compared to Scandinavian and liberal (Anglo-Saxon) countries. For a more detailed description, see Esping-Andersen 1990.

10 Although the administration of public pensions is mostly consensual, as it involves the application of current legislation, its membership reflects the importance of specific actors within this policy field. The involvement of social partners legitimates their activity in this field. As a result, they have developed their own expertise and often present detailed proposals to reform public pensions.

11 Budget item documents are distinguished by different colours. *Les jaunes* are general appendixes to the national budget (referred to as *les bleus*). *Les jaunes* do not follow the same procedural rules, as they are usually just additional information for parliamentarians (Mekhantar 1996: 37).

12 In southern European countries, social contributions have also been employed as a means to fight tax evasion. Those who work in the black market do not earn entitlements to public programmes, rendering those jobs less attractive.

13 The government is an integral part of this dialogue since it also finances social benefits, including pension plan benefits, albeit less significantly than in the Parliamentary Integration model. The benefits, despite being based on occupational status and being managed by social partners, are also considered to be public and are treated as such in political debates, with the government legislating on the parameters regarding how benefits are granted. Thus, this is very different from British and Swedish occupational plans, which 'top up' the benefits received from public pension plans; the amount received in addition to what members receive from the public plan is negotiated within collective agreements. In both cases, the government does not have a say with regard to entitlement conditions and levels of benefits paid. Thus, they remain truly private benefits.

14 In Belgium, civil servants usually receive their lost wages following a strike as part of the negotiated agreement with the state.

15 The major difference relevant to this discussion concerns the role of the state in terms of social responsibilities. It is minimal in the liberal countries where reliance on the private sector is relatively strong. In Scandinavia, the state plays an important role in providing universal social protection.

16 One possible exception could be mandatory public occupational pension schemes, which are an off-budget item. Nevertheless, Parliament has much greater oversight power than in continental countries with regards to their development. It can alter the ceiling and can easily play with the value of their indexation. Parliament has full budgetary control of the non-contributory pension.

17 For a more detailed explanation, see Chapter 4.

18 'City belt' is Rokkan's terminology to describe the strength and powers of the cities and their trade networks prior to the establishment of states in Europe; it is a geographical territory stretching northward from the Mediterranean and encompassing all of Italy and Germany and the surrounding territories. He claims that the strong powers of cities and their attached territories is the reason why it was so difficult to unify Italy and Germany.

19 This is also consistent with recent research in the field (for examples, see Hallerberg and von Hagen 1999; Powell 2000).

20 The bibliography contains the exact sources consulted.

21 In Belgium, the analysis was based on French sources. However, some interviews were conducted with both French and Flemish leaders to ensure appropriate representation. Many interviews in Sweden were conducted in English.

2 France: still a 'société bloquée'?

1 Force Ouvrière.

2 Confédération Française Démocratique des Travailleurs.

3 Confédération Française de l'Encadrement – Confédération Général des Cadres.

4 Caisse Nationale de Retraites des Agents des Collectivités Locales.

5 This does not mean that the Ministry of Social Affairs and its bureaucrats are totally excluded. During the writing of *L'Avenir de nos retraites* (i.e. the Charpin Report) in 1998–9, Charpin consulted many offices within the Social Ministry (especially the *Direction de la Sécurité Sociale*, DSS). Nonetheless, it is worth stating that documents and notes written by the DSS had to be validated by the cabinet prior to their release. The same process was in place for the work of the *Conseil d'Orientation des Retraites* (COR).

6 This fact has been stated on numerous occasions in various articles of *Le Monde* (1990–2002) and during the interviews conducted with politicians and social partners. The chief exception is the CGT, which argues that benefits should be maintained. In order to finance pensions, new funds should come from the profit earned by private companies and from economic growth.

7 *Contribution sociale généralisée* – a tax of 1.1 per cent on all income.

8 Author interview, 13 December 2001.

9 Author interview, 13 December 2001.

10 Author interview, 13 December 2001.

11 For example, in the 17 April 1991 edition discussing the release of the *Livre blanc*, it is stated that 'leurs dirigeants [i.e. unions] admettent en privé, que les problèmes sont réels mais que la surenchère des plus 'durs' – entendre FO et la CGT – voire l'état d'esprit de leurs propres adhérents les incitent, pour le moment, à dégager en touche' (29 August 1993). Following the Balladur reform, the author stated that '[l]es syndicats les plus réalistes n'ont soulevé que de timides objections de fond, alors que la CGT n'est pas parvenu à mobiliser ses troupes' (29 August 1993).

12 Author interview, 13 December 2001.

13 By 2020 the financial commitment would reach 99.5 billion francs (15.2 billion euros) in the worst-case scenario and 71.7 billion francs in the best-case scenario (10.9 billion euros) (COR 2001: Annex 8).

14 According to a study by the CNAV in 1992, 66 per cent of men and 40 per cent of women had contributed for more than 40 years by the time they collected their first pensions. In addition, 77 per cent of men and 51.5 per cent of women had contributed for more than 37.5 years (Ruellan 1993: 919).

15 Unless these individuals can claim non-contributory benefits (e.g. unemployment or illness).

16 The pension is calculated as follows: $P = \text{Avg Sal.} \times R \times D/160$ as of 2003. R is the rate (50 per cent for a full career, but it is reduced incrementally for incomplete careers) and D is the duration of contribution in quarters. Thus, someone who works 38 years instead of 40 obtains an R of 0.4 and $D/160 = 152/160$. Thus, with an average wage of 1,000 euros, the person with a full 40-year working period receives a pension of 500 euros. The individual with a career of 38 years with the same average wage receives a pension of 380 euros, or 76 per cent of the pension amount received by the individual who received the full rate.

17 From 50.3 per cent to 45.7 per cent for those at the SMIC (salaire minimum interprofessionnel de croissance, pretty much the standard minimum wage), and from 23.44 per cent to 21.26 per cent for those at the ceiling; both experience a reduction of 9.3 per cent.

18 Since the civil servants *régime* does not have a *caisse* (i.e. fund/administration), the CGP claims 1993 to be year zero and demonstrates the kind of increase in contributions points that would be required by civil servants to maintain the *régime*'s financial stability. The study also assumed that the contribution/state financing remained constant throughout the period. Since there is no contributory scheme for civil servants, the state collects the contributions of its

employees and adds the necessary amount. Pensions for civil servants function much more like a continuous wage would – with parameters focusing on the length of a career and the final salary – in its financial books.

19 Union Nationale des Syndicats Autonomes (active mostly in the public sector).
20 Fédération Syndicale Unitaire.
21 RDS stands for *remboursement de la dette de la sécurité sociale* and amounts to 0.5 per cent of all income for a period of 13 years to erase social security's accumulated debt.
22 The strike was originally planned for 28 November by the FO and the CGT, and the CFDT did not plan to attend. However, following the announcement of the Juppé plan, the CGT and other unions (including the CFDT) decided to have it on the 24th, making that the day of defence for social security. However, the FO decided to stick to the 28th. Unions in the private sector decided not to participate in the strike efforts at all.
23 Fédération de l'Éducation Nationale – part of UNSA.
24 Its resources come mainly from the RDS.
25 Agriculture and Fisheries, Economy, Finance and Industry, Employment and Solidarity, Equipment, Transport and Housing, and Public Service, state reform and decentralization. This high number is partly the result of the specificities of certain *régimes*. For example, the ministries of agriculture and fisheries are viewed as legitimate actors because farmers have their own pension *régime*.
26 These figures assume an unemployment rate of 6 per cent. Citing a study from INSEE, Charpin claimed that a decrease in the working population does not necessarily translate into a lower unemployment rate. Thus, in order to achieve an unemployment rate of either 3 per cent or 6 per cent an active employment policy would have to be in place (Charpin 1999: ch. 5).
27 For details of this commission report, see Taddei (2000).
28 It is worth noting that the MEDEF changed president in 1997 and adopted a more confrontational strategy with the other social partners and the government.
29 They also stated that employee's contributions in the public sector averaged 7.85 per cent while they averaged 10.35 per cent in the private sector (Charpin 1999: 256).
30 With the exception of the CFDT, which abstained (see reasons outline on p. 69).
31 Author interviews, December 2001.
32 Author interviews, December 2001.
33 Few federations even continued their actions until 14 May.

3 Belgium: seeking to adapt in a crumbling consensual world, one small step at a time

1 Author interview, 24 May 2002.
2 For example, the Socialists have tended to be quite strong in the French part of the country, while the Christian Democrats and Liberals have had more success in the Flemish part. Interestingly, Witte argues that the French Socialists supported the idea of a federal Belgium. Essentially, they wanted to increase their power within Wallonia and promote socialist ideas independent of Flanders, which in turn would increase the party's importance at the national level (Witte 1992: 96–7). It is an unwritten rule to have the sister party join the government, meaning that the French Socialists could not join a government without their Flemish counterpart.
3 It is worth stating that, as in France, unions have included pensioners within their organization, although to a much lesser extent. From the data gathered, in all cases these figures do not exceed 10 per cent.
4 Union des Travailleurs Manuels et Intellectuels.

5 Prior to World War II, unions did not mind getting closer to the state since they were also given control of social insurance, which they used to boost their membership. This was particularly true of the Catholic unions and unemployment insurance. Nonetheless, it benefited the Socialists, as well, and ensured that social protection became the realm of social partners rather than the state.

6 Seven members represent the employers and seven represent the workers (3 ACV/CSC, 3 ABVV/FGTB, 1 ACLV/CGSLB).

7 Interestingly, the DGII also asked that the plan adopt more realistic assumptions.

8 The strategy was to change names from PVV to VLD. Their rationale was to adopt a more neo-liberal tone in an attempt to integrate Flemish nationalists. It failed to fuse with the VU, but nonetheless attracted important VU politicians, such as the former president of the party (Swyngedouw 1998: 50).

9 Despite the weak link between benefits and contributions, the perception remains firmly anchored. Contributions were preferred to general taxation as a policy tool, since they result in less visible transfers between the regions.

10 All interviewees were asked whether or not pensions were part of the debate on the regionalization of social security. A vast majority of those questioned presented the argument sketched in this paragraph, including two cabinet members within the Ministry of Pensions, unions, experts with the *Bureau Fédéral du Plan* and the Central Bank, French liberal representatives and a member of the PSC.

11 It was 40 years for women.

12 *Une Exploration à long terme de la Sécurité sociale (1987–2040): Comment l'Avenir se présente-t-il et comment le politique peut-il s'y préparer?* (BFP 1990).

13 An article in *Le Soir* stated that 13 court rulings had been brought in an attempt to change the 45-year criterion, and that 65 men also brought forward judicial requests that their pensions be calculated on the basis of a 40-year working career instead of 45 (*Le Soir*, 6 January 1995).

14 The average married woman earned 59.5 per cent of men's pensions, while the average single woman earned 82 per cent (*Le Soir*, 16 February 1994).

15 This date was used because employers have not been allowed to discriminate since 1975, thus a 45-year career commencing in 1975 officially ends in 2020.

16 Bureau du Conseil de l'Égalité des Chances entre Hommes et Femmes.

17 The basic calculation for a pension in the public service is 1/60 × reference salary × number of years of service. 1/60 is the so-called *tantième*.

18 Other professions that need a lower *tantième* than 60 include teachers, postal workers, customs agents, railway workers and labourers.

19 For example, one restriction is that workers who move to another company cannot bring their pensions with them. This was a tactic used by employers to ensure that workers would remain faithful to the company. Prior to his departure, Willockx presented a plan to make pensions transferable, which was later adopted.

20 Melchior was no junior minister. He was one of the three vice prime ministers, and he was also responsible for economic affairs.

21 Reducing or harmonizing the *tantièmes* would have hurt them a lot because many members of the magistrate had a *tantième* of 1/30, so the passage to 1/60 would have meant a 50 per cent reduction in their pensions.

22 A key difference was that the French Liberals promised to guarantee the value of current pensions. They proposed the creation of a minimal pension financed via general taxation complemented by a funded scheme (*Le Soir*, 12 December 1994).

23 Pension funds do not even exist within the pension system, which relies exclusively on redistributive aspects.

24 The PVV received 12 per cent of the votes in the 1991 election, while the VLD (which was also counting on the support of large segments of the VU) gathered

13.1 per cent. That was 4 per cent less than the CVP, which had led in the polls for a long time prior to the elections.

25 Author interviews, 29 May 2000 and 5 June 2000.

26 Author interviews, 21 and 22 May 2002.

27 It also objected to a reconsideration of the positive adjustments made to contributions between 1955 and 1974 by previous governments, and altering the method used to calculate non-contributory periods.

29 *Comité d'avis pour l'émancipation sociale.*

30 Earlier government proposals suggested an implementation period lasting until 2006.

31 For example, someone who stops working at 62 with a career of 43 years would obtain a pension reflecting his average wage × 60 per cent × 43/45, and not 45/45, the latter representing a complete career. This system remains more advantageous than the actuarial mechanism incorporated by the new Swedish pension system. See Chapter 5.

32 Other assumptions include: an increase in the fertility rate from 1.55 in 1995 to 1.75 in 2010, and remaining constant afterwards; an increase in life expectancy and a decline in net migration from 10.638 in 1996 to 2.897 in 2050 (probably caused by a decline in the population due to ageing, rather than a reduction in immigration).

33 Author interview, 22 May 2002.

34 In an interview, Vandenbroucke claimed that it was an easy point to negotiate with the Liberals, who were strong advocates of pension reform within the public sector (*Le Soir*, 14 September 1999).

35 This is for single pensions; for couples, it affects pension amounts over 55,204 BF.

4 Sweden: do unions still matter? Committees instil a radical pension reform

1 *Allmän tilläggspension* (i.e. universal earnings-related pension).

2 A few changes were implemented, such as reducing the retirement age from 67 to 65 in 1976 and removing distinctions based on gender and marital status.

3 On the latter, see Lindqvist (1990) and Rothstein (1996).

4 Rothstein claims that the state was not strong enough to incorporate the working class as was done in France, and that it was not so weak as to prevent any form of corporatism like in Britain. It was *'lagom'*, meaning just right (Rothstein 1991: 168).

5 *Statens Offentliga Utredningar* (i.e. State Public Inquiry).

6 Wiklund retired and left his seat to Frebran.

7 Such as retirement (for example Wiklund [kd] was replaced by Frebran [kd]), negative election results (Bergdahl [nd], Westerholm [fp]) or positive election results (most Social Democrats in the Implementation Group), 'promotions' (for example Anna Hedborg [s] was appointed as general director of the National Social Insurance Board in 1996) or because his/her party refused to participate further (Ulla Hoffmann [v]).

8 The RFV and 21 general insurance boards were centralized within a single state agency, *Försäkringskassan* (Swedish Social Insurance Agency), in 2004. Nonetheless, each risk maintains its own operating rules, meaning that pension contributions are not used to offset deficits in other areas and vice versa. Even though the RFV no longer exists, all events described in this chapter occurred while it was still operational. Thus, no references are made to *Försäkringskassan*.

9 www.lo.se (accessed on 9 May 2002).

10 According to Aylott, it was a 'divorce' that was convenient for both sides. On one hand, the LO's attachment to an unpopular Social Democratic Party was

hurting its recruitment efforts in an increasingly competitive environment, while, on the other, the Social Democrats were seeking to become more of a 'catch all' party (Aylott 2001: 4).

11 See, for example, Rothstein (1991) on the importance of the state in the creation of corporatism in Sweden. He challenges the economic factors emphasized by Katzenstein (1985).

12 The latter point is challenged by Huber *et al.* (1993) who claim that Christian democratic parties in Belgium and the Netherlands performed a role similar to that of social democratic parties in Scandinavia.

13 This is why this issue was first sent to the Commerce Ministry and was part of a commission that lacked political participation.

14 Author interview, 6 December 2000.

15 This is in direct contrast to Belgium and France, where the Left was never able to obtain sufficient support to introduce a public pension system within the state, leading to a fragmented system where the social partners' role remains substantial.

16 'Dags för en ny ATP-Strid', title of a special article written in *Veckans Affärer* on 10 October 1990.

17 It stated that contribution rates could reach 15 per cent by the end of the 1980s and more than 20 per cent by the year 2000.

18 The ATP system worked on a 'base amount', the ceiling of which was fixed at 7.5.

19 The LO was one of the actors that had been pushing for the creation of such a committee starting at the end of 1982.

20 With 3 per cent growth, these figures increased to 87 per cent and 81.7 per cent, respectively (RFV 1987: 87).

21 The director-general was appointed by the minority Centre government of 1982. Interestingly, as a bureaucrat, he sought to maintain the system rather than see it become like a strong basic pension, the traditional position of the Centre Party (see Marier 2001).

22 Many members of the Working Group on Pensions acknowledged that this book greatly influenced their thinking with respect to reforming the ATP system. Many experts on the committee expressed similar views.

23 Author interview, 21 April 2002.

24 In order to facilitate the understanding of the political compromise among the five parties and the opposition to it, it was decided to tackle them separately. Thus, an overview of the negotiations among the five parties is presented in the following two sections (pp. 121–7 and pp. 127–33), which are followed by a full section on the opposition to the compromise (pp. 133–9).

25 Author interview, 17 November 2000.

26 Author interview, 20 November 2000.

27 The members of the Working Group on Pensions were: Bo Könberg (fp), Leif Bergdahl (nyd), Per Lennart Börjesson (v; until the end of 1992), Ulla Hoffmann (v; replacing Börjesson), Margit Gennser (m), Anna Hedborg (s), Åke Pettersson (c), Ingela Thalén (s), Barbro Westerholm (fp) and Pontus Wiklund (kd). The Liberals (fp) had two representatives because Könberg sat as minister/chair rather than as a party representative. To learn more about the reasons behind the selection of the two SAP representatives, see Lundberg 2001: 25.

28 She was explicit about this inspiration in an article written for the Taxpayers' Association (*Skattebetalarnas Förening*) in 1991. In that article, she also proposed the creation of a new law that would force individuals to put aside 21 per cent of their income for pension purposes. Two-thirds of these contributions would have to go into an individual ATP system, with the rest invested elsewhere. She also advocated transferring earlier ATP points into a private account; pensions paid from individual accounts would be granted according to insurance principles. For more information about the British reform, see Chapter 6.

29 All committee members stated that good chemistry existed within the group, and that they were truly open to suggestions and ideas from other individuals. This point is also stressed in an article in *Äffärsvärlden*: 'most of them in the group had been department's secretary or secretary of state and was an expert within the field ... the atmosphere was an academic seminar. The group could resolve a problem and the members came to trust each other, listen to each other, and believe in each other's word' (*Äffärsvärlden*, 15 November 2000).

30 Interestingly, this measure was taken for administrative simplicity. Very few individuals at that time had contributions above the ceiling, and collecting such contributions made it easier for employers. That is, they did not have to worry about which employees were over the ceiling, or by how much.

31 The Centre Party and the Christian Democratic Party were also opposed to contributions above the ceiling, but they attached far less importance to this issue than the other two bourgeois parties.

32 Author interview, 12 December 2000.

33 According to Lindbom, the Christian Democrat representative withdrew its support once it became clear that such an alternative would be extremely expensive (17 billion SEK per year – roughly US$0.17 billion). Worse, such a stance would have been difficult to support with Sweden experiencing a strong recession (Lindbom 2001: 74).

34 However, the guaranteed pension in the new system is taxed (*Dagens Nyheter*, 13 January 1994). As such, this increase is more symbolic than anything else.

35 The three federations were Kommunal Förbundet (regional government – and the largest LO federation), Handelsförbundet (retail) and the union for hotels and restaurants.

36 In protest, the writer Sven Lindqvist quoted some of the responses offered by some party districts in *Dagens Nyheter*, all of which were negative. He also cited one of the LO's newspaper articles, which used the title 'Are 95 Per Cent of the Replies Critical of the Five Party Agreement?' (*Dagens Nyheter*, 18–19 August 1997).

37 Author interview, 12 December 2000.

38 Author interview, 6 December 2000.

39 Author interview, 15 November 2000.

40 Author interview, 20 November 2000.

41 Author interview, 12 December 2000.

5 United Kingdom: a marriage with the private sector?

1 It was previously the Department of Social Security (DSS), which originated from the DHSS.

2 Unless wages decline, as was noted in Chapter 4.

3 Author interview, July 2006.

4 According to Nesbitt, employers were also provided with a strong incentive to soften their objections to the introduction of personal pensions, as they preferred to strengthen occupational pensions while decreasing the value of SERPS. The incentive also helped make personal pensions attractive to employers contributing to SERPS even as it eliminated potential opposition from employers for their loss of members in occupational plans (Nesbitt 1995: 95).

5 The first estimates claimed that one million people lost pension income by leaving SERPS, a figure reduced to between 43,000 and 238,000 after further analysis and consideration of the impact of the 2 per cent rebate (Ward 2000: 142).

6 As we saw in Chapter 3, Guillemard (1986) does the same for the French case.

7 Author interviews, April and July 2006.

8 Similar figures were obtained from other sources. According to the Institute for Fiscal Studies, 73 per cent of households will be eligible for the Pension Credit in 2025, as opposed to the current 58 per cent.

9 Only 14 per cent of individuals trust the government to deliver on its pension promises a great deal, as opposed to 52 per cent and 67 per cent who trust the pension provider and employer, respectively (Pensions Commission 2004: 215).

10 Blair strongly endorsed compulsion to increase the savings rate of low- to middle-wage earners. He held out until the very last minute when the 1998 Green Paper was published. Brown is more sensitive to the political implications of imposing compulsion (which would be immediately criticized as a tax by the Conservatives), and has shied away from this solution.

6 Conclusion: comparative tests of the hypotheses and their application to other industrialized countries

1 It is acknowledged that they had seats within the administration board of the social insurance agency, but they did not have a majority similar to Belgium's and France's. Further, union and employer representatives left the board in the early 1990s.

2 Of course, few individuals criticized the work of the committee and the assumptions the RFV made for evaluating the pension system. However, these individuals decided this on a personal basis and did not have the backing of a powerful group within Swedish society such as a political party or a union. The Left was highly critical of many sections of the five-party agreement, but did not challenge the basis (projections provided by state offices) upon which these decisions were made.

3 Here it is important to differentiate between consensus regarding the need to reform the system and actual agreement about the reform itself. The latter was less consensual, but was simply not discussed during both the 1994 and 1998 elections.

Bibliography

Official documents

Bureau Fédéral du Plan (BFP) (1990) *Une Exploration à long terme de la sécurité sociale (1987–2040): Comment l'Avenir se presente-t-il et comment le politique peut-il s'y préparer*, Brussels: BFP.

Conseil d'Orientation des Retraites (COR) (2001) *Retraites: Renouveler le Contrat social entre les générations*, Paris: La Documentation Française.

Department for Work and Pensions (2005) *The Pensioners' Incomes Series 2003/4*, London: DWP.

—— (2006a) *Income Related Benefits Estimates of Take-Up in 2003/2004*, London: DWP.

—— (2006b) *Security in Retirement: Towards a New Pensions System*, London: DWP.

Department of Social Security (1998) *A New Contract for Welfare: Partnership in Pensions*, London: Stationery Office.

Ds (1992[89]) *Ett Reformerat Pensionssystem-bakgrund, Principer och Skiss, en Promemoria av Pensionsarbetsgruppen*.

—— (1997[66]) *Garantipension och Samordningsfrågor*.

—— (1998[7]) *AP-Fonden i det Reformerade Pensionssystemet*.

—— (1999[43]) *Automatisk Balansering av Ålderspensionssystemet*.

Economic Policy Committee (2000) *Progress Report to the Ecofin Council on the Impact of Ageing Populations on Public Pension Systems*, European Union: European Commission.

Ministry of Health and Social Affairs (1994) *Pension Reform in Sweden*, Stockholm: Ministry of Health and Social Affairs.

—— (1998) *The Pension Reform: Final Report*, Stockholm: Ministry of Health and Social Affairs.

NOU (2004[1]) *Modernisert Folketrygd: Bærekraftig Pensjon for Framtida*, Oslo: Finansdepartementet and Socialdepartementet.

Office National des Pensions (ONP) (1999) *Annual Report*, Brussels: Office National des Pensions.

Pensions Commission (2004) *Pensions: Challenges and Choices – The First Report of the Pensions Commission*, London: Stationery Office.

—— (2005) *Executive Summary: Overlay Conclusions and Outline Recommendations*, London: Stationery Office.

Pensions Policy Institute (2006) *Initial Analysis of the Pensions Commission's Second Report*, London: Pensions Policy Institute.

Proposition (1990/1[100]) *Förslag till Statsbudget för Budgetåret 1991/92.*

Riksförsäkringsverket (1987) 'ATP och dess finansiering i det medel – och långsiktiga perspektivet', *RFV Anser*: 9.

—— (1991) 'En strategi för ATP-systemets framtid', *RFV Anser*: 15.

SOU (1990[76]) *Allmän Pension*, Stockholm: Allmäna Förlaget.

—— (1994[20]) *Reformerat Pensionssystem*, Stockholm: Fritzes.

—— (1994[21]) *Reformerat Pensionssystem. Kostnader och individeffekter*, Stockholm: Fritzes.

—— (1994[22]) *Reformerat Pensionssystem: Kvinnors ATP och avtalspension*, Stockholm: Fritzes.

—— (2004[105]) *Utdelning av Överskott i Inkomstpensionssystemet*, Stockholm: Fritzes.

Non-academic documents from unions and employers

Belgium

Documents from ABVV/FGTB, ACV/CSC and VOB/FEB.

France

Documents from CFDT, MEDEF, FO and CGT
CFDT (1999) 'Retraites: Première discussions', *Syndicalisme hebdo*, 2758: 5.

Periodicals

Affärsvärlden
Dagens Nyheter
L'Écho
L'Express
Expressen
Financial Times
Göteborgs Posten
Libération
Le Monde
Le Soir
Standaard
Veckans Affärer

Secondary sources

Abrahamson, P. (1999) 'The welfare modeling business', *Social Policy & Administration*, 33 (4): 394–415.

Alaluf, M. (1999) 'Le Modèle social Belge', in P. Delwit, J.-M. De Waele and P. Magnette (eds) *Gouverner la Belgique: Clivages et compromise dans une société complexe*, Paris: Presses Universitaire de France.

Alesina, A. and Perotti, R. (1995) 'Fiscal expansions and adjustments in OECD countries', *Economic Policy*, 21: 205–48.

Anderson, K.M. (2001) 'The politics of retrenchment in a social democratic welfare state. Reform of Swedish pensions and unemployment insurance', *Comparative Political Studies*, 34: 1,063–91.

Anderson, K.M. and Immergut, E. (2006) 'Sweden: after social democratic hegemony', in K.M. Andersen, E. M. Immergut and I. Shulze (eds) *The Oxford Handbook of West European Pension Politics*, Oxford: Oxford University Press.

Anderson, K.M., Immergut, E.M. and Schultze, I. (2006) *The Oxford Handbook of West-European Pension Politics*, Oxford: Oxford University Press.

Araki, H. (2000) 'Ideas and welfare: the conservative transformation of the British pension regime', *Journal of Social Policy*, 29: 599–621.

Arcq, E. and Chatelain, E. (1994) 'Bref Survol des relations collectives, des origines au plan global', *Pour un Nouveau Pacte social*, Brussels: Éditions Vie Ouvrière.

Arter, D. (1990) 'The Swedish Riksag: the case of a strong policy-influencing assembly', *West European Politics*, 13: 120–42.

Ashford, D.E. (1986) *The Emergence of the Welfare States*, Oxford: Basil Blackwell.

—— (1991) 'Advantages of complexity: social insurance in France', in J.S. Ambler (ed.) *The French Welfare State: Surviving Social and Ideological Change*, New York: New York University Press.

Aylott, N. (2001) 'After the divorce: intra-party power and organizational change in Swedish social democracy', Keele European Parties Research Unit, Working Paper 1, Keele.

Baldwin, P. (1990) *The Politics of Social Solidarity: Class Bases of the European Welfare State 1875–1975*, Cambridge: Cambridge University Press.

Bashevkin, S.B. (2002) *Welfare Hot Buttons: Women, Work, and Social Policy Reform*, Toronto: University of Toronto Press.

Béland, D. (2001) 'Does labor matter? Institutions, labor unions and pension reform in France and the United States', *Journal of Public Policy*, 21: 153–72.

—— (2005) *Social Security: History and Politics from the New Deal to the Privatization Debate*, Lawrence, KS: University Press of Kansas.

—— (2006) 'The politics of social learning: finance, institutions and pension reform in the United States and Canada', *Governance: An International Journal of Policy, Administration and Institutions*, 19 (4): 559–83.

Béland, D. and Marier, P. (2006) 'Avoiding protest: labor mobilization and welfare state politics in France', *Mobilization*, 11(3): 297–311.

Bendz, A. (2004) *I Välfärdsstatens Hägn: Autonomi Inom Arbetslöshetsförsäkringen*, Kungälv: Grafikerna Livréna.

Bichot, J. (1999) *Retraites en Péril*, Paris: Presses de Sciences Po.

Birnbaum, P. (1988) *States and Collective Action: The European Experience*, Cambridge: Cambridge University Press.

Bonoli, G. (2000) *The Politics of Pension Reform*, Cambridge: Cambridge University Press.

—— (2001) 'Political institutions, veto points, and the process of welfare state adaptation', in P. Pierson (ed.) *The New Politics of the Welfare State*, New York: Oxford University Press.

—— (2003) 'Two worlds of pension reform in Western Europe', *Comparative Politics*, 35 (4): 399–416.

Bonoli, G. and Palier, B. (2000) 'How do welfare states change? Institutions and their impact on the politics of welfare state reform', *European Review*, 8 (2): 333–52.

Bouget, D. (1998) 'The Juppé plan and the future of the French social welfare system', *Journal of European Social Policy*, 8: 155–72.

Cameron, D. (1984) 'Social democracy, labour quiescence and the representation of economic interest in advanced capitalist society', in J. Goldthorpe (ed.) *Order and Conflict in Contemporary Capitalism*, Oxford: Oxford University Press.

Campbell, A.L. and Lynch, J. (2000) 'Whose gray power? Elderly voters, elderly lobbies, and welfare reform in Italy and the US', *Italian Politics and Society* 53 (Summer).

Charpin, J.-M. (1999) *L'Avenir de nos retraites*, Paris: La Documentation Française.

Clayton, R. and Pontusson, J. (1998) 'Welfare-state retrenchment revisited: entitlement cuts, public sector restructuring, and inegalitarian trends in advanced capitalist societies', *World Politics*, 51: 67–98.

Cox, R.H. (2001) 'The social construction of an imperative: why welfare reform happened in Denmark and the Netherlands but not in Germany', *World Politics*, 53 (3): 463–98.

Crozier, M. (1970) *La Société bloquée*, Paris: Le Seuil.

David, P.A. (1985) 'Clio and the economics of Qwerty', *American Economic Review*, 75 (2): 332–37.

Delwit, P., De Waele, J.-M. and Magnette, P. (eds) (1999) *Gouverner la Belgique: Clivages et compromis dans une société complexe*, Paris: Presses Universitaire de France.

Dempster, M.A. and Wildavsky, A. (1980) 'On change, or there is no magic size for an increment?' *Political Studies*, 27: 371–89.

Dierickx, G. (2003) 'Senior civil servants and bureaucratic change in Belgium', *Governance: An International Journal of Policy, Administration, and Institutions*, 16 (3): 321–48.

Duverger, M. (1980) *Les Partis politiques*, Paris: Seuil.

Esping-Andersen, G. (1985) *Politics against Markets: The Social Democratic Road to Power*, Princeton: Princeton University Press.

—— (1990) *The Three Worlds of Welfare Capitalism*, Princeton: Princeton University Press.

—— (1996) 'After the golden age? Welfare state dilemmas in a global economy', in G. Esping-Andersen (ed.) *Welfare State in Transitions: National Adaptations in Global Economies*, London: UNRISD.

Eurostat (1999) *Social Protection: Expenditure and Receipts*, Brussels: Eurostat.

Fawcett, H. (1995) 'The privatisation of welfare: the impact of parties on the private/public mix in pension provision', *West European Politics*, 18: 150–69.

—— (2002) 'Pension reform in the UK: re-casting the public/private mix in pension provision, 1997–2000', Turin, Italy: ECPR Workshop.

Ferrera, M. and Rhodes, M. (2000) 'Building a sustainable welfare state', *West European Politics*, 23: 257–82.

Festjens, M.J. (1997) 'La Réforme des pensions: Une Nouvelle Génération et un nouveau contrat', Planning Paper 82, Brussels: Bureau Fédéral du Plan.

Foley, M. (2000) *The British Presidency*, Manchester: Manchester University Press.

Fondation Copernic (1999) *Les Retraites au péril du libéralisme*, Paris: Éditions Sylleps.

Friot, B. (1998) *Puissances du salariat: Emploi et protection sociale à la française*, Paris: La Dispute.

Gamble, A. (1994) *Britain in Decline: Economic Policy, Political Strategy, and the British State*, London: Macmillan.

Garrett, G. (1998) *Partisan Politics in the Global Economy*, Cambridge: Cambridge University Press.

Garrett, G. and Lange, P. (1991) 'Political responses to interdependence: what's left for the Left', *International Organization*, 45: 539–64.

Gilpin, R. (1987) *The Political Economy of International Relations*, Princeton: Princeton University Press.

Green-Pedersen, C. (2001) 'Welfare-state retrenchment in Denmark and the Netherlands, 1982–98: the role of party competition and party consensus', *Comparative Political Studies*, 34: 963–85.

Green-Pedersen, C. and Haverland, M. (2002) 'The new politics and scholarship of the welfare state', *Journal of European Social Policy*, 12 (1): 43–51.

Green-Pedersen, C. and Lindbom, A. (2006) 'Politics within paths: the trajectories of Danish and Swedish earnings-related pensions', *Journal of European Social Policy*. 16 (3): 245–58.

Guillemard, A.-M. (1980) *La Vieillesse et l'état*, Paris: Presses Universitaire de France.

—— (1986) *Le Déclin du Social*, Paris: Presses Universitaire de France.

Hallerberg, M. (1999) 'The role of parliamentary committees in the budgetary process within Europe', in R. Strauch and J.V. Hagen (eds) *Institutions, Politics and Fiscal Policy*, Boston: Kluwer Academic Publishers.

—— (2004) *Domestic Budgets in a United Europe: Fiscal Governance from the End of Bretton Woods to EMU*, New York: Cornell University Press.

Hallerberg, M. and von Hagen, J. (1999) 'Electoral institutions, cabinet negotiations, and budget deficits in the European Union', in J.V. Hagen (ed.) *Fiscal Institutions and Fiscal Perfomance*, Chicago: University of Chicago Press.

Hancke, B. (1991) 'The crisis of national unions: Belgian labor in decline', *Politics and Society*, 19 (4): 465–87.

Haverland, M. (2001) 'Another Dutch miracle? Explaining Dutch and German pension trajectories', *Journal of European Social Policy*, 11: 308–23.

Heclo, H. (1974) *Modern Social Politics in Britain and Sweden*, New Haven, CT: Yale University Press.

Heffernan, R. (2005) 'Why the prime minister cannot be a president: comparing institutional imperatives in Britain and America', *Parliamentary Affairs*, 58: 53–70.

Hennessy, P. (2005) 'Rulers and servants of the state: the Blair style of government 1997–2004', *Parliamentary Affairs*, 58: 6–16.

Herbertsson, T.T., Orszag, J.M. and Orszag, P.R. (2000) *Retirement in the Nordic Countries: Prospects and Proposals for Reform*, Copenhagen: Nordic Council.

Hermansson, J. (1993) *Politik som Intressekamp*, Stockholm: Norstedts Juridik.

Hermansson, J., Svensson, T. and Öberg, P.O. (1997) 'Vad blev av den svenska korporativismen', *Politica*, 29: 365–84.

Hinrichs, K. (2000) 'Elephants on the move: patterns of public pension reform in OECD countries', *European Review*, 8: 353–78.

Hinrichs, K. and Kangas, O. (2003) 'When is a change big enough to be a system shift? Small system-shifting changes in German and Finnish pension policies', *Social Policy and Administration*, 37: 573–91.

Huber, E., Ragin, C. and Stephens, J. (1993) 'Social democracy, Christian democracy, constitutional structure, and the welfare state', *American Journal of Sociology*, 99: 711–49.

Huyse, L. (1980) *De Gewapende Vrede*, Leuven: Kritak.

Immergut, E.M. (1992) *Health Politics: Interests and Institutions in Western Europe*, Cambridge: Cambridge University Press.

Jobert, B. (1981) *Le Social en plan*, Paris: Les Éditions Ouvrières.

Katzenstein, P.J. (1985) *Small States in World Markets*, Ithaca, NY: Cornell University Press.

King, D. (1995) *Actively Seeking Work? The Politics of Unemployment and Welfare Policy in the United States and Great Britain*, Chicago: University of Chicago Press.

King, G., Keohane, R.O. and Verba, S. (1994) *Designing Social Inquiry*, Princeton: Princeton University Press.

Korpi, W. (1983) *The Democratic Class Struggle*, Boston: Routledge.

Korpi, W. and Palme, J. (1998) 'The paradox of redistribution and strategies of equality: welfare state institutions, inequality and poverty in the western countries', *American Sociological Review*, 63: 661–87.

Krasner, S.D. (1976) 'State power and the structure of international trade', *World Politics*, 28: 317–47.

Kuhnle, S. and Alestalo, M. (2000) 'Introduction: growth, adjustments and survival of European welfare states', in S. Kuhnle (ed.) *The Survival of the European Welfare State*, London: Routledge.

Legros, F. (2001) 'Pension reform between economic and political problems', paper presented at the 8th French–German Economic Forum, Berlin, January.

Lentzen, É. (1998) 'Le Processus de fédéralisation', in M. Swyngedouw and M. Martiniello (eds) *Où Va La Belgique?* Paris: Éditions L'Harmattan.

Levy, J.D. (1999) 'Vice into virtue? Progressive politics and welfare reform in continental Europe', *Politics and Society*, 27: 239–73.

—— (2001) 'Partisan politics and welfare adjustment: the case of France', *Journal of European Public Policy*, 8 (2): 265–85.

Lijphart, A. (1968) 'Typologies of democratic systems', *Comparative Political Studies*, 1 (1): 46–80.

—— (1984) *Democracies: Patterns of Majoritarian and Consensus Government in Twenty-One Countries*, New Haven, CT: Yale University Press.

Lindbom, A. (2001) 'De borgerliga partierna och pensionsreformen', in J. Palme (ed.) *Hur blev den stora kompromissen möljig? Politiken bakom den svenska pensionsreformen*, Stockholm: Pensionsforum.

Lindqvist, R. (1990) *Från Folkrörelse Till Välfärdsbyråkrati: Det Svenska Sjukförsäkirngssystemets Utveckling 1900–1990*, Lund: Arkiv.

Lowi, T.J. (1972) 'Four systems of policy, politics, and choice', *Public Administration Review*, 32: 298–310.

Lundberg, U. (2001) 'Socialdemokratin cch 1990-talets pensionsreform', in J. Palme (ed.) *Hur blev den stora kompromissen möjlig? Politiken bakom den svenska pensionsreformen*, 8–49, Stockholm: Pensionsforum.

Lynch, J. (2001) 'The age-orientation of social policy regimes in OECD countries', *Journal of Social Policy*, 30: 411–36.

March, J.G. and Olsen, J.P. (1989) *Rediscovering Institutions: The Organizational Basis of Politics*, New York: Free Press.

Marier, P. (2001) 'Buråkratiernas roll i pensionsreformprocessen', in J. Palme (ed.) *Hur Blev den Stora Kompromissen Möljig? Politiken Bakom den Svenska Pensionsreformen*, Stockholm: Pensionsforum.

—— (2005) 'Where did the bureaucrats go? Role and influence of the public bureaucracy in the Swedish and French Pension reform debate', *Governance: An International Journal of Policy, Administration and Institutions*, 18: 521–44.

—— (2006) 'Bureaucrats and welfare reform: a comparative analysis of 6 industrialized countries', paper presented at the American Political Association Meeting, Philadelphia, 30 August 30–2 September.

—— (2007) 'Affirming, transforming, or neglecting gender? Conceptualizing gender in the pension reform process', *Social Politics: International Studies in Gender, State & Society* 14 (2): 182–211..

Mattson, I. (1996) *Förhandlingsparlamentarism – en Jämförande Studie av Riksdagen och Folketinget*, Lund: Lund University Press.

Mayhew, D.R. (1974) 'Congressional elections: the case of the vanishing marginals', *Polity*, 6 (3): 295–317.

Mekhantar, J. (1996) *Finances publiques*, Paris: Hachette.

Merrien, F.-X. (1991) 'L'État par défaut', in J.-P. Durand and F.-X. Merrien (eds) *Sortie de siècle: La France en mutation*, Paris: Éditions Vigot.

Mishra, R. (1990) *The Welfare Stare in Capitalist Society*, Toronto: University of Toronto Press.

Montagne, S. (2000) 'Les Conséquences de la nouvelle politique budgétaire sur le système de retraite', *Chronique international de l'IRES*, 67: 1–8.

Myles, J. and Pierson, P. (2001) 'The political economy of pension reform', in P. Pierson (ed.) *The New Politics of the Welfare State*, Oxford: Oxford University Press.

Natali, D. and Rhodes, M. (2004) 'Trade-offs and veto players: reforming pensions in France and Italy', *French Politics*, 2: 1–23.

Nesbitt, S. (1995) *British Pension Policy Making in the 1980s: The Rise and Fall of a Policy Community*, Aldershot: Avebury.

OECD (2005) *Pensions at a Glance*, Paris: OECD Publishing.

Ogus, A.I. (1982) 'Great Britain', in P.A. Köhler and H.F. Zacher (eds) *The Evolution of Social Insurance 1891–1981: Studies of Germany, France, Great Britain, Austria and Switzerland*, London: Frances Pinter.

Olsen, J.P. (1983) *Organized Democracy: Political Institutions in a Welfare State – The Case of Norway*, Bergen: Universitetsforlaget.

Olson, M. (1965) *The Logic of Collective Action*, Cambridge, MA: Harvard University Press.

Olson, S. (1988) 'Sweden', in P. Flora (ed.) *Growth to Limits*, vol. 1, New York: Walter de Gruyter.

Palme, J. (2005) 'Features of the Swedish pension reform', *Japanese Journal of Social Security Policy*, 4 (1): 42–53.

Palmer, E. (2000) 'The Swedish pension reform model: framework and issues', World Bank's Pension Reform Primer Social Protection Discussion Paper No. 0012, Washington, DC: World Bank.

Pasture, P.T. (1993) 'The April 1944 "Social Pact" in Belgium and its significance for the post-war welfare state', *Journal of Contemporary History*, 28: 695–714.

Peeters, P. (1996) 'Les Pensions l/gales: la peu, bonne ou mauvaise conseillère?', *Reflets et perspectives de la vie économique*, 35(2).

Pensions Policy Institute (PPI) (2006) 'Initial analysis of the Pensions Commission's second report', PPI Discussion Paper, London: PPI.

Pestieau, P. and Stijns, J.-P. (1997) 'Social security and retirement in Belgium', NBER Working Paper Series, Cambridge, MA: NBER.

Peters, B.G. (1995) *The Politics of Bureaucracy*, White Plains, NY: Longman.

—— (1997) 'Policy transfers between governments: the case of administrative reforms', *West European Politics*, 20 (4): 71–88.

—— (1999) *Institutional Theory in Political Science: The 'New Institutionalism'*, New York: Continuum.

—— (2005) 'I'm OK, you're (not) OK: the private welfare state in the United States', *Social Policy and Administration*, 39: 166–80.

Pierre, J. (1995) 'Comparative public administration: the state of the art', in J. Pierre (ed.) *Bureaucracy in the Modern State: Introduction to Comparative Administration*, Aldershot: Edward Elgar.

Pierre, J., Peters, B.G. and King, D. (2005) 'The politics of path dependency: political conflict in historical institutionalism', *Journal of Politics*, 67(4): 1275–300.

Pierson, P. (1993) 'When effect becomes cause: policy feedback and political change', *World Politics*, 45 (4): 595–628.

—— (1994) *Dismantling the Welfare State?* Cambridge: Cambridge University Press.

—— (1996) 'The new politics of the welfare state', *World Politics*, 48 (2): 143–79.

—— (1998) 'Irresistible forces, immovable objects: post-industrial welfare states confront permanent austerity', *Journal of European Public Policy*, 5: 539–60.

—— (2000) 'Increasing returns, path dependence, and the study of politics', *American Political Science Review*, 94 (2): 251–67.

—— (ed.) (2001) *The New Politics of the Welfare State*, Oxford: Oxford University Press.

Pierson, P. and Smith, M. (1993) 'Bourgeois revolution? The policy consequences of resurgent conservatism', *Comparative Political Studies*, 25: 487–520.

Pierson, P. and Weaver, R.K. (1993) 'Imposing losses in pension policy', in B. Rockman and R.K. Weaver (eds) *Do Institutions Matter? Government Capabilities in the United States and Abroad*, Washington, DC: Brookings Institution.

Pitruzzello, S. (1997) 'Social policy and the implementation of the Maastricht fiscal convergence criteria: the Italian and French attempts at welfare and pension reforms', *Social Research*, 64: 1,589–642.

Polanyi, K. (1944) *The Great Transformation*, New York: Rinehart.

Pontusson, J. (1993) 'The comparative politics of labor-initiated reforms', *Comparative Political Studies*, 25: 548–78.

Powell Jr, G.B. (2000) *Elections as Instruments of Democracy: Majoritarian and Proportional Visions*, New Haven, CT: Yale University Press.

Quermonne, J.-L. (1991) *L'Appareil administratif de l'état*, Paris: Éditions du Seuil.

Rake, K., Falkingham, J. and Evans, M. (2000) 'British pension policy in the twenty-first century: a partnership in pensions or a marriage to the means test?' *Social Policy and Administration*, 34: 296–317.

Reman, P. (1994) 'Du Pacte social de 1944 au plan global de 1993: Évolution de la notion de solidarité', *Pour un Nouveau Pacte social*, Brussels: Éditions Vie Ouvrière.

Reynaud, E. (1997) 'Le New Labour face aux retraites après dix-huit ans de libéralisme', *Chronique international de l'IRES*, 48: 57–64.

—— (1998) 'Pensions in the European Union: adapting to economic and social changes', *International Social Security Review*, 51 (1): 31–46.

—— (ed.) (2000) *Social Dialogue and Pension Reform*, Geneva: International Labour Office.

Richardson, J., Gustafsson, G. and Jordan, G. (1982) 'The concept of policy style', in J. Richardson (ed.) *Policy Styles in Western Europe*, London: George Allen and Unwin.

Rhodes, M. (2001) 'The political economy of social pacts: Competitive corporatism and European welfare reform', in P. Pierson (ed.) *The New Politics of the Welfare State*, Oxford: Oxford University Press.

Rokkan, S. (1999) 'State formation and nation-building', in P. Flora, S. Kuhnle and D. Urwin (eds) *State Formation, Nation-Building, and Mass Politics in Europe*, Oxford: Oxford University Press.

Rosanvallon, P. (1995) *La Nouvelle Question sociale*, Paris: Éditions du Seuil.

Ross, F. (2000a) 'Beyond Left and Right: the new partisan politics of welfare', *Governance: An International Journal of Policy and Administration*, 13: 155–83.

—— (2000b) 'Interests and choice in the "not quite so new" politics of welfare', *West European Politics*, 23 (4): 11–34.

Rothstein, B. (1991) 'State structure and variations in corporatism: the Swedish case', *Scandinavian Political Studies*, 14: 149–71.

—— (1992) 'Labor-market institutions and working-class strength', in S. Steinmo, K. Thelen and F. Longstreth (eds) *Structuring Politics: Historical Institutionalism in Comparative Analysis*, Cambridge: Cambridge University Press.

—— (1996) *The Social Democratic State: The Swedish Model and the Bureaucratic Problem of Social Reforms*, Pittsburgh: University of Pittsburgh Press.

—— (1998) 'State building and capitalism: the rise of the Swedish bureaucracy', *Scandinavian Political Studies*, 21: 287–306.

—— (2001) 'The universal welfare state as a social dilemma', *Rationality and Society*, 13: 213–33.

Ruellan, R. (1993) 'Retraites: L'Impossible Réforme est-elle achevée', *Droit social*, 12: 911–29.

Scarborough, E. (2000) 'West European welfare states: the old politics of retrenchment', *European Journal of Political Research*, 38: 225–59.

Scharpf, F.W. (1988) 'The joint decision trap: lessons from German federalism and European integration', *Public Administration*, 66: 239–68.

—— (1997) *Games Real Actors Play*, Boulder, CO: Westview.

Schludi, M. (2002) 'The politics of pensions in European social insurance countries', paper presented at ECPR, Turin, Italy.

Sefton, J., van de Ven, J. and Weale, M. (2005) 'The effects of means-testing pensions on savings and retirement', Discussion Paper No. 265, London: National Institute of Social Economic Research.

Seiler, D.-L. (1999) 'Un État entre importation et implosion: Consociativité, partitocratie et lotissement dans la sphère publique en Belgique', in P. Delwit, J.-M. De Waele and P. Magnette (eds) *Gouverner la Belgique: Clivages et compromise dans une société complexe*, Paris: Presses Universitaire de France.

Steinmo, S. (1993) *Taxation and Democracy: Swedish, British and American Approaches to Financing the Modern States*, New Haven, CT: Yale University Press.

Svensson, T. (1994) *Socialdemokratins Dominans: En Studie av Den Svenska Socialdemokratins Partistrategi*, Uppsala: Acta Universitatis Upsaliensis.

Swank, D. (2002) *Global Capital, Political Institutions, and Policy Change in Developed Welfare States*, Cambridge: Cambridge University Press.

Swyngedouw, M. (1998) 'Les Rapports de force politiques en Belgique', in M. Swyngedouw and M. Martiniello (eds) *Où Va La Belgique?* Paris: Éditions L'Harmattan.

Taddei, D. (2000) *Retraites choisies et progressives*, Paris: La Documentation Française.

Tamburi, G. (1999) 'Motivation, purpose and processes in pension reform', *International Social Security Review*, 52: 15–44.

Taylor-Gooby, P. (2005) 'Uncertainty, trust and pensions: the case of the current UK reforms', *Social Policy and Administration*, 39: 217–32.

Teulade, R. (2000) *L'Avenir des systèmes de retraite*, Paris: Les Éditions des Journaux Officiels.

Tsebelis, G. (1995) 'Decision making in political systems: veto players in presidentialism, parliamentarism, multicameralism and multipartyism', *British Journal of Political Science*, 25 (3): 289–325.

—— (1999) 'Veto players and law production in parliamentary democracies: an empirical analysis', *American Political Science Review*, 93: 591–608.

—— (2002) *Veto Players: How Political Institutions Work*, Princeton: Princeton University Press.

Vaes, B. (1998) 'Un Divorce de la sécurité sociale?' in M. Swyngedouw and M. Martiniello (eds) *Où Va La Belgique?* Paris: Éditions L'Harmattan.

Vail, M.I. (1999) 'The better part of valour: the politics of French welfare reform', *Journal of European Social Policy*, 9: 311–29.

van den Brande, A. (1987) 'Neo-corporatism and functional-integral power in Belgium', in I. Scholten (ed.) *Political Stability and Neo-Corporatism: Corporatist Integration and Societal Cleavages in Western Europe,* London: Sage.

van den Bulck, J. (1992) 'Pillars and politics: neo-corporatism and policy networks in Belgium', *West European Politics* 15: 35–53.

Vanthemsche, G. (1994) *La Sécurité sociale*, Brussels: De Boeck.

Vermeylen, Y. (2004) 'The new pension law in Belgium', *Benefits and Compensation International*, 33: 7–9.

von Hagen, J. (1992) *Budgeting Procedures and Fiscal Performance in the European Communities*, Brussels: Commission of the European Communities.

Walker, A. (1991) 'Thatcherism and the new politics of old age', in J. Myles and J. Quadagno (eds) *States, Labor Markets, and the Future of Old-Age Policy*, Philadelphia: Temple University Press.

Ward, S. (2000) 'Personal pensions in the UK, the mis-selling scandal and the lessons to be learnt', in J. Stewart and G. Hughes (eds) *Pensions in the European Union: Adapting to Economic and Social Change*, Boston: Kluwer Academic.

Weaver, R.K. (1986) 'The politics of blame avoidance', *Journal of Public Policy*, 6 (4): 371–98.

—— (1999) *The Politics of Pension Reform in Canada and the United States*, Boston, MA: Center for Retirement Research at Boston College.

—— (2004) 'Design and implementation issues in Swedish individual pension accounts', *Social Security Bulletin*, 65: 38–56.

Wilensky, H.L. (1974) *The Welfare State and Equality: Structural and Ideological Roots of Public Expenditures*, Berkeley, CA: University of California Press.

Williamson, J.B. and Pampel, F.C. (1993) *Old-Age Security in Comparative Perspective*, New York: Oxford University Press.

Wilson, W.J. (1987) *The Truly Disadvantaged: The Inner City, the Underclass, and Public Policy*, Chicago: University of Chicago Press.

Witte, E. (1992) 'Belgian federalism: towards complexity and asymmetry', *West European Politics*, 15: 95–117.

Websites

Centre de Recherche et d'Information Socio-Politiques (CRISP). Online. Available at www.crisp.be/ (accessed 5 December 2005).

Landsorganisationen i Sverige (LO). Online. Available at www.lo.se/ (accessed 9 May 2002).

Index

eBooks – at www.eBookstore.tandf.co.uk

A library at your fingertips!

eBooks are electronic versions of printed books. You can store them on your PC/laptop or browse them online.

They have advantages for anyone needing rapid access to a wide variety of published, copyright information.

eBooks can help your research by enabling you to bookmark chapters, annotate text and use instant searches to find specific words or phrases. Several eBook files would fit on even a small laptop or PDA.

NEW: Save money by eSubscribing: cheap, online access to any eBook for as long as you need it.

Annual subscription packages

We now offer special low-cost bulk subscriptions to packages of eBooks in certain subject areas. These are available to libraries or to individuals.

For more information please contact webmaster.ebooks@tandf.co.uk

We're continually developing the eBook concept, so keep up to date by visiting the website.

www.eBookstore.tandf.co.uk

For Product Safety Concerns and Information please contact our EU
representative GPSR@taylorandfrancis.com Taylor & Francis Verlag GmbH,
Kaufingerstraße 24, 80331 München, Germany

Printed and bound by CPI Group (UK) Ltd, Croydon, CR0 4YY
12/05/2025
01867574-0001